C000216855

'If reading the New Testament [...]
read this book! As Richard Po[...]
understand the New Testament [...]
came before it." Porter is a guid[...]
reader for whom it makes no s[...]
funny, but always compelling, *The Kingdom of God – The Director's Cut* challenges the church to demonstrate the kingdom of God before a watching world. No longer a hippie, Porter is still a nonconformist and one from whom the church can learn a great deal!'

Stephen Katz
North American Director of Jews for Jesus

'Richard has diverse life experience, having lived on three continents, served in the military and spent decades in pastoral ministry. In this book, Richard helps us to rethink biblically and theologically about the kingdom of God and our place in it. If we pray "thy kingdom come on earth as it is in heaven" perhaps it's time to understand more fully what that means. *The Kingdom of God – The Director's Cut* will help deepen your love for the Father and will encourage you to partner with the Father, Son and Holy Spirit to see his kingdom come, and the Great Commission fulfilled.'

Tommy Stewart
Founder of Christians Who Lead and International
Christian Leadership Advisor and Consultant

'This book is full of personality, warmth, humour, possibility, impossibility all with a sting in its tale (spelling intended!). Richard writes simply, loaded with story and illustration and sucks you into the joy and abundance of his love for the gospel and the kingdom – and then hits hard with reminder after reminder that true following of Jesus takes us into an unexpected kingdom. The world described is full of prayer, encounter, transformation, obedience and radical action. Drawn from a wealth of experiences it is part testimony, part theology, part a practical call to action, and in the weaving together of these things it is 100 per cent inspiring. Don't read this book if you value your comfort. Read this book if you want to join in a story that changes lives – including your own!'

Revd Deirdre Brower Latz
Principal and Senior Lecturer in Pastoral and
Social Theology, Nazarene Theological College, Manchester

'*The Kingdom of God – The Director's Cut* is original on many levels. Presenting the kingdom as a theatre production or a cinema event gives clarity to a somewhat nebulous subject. I especially appreciate the chapters highlighting the message and ministry of Jesus. He only preached one gospel: the gospel of the kingdom. Richard asks: "Do we believe that the good news for the world is something different from what Jesus proclaimed and believed it to be?" This book will get you to think outside the box. It will help you to hear the parts of the Bible we tend to ignore. This book is revolutionary yet firmly founded on Scripture. It is humorous and passionate and presents a real challenge to the church. As Richard wrote, "This orphaned planet has enough dysfunctional families. Jesus never intended his church to be one of them." I highly recommend this book. It will help any reader to seek first the kingdom of God and to know why Jesus told us to do it.'

Debra Green
Executive Director, Redeeming Our Communities, and author

'I once heard a preacher challenge a crowd of men: "This world needs men and women who are willing to climb and, if needs be, crawl up the mountain of prayer to grab heaven by the lapels and trail it back down to earth." This preacher was Richard Porter and to know him is to know that these are the words he and his incredible wife live by every day – to see heaven come down and invade our hearts, our lives, our churches, our streets and our nations. This book is a compelling story of life's greatest adventure from a prayer warrior that I love, admire and have the honour to call my friend and brother. If you want a revelation of the kingdom of God and where you fit into this great adventure, read this book. It will impact the direction of your life!'

Revd Gareth (Spud) Murphy
Chief Executive, CVM Ireland

'I met Richard recently on my first time in Northern Ireland. Little did I know that on this trip I was going to meet possibly the nicest and most sincere man I've ever met. His love for people and, more importantly, his love for God is remarkable. It was so shocking that, before I said anything about the book, I wanted to let you know about the heart of the man whose book you have in your hand: *The Kingdom of God – The Director's Cut*. Richard has been so captured with the love of God, and what it looks like in his kingdom, that it makes perfect sense for him to unpack the story. My prayer is that you, too, are caught up in the greatest story that has ever been, and is still being, told.'

Eric B. Johnson
Senior Pastor of Bethel Redding and author

'Richard Porter has written a book earnestly inviting you to consider your place in the divine story unfolding all around you, each and every day. From where we stand in this moment, many things about this story remain a deep mystery – but as we wait for the glorious unfolding of the hidden plans of God, we know that our part lies in obedient humility, in service to one another, and in loving intimacy with our heavenly Father. May you always walk through the great drama of creation with each of these treasures held joyously in your heart!'

Heidi G. Baker
Co-founder and Executive Chairman of the Board, Iris Global

'Richard Porter's writing is a unique mix of passion and groundedness. From his embracing of the Christian faith in the days of flower-power and the Jesus movement in the United States of the 1970s, to his present life in post-troubles Northern Ireland, he brings a wealth of life-experience to his writing. This book shows an incredible imagination and originality, a deep and thorough knowledge of the Bible, and a rootedness in humanity. These, brought together through the prism of kingdom-values, make it engaging, surprising and challenging. I got to know Richard through his role as a chaplain in the Dock Cafe, part of the newly emerging Titanic Quarter in Belfast. He is a godly, humble-hearted follower of Jesus, and he has much to teach us.'

Bishop Harold Miller
Church of Ireland

'I have had the privilege of knowing Pastor Richard Porter for many years now. The moment I met him, I knew he was a man who had a heart for Christ and the things of God. Richard has a great desire to see God's church united, walking in the power of the Holy Spirit and demonstrating the heart of God the Father. Pastor Richard became an incredible influence and mentor in my life. His desire to see God's people walking in freedom and purpose was both refreshing and contagious. As you read this book you will be captured by the heart of Pastor Richard as he lays out in great detail the plan of God as it unfolds before our eyes. Yet Richard compels us; this is not about being a spectator but a participator in the kingdom of God.'

Pastor Lee McClelland
The Ark Church Belfast

The Kingdom of God
The Director's Cut

Understanding the Greatest Show on Earth

God Bless you Debra
Thank you for your
Contribution and support

Richard Porter

Richard Porter

Authentic

First published 2021 by Authentic Media Limited,
PO Box 6326, Bletchley, Milton Keynes, MK1 9GG.
authenticmedia.co.uk

British Library Cataloguing in Publication Data
A catalogue record for this book is available from the British Library.
ISBN: 978-1-78893-169-4
978-1-78893-170-0 (e-book)

Cover design by Hamar
Printed and bound by CPI Group (UK) Ltd, Croydon, CR0 4YY

I dedicate this book to my family, the family of God: the kingdom is within you.

I dedicate this book to all the raving charismatic loonies out there looking for a chandelier to swing from: you challenge me.

I dedicate this book to all the conservative, respectable, traditionalists who love to sit on pews and listen to the pipes: you keep me grounded.

I dedicate this book to all the holy isolationists who have a monopoly on the truth: you unswervingly correct me.

I dedicate this book to all the creative radicals, who break the mould and step out of the boat: you inspire me.

I have lived and have participated in all of these worlds at one time or another. I have found the love of God in each one of them. So, with great fanfare, I dedicate this book to all of my brothers and sisters in the kingdom of God and to Jesus Christ the King, my saviour and my friend.

Oh, and I also dedicate this book to my long-suffering wife who puts up with more than you'll ever know, and my two grown boys who often roll their eyes and exclaim: 'Dad!'

Love has invaded an orphaned planet. The kingdom of God is the greatest show on earth. I dedicate this book to that kingdom.

Contents

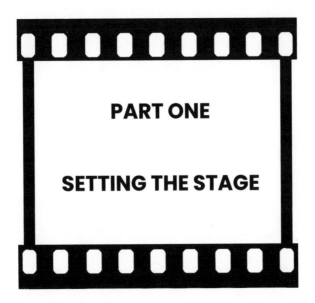

PART ONE

SETTING THE STAGE

First Contact

I met Jesus before I knew much about him. I often thought I'd become a Buddhist or a follower of Paramahansa Yogananda before I'd become a Christian.[1] Carlos Castaneda and his series of books popularising drug-induced shamanism were more attractive than yawning my way through a Sunday morning church service.[2] Being strapped in a suit, sitting on a pew, singing religious songs to the droning of a pipe organ wasn't a world or a culture I could readily accept. It was painful singing 'Beulah Land' while living on a diet of Jimi Hendrix, Jefferson Airplane, and Led Zeppelin. To me, Christianity was for old ladies and little children. It was part of the establishment I was trying to escape.

Like so many young people during the 1960s and early 1970s, I questioned capitalism. I didn't trust the government or organised religion. Life had to be more than owning a house, paying off a mortgage and driving a family car. It all seemed so shallow with the spectre of world annihilation lurking in the background. Nothing through that window attracted me.

My world, at that time, revolved around peace, love, dope, Woodstock, psychedelic drugs, free sex, dropping out, *A Child's Garden of Grass*,[3] *The Electric Kool-Aid Acid Test*,[4] and Robert

Crumb.[5] However, the deeper I descended into that psyche-delic maze, the more I hated it. It wasn't my friend. Then add to that four years of military service working for the National Security Agency and twelve months of madness in Vietnam, and I floundered like a ship without a rudder or an anchor.

The day I was able to clutch my discharge papers, I ran. I ran away from everything like a scared rabbit. It was difficult to readjust and relate to the people back home in the States. I had panic attacks, but I didn't know what they were, which only made it worse. All the drugs (LSD, marijuana, psilocybin and speed) accentuated my fear and social ineptness.

By 1974 I was living in a tepee on two acres of land in the middle of nowhere in Kansas. I took baths in a stream a mile down the road. Drinking water was from an old well. The only connection I had with the so-called system was Derby Oil Refinery in Wichita. I worked there for two days a week. It provided enough money to keep me in drugs, a bit of food, and fuel for the truck (an old 1959 Ford). I was off the grid, but I wasn't living. I had isolated myself in a virtual reality without purpose or direction; broken.

I remember one day standing in a wheat field across the dirt road from the tepee, desperately talking towards the sky: 'God, I don't know who you are, or even if you're there, but if you hear me, could I please get some help? If you are real, show me? I'm not playing around. I am serious. Here I am. I want to know you.'

God answered that prayer. A month later, in 1975, I was in Lindsborg, Kansas. The room of the house was full of Christians. Why I was there, I don't know. A friend had invited me, so I went. All I remember was everyone sitting in a circle singing worship songs. They sang; I watched. At that time, I had a ZZ Top beard hanging on my chest, hair past my shoulders, jeans with more patches than original fabric, and shoes held together with duct tape. Fortunately, no one rejected me at the door.

Little did I know I was going to have an encounter with God. That night he was going to answer my prayer. The first thing he did was open my eyes to the people around me. As they sang their songs, I sat there, silent, looking at their faces. I was surprised by how pure and wholesome they all looked. They were so attractive, and I wanted to be like them. I aspired to be virtuous and unpolluted, but I knew there was nothing noble or innocent in my life. The drugs dropped me in a social and spiritual cesspit I couldn't escape.

I don't remember anyone in that meeting reading from the Bible or speaking from it. They just sang, but for me, it was enough. God came. He didn't just open my eyes to the Christians around me, but he revealed himself. Did I see him? No. Did I hear an audible voice? No. I just sensed his presence. He enveloped me. The Holy Spirit revealed Jesus to me in a way I can't explain, but the reality of his arrival and his existence right there in front of me was overwhelming. I didn't know what to do. I wasn't emotional. I didn't feel like laughing or crying. I was awestruck by the purity and the reality of Jesus Christ.

At the end of that meeting, everyone got up to make their way to another room for refreshments. When I stood, I went over to a man who was still sitting there. I tried to explain what was happening to me. He didn't say a lot, but he asked me if I'd like to pray and ask Jesus into my life. I said, yes. I didn't have a revelation of doctrine; I had a revelation of Jesus. That was all I needed. The rest would come later. Like most people, I was searching for him, not a doctrine about him.

I had prayed many times in my life. As a child, I knew that Christmas celebrated the day Jesus was born, so I made it a point to go to my room and wish him a happy birthday. Whenever I took a hit of acid (LSD), I would say a simple prayer: 'God, please help me to have a good trip.' But most of the time, I would pray for reality.

- Who are you God?
- What are you like?
- Where are you?
- What's the purpose of this life?
- What religion do you hide in?
- Which one was your idea?

Those prayers were sincere, but the prayer I prayed in Lindsborg that night was different. I didn't question God. I was responding to a real-life encounter. It was a dialogue that went beyond words. My new Christian friend told me what to pray, but I knew I was talking directly to God. 'Jesus, please forgive me of my sins. I invite you into my life. I commit myself to you.'

As soon as the words left my mouth, I knew I was going on with Jesus. The conviction was rooted in me. I knew from that moment, nothing was going to be the same again, and it wasn't. Even though I was parroting the words of this Christian, I sincerely meant each one of them, and I was changed; not by the prayer but by God. Jesus was the reality that stilled all my questions.

I had no idea the impact that night would have on me. A couple of days later, I realised my desire for drugs was gone. I had tried to quit many times, but now I knew I was free. I got rid of all the pipes, needles, pills and weed and never touched them again. That empty, lying nightmare was over. I knew it. I was leaving it behind. Jesus lifted me out of that pit, and I was following the one who lifted me.

No one told me this would be part of the package. I thought Jesus himself was enough. To know him, know he was real, to know he was there and that I was now spiritually connected to him was more than I hoped possible. I wasn't thinking about eternal life, divine promises, judgement or any of the other aspects linked to the faith. I just wanted a hold on reality, and I found it in Jesus.

During those first few months, I'd have recurring dreams of shooting up speed or dropping acid. In those dreams, I'd be asking, 'Why am I still doing this? I don't need these drugs anymore.' Then I would wake up and thank God it was only a dream. I was free. The new freedom wasn't an act of personal willpower; it was the grace and mercy of God. 'It is for freedom that Christ has set us free' (Gal. 5:1).

A Bona Fide Mission

Fast forward one year. It is 1976. I now attend a young, independent church in Colorado. It is full of converted hippies: long hair, beards, beads, bare feet resting on the back of pews, guitars, drums, no suits, no ties, just Bibles in hand and a strong belief in Jesus Christ. On reflection, we can either thank or curse the redeemed hippies for the musical shift in church culture, but without it, many of my generation would've floundered.

Historically it is now called the Jesus Movement. It was God's answer to the prayers of the mothers and fathers who were losing their children to drugs, sex and the unmooring of Christian principles. During my first year in the faith, I was living on a diet of *Rees Howells: Intercessor*;[6] *The Late Great Planet Earth*;[7] *The Cross and the Switchblade*;[8] Keith Green; Love Song; Randy Matthews; Larry Norman and Randy Stonehill.[9]

The emphasis during those years was just like the early church: evangelism and the imminent return of Christ. Hal Lindsey warned that the apocalypse was just around the corner, while Larry Norman sang, 'I Wish We'd All Been Ready.'

John, a friend in the hippie church, told me that Christians were supposed to go out and tell others about Jesus. I often told people what Jesus did for me, but I didn't know the details of the faith, and I couldn't answer any doctrinal questions. All I knew was that Jesus was real, and he saved me.

John said the best way to do a legitimate, bona fide mission was to wear a sandwich board and hand out tracts. I never heard of a tract, and I never wore a sandwich board, but who was I to argue with a 4-year-old Christian. So that Saturday morning we wrote our message on the white cardboard sheets. My text was simple. The one hanging over my chest shouted. 'Jesus Loves You'. The one hanging on my back read, 'Jesus Died for Your Sin'. So, armed and ready, with our hands full of tracts, the two walking billboards hit the town.

It was a learning experience. Most people crossed the street before we got to them, so we went to the local grocery store and accosted people there. We handed out quite a few tracts before the management asked us to leave. Some weeks later, we decided to drop the sandwich-board idea. People just weren't ready for it. It was too intense and in your face, but it sure helped us break the ice for getting on to the streets with our faith. We were zealous, but we didn't have a lot of savvy or understanding, biblically or socially.[10]

Krishna

I remember one evening talking to a Hare Krishna follower. The person wore a saffron robe and was handing out copies of the *Bhagavad Gita*.[11] Others were standing around chanting, '*Ramah, Ramah, Krishna, Krishna, Ramah, Ramah.*'

I approached them, armed with a small Gideon New Testament. The Bible says the word of God is a mighty, two-edged sword, but that evening, I might as well have been standing there with a dull pocket knife.[12] I only had half the text, and I didn't know how to navigate or use it.

They tried to convince me that Krishna was the answer, and Krishna was in the Bible. I knew that wasn't right, but I didn't know how to refute it, so I asked them to show me. They opened up my New Testament to Matthew 2:18 and read, 'A voice is heard in Ramah.' Then they continued chanting, '*Ramah, Ramah, Krishna, Krishna, Ramah, Ramah.*'

The word *Ramah* was the proof text. I was shocked. I didn't know what to say. 'That's not in the Bible!' I exclaimed. They then pointed to it and had me read it.

My witness to the reality of Jesus was falling apart. My blade was dull and needed sharpening. Not wanting to admit defeat I blurted out: 'This must not be a real Bible. Some Krishna person must have had this printed and added that verse in there.' They just looked at me and said, 'But this is your book!'

Well, I still denied Krishna was in the Bible. It didn't matter how many times the word *Ramah* was in the pages. I had found reality, and Krishna was not part of the picture. I didn't care who tried to convince me otherwise. I went home feeling defeated on the battlefield, but still holding on to my Commander in Chief, Jesus Christ.

The Warlock

Daryl was another friend who started attending the hippie church. He said he once made a giant, 20-foot, wax dragon.

I'm sure it was impressive because Daryl was one of the most realistic and talented artists I had ever met. To Daryl, though, that dragon was more than a work of art. He said the thing talked to him. It told him it would come to life and walk with him down the street. I thought this guy took one hit of LSD too many. But after he told me of his occult involvement and that he was training to be a warlock, a talking dragon seemed a bit more credible.

The year Daryl became a Christian he turned away from that warlock thingy and destroyed the dragon. One day when I visited him in the studio, he was working on a portrait of Jesus. It was emotive, realistic and big. Of course, he didn't have a clue what Jesus looked like, but Daryl painted him anyway. I had no problem with this. It was better than making a talking, demon-possessed dragon.

Daryl never joined our bona fide mission, and he refused to wear a sandwich board. He was too cool for that. Instead, my artist friend would visit the local sauna and make it unbearably hot by pouring water on the stones to increase the steam. Then he turned off the light and shut the door with everyone inside. It was pitch black in there as he announced, 'Now let me tell you what hell is going to be like.'

Everyone freaked out, but before a hand groped for the door, he continued his semi-bona fide mission telling them how Jesus saved him. I don't know how effective this evangelism was, but at least it was creative and dramatic. It was something only Daryl would do.

The Latter-day Saints

Two other friends from the hippie church and I once encountered a couple of Latter-day Saints (Mormons) on the street.

They wanted us to join their church. The discussion went on for quite a while. My friend Roger, who was more knowledge-able than me, was doing most of the talking, but the debate wasn't shifting anyone's doctrinal position. So Roger, who had a lot of faith, said to them:

> You know this is getting us nowhere. Let's pray and ask God to show us who is right. I'm going to flip a coin, and if it comes up heads, God is telling you that we are right and you will leave your church and join our congregation. On the other hand, if it comes up tails, then God is telling us that you are correct and we will leave our church and become Mormons.

Whoa! I found this a bit scary. I don't know if God wants us to evangelise like this or not, but I knew I wasn't going to join the Latter-day Saints on the flip of a coin. They weren't going to join our congregation either; they just shook their heads and walked away. Afterwards, I found what Roger did wasn't entirely unprecedented or unbiblical. Instead of flipping a coin, the Bible calls it casting lots.[13] It takes a lot of faith to flip a coin and trust God to direct the outcome.

The Big Question

I now look back over those early, formative years as a Christian and can't help but smile. We stepped into the kingdom of God like little children visiting Disneyland for the first time. We couldn't wait to tell others the good news as the word 'gospel' quickly entered our vocabulary. It was one of those religious words every Christian values, but what exactly is the gospel?

The more I read the statements of Jesus, the more I real-ised there was a disconnect. I wasn't proclaiming what Jesus proclaimed as the gospel, and neither were my friends. The gospel Jesus proclaimed was the gospel of the kingdom. It was the only gospel Jesus preached.

I find it strange that when the gospel is spoken of in many congregations, or on the streets, the kingdom rarely gets a mention. Do we believe that the good news for the world is something different from what Jesus proclaimed and thought it to be? In almost every town, city, country and continent, we hear people pray:

> your kingdom come,
> your will be done,
>   on earth as it is in heaven. (Matt. 6:10)

Two thousand years on, Christians still pray this, and we know it's the will of God because Jesus told us to do it. Has God ever answered that prayer? How would we know if he answered that prayer? How much of the kingdom should we expect without slipping into an over-realised or under-realised theology?

As a disciple, I needed to know what the gospel of the kingdom was about because I want to value what Jesus values. As a pastor, I needed to know because of the divine responsibility entrusted to me. As an Old Testament lecturer, I needed to know because this is the overarching theme of the Bible. If I am to 'seek first the kingdom of God and his righteousness', I need to know what I'm looking for and what it looks like when I encounter it.[14] The main question is, what did Jesus have in mind when he spoke of the kingdom of God?

Like a jigsaw puzzle, I had all these scriptural pieces of the kingdom laid out in front of me, but I didn't know how to put them together. I needed to see the picture on the box. So I prayed and studied, read and prayed. Then over the months and years, the various pieces started to come together. This completed picture has revolutionised my theology, life and praxis. To me, the revelation of the kingdom is a heart transformation that I have been building on ever since. I now understand why the kingdom of God is good news for our towns, our cities, our homes and families. I see why Jesus and the twelve disciples proclaimed this message. It's an incredible story – love invades an orphaned planet. It is the greatest show on earth. This book is my attempt to articulate this revelation.

Sinking the Ship

The most notorious maritime disaster of the twentieth century is the sinking of the *Titanic*. We write about it. We talk about it on the radio. We watch it on the television and our movie screens. It's embedded in our psyche. Who hasn't heard of, or commented on, the *Titanic*? It was constructed in the city of Belfast, Northern Ireland, and it sank.

Thousands of shipyard workers at Harland and Wolff applied their particular skills to make this the greatest luxury ship to sail the Atlantic. With pride, the city of Belfast paid close attention to that maiden voyage. The day it went down, the city mourned. For years the *Titanic* was rarely mentioned on the streets; it was too painful.

Eight decades later, I ministered as a pastor on the Newtownards Road in East Belfast. The church is less than a mile from the Harland and Wolff Shipyard. Almost every great-grandfather in this city pounded rivets, welded or worked with wood to build that ship. The local street artists still paint murals depicting it. When I heard Belfast was going to transform the acreage surrounding the shipyard into a world tourist attraction, my immediate response was: 'What? Why would you want to draw attention to one of the city's greatest disasters? Why open up and memorialise one of our deepest wounds? Why not do something more positive? Perhaps commemorate a ship that's still floating.' At that time, only an American like me would have asked such questions. I just didn't get it.

Today the Titanic Quarter of Belfast is thriving. It's attracting people from all over the planet. In 2016 the Titanic museum was voted the best tourist attraction in the world.[1] I even worked in the Titanic Quarter as a chaplain, but that's not when I got it. The day I understood what the *Titanic* meant to the city and the families of Belfast was when a local person on the street said to me, 'Richard, it may have sunk, but when it left this dock it was perfect.'

That's when I got it. The city didn't want to sensationalise the disaster. Instead, the people of Belfast took great pride in the artistry, the labour, the dedication, the vision to create a luxury ship so big and grand the world would stand in awe.

That ship didn't sink because the work was shoddy; it went down due to navigational errors and poor handling at sea. The captain and crew had all the training and ability they needed to make that maiden voyage a success. There was nothing to prevent a safe and joyful entry into New York Harbour. All the captain and crew had to do was follow their training and pay attention to the manual.

I tell this story because the imagery helps communicate the heart and history of the kingdom of God. The origins of the kingdom in the first three chapters of Genesis are surprisingly similar to the *Titanic* story. People can be quick to point the finger and blame the Creator for all the wrongs in this world, but many times, we just don't get it.

First Creation Story

The creation story of Genesis is a divinely inspired work of literary genius. The fact that there are two creation stories set side by side without warning or explanation is part of that genius. The first creation story beginning at Genesis 1:1 is written from a heavenly perspective. God is outside of creation, speaking things into being. The second creation story starts at Genesis 2:4. Here the account is repeated but from ground level. It's the human viewpoint. God bends down and works with the soil, physically forming, shaping and breathing life into the creatures. These two narratives give us the initial picture of the kingdom of God. The first one shows us what the kingdom looked like before it left the harbour. The second one tells us what happened after Adam and Eve took the helm.

Some may be surprised to find the first creation story does more than outline a series of events; it's communicating a much deeper truth. We focus upon the seven-day timescale, and rigorously defend it, because of the questions we ask and the ideological battles we fight.[2] Our English versions of the Bible also invite this interpretation of the text, as though the timescale is the first truth the inspired writer is trying to communicate.[3]

Unfortunately, the part we miss is untranslatable. It doesn't mean the words of our translations are inaccurate. However, it is a challenge to transpose the words of one language to another and still maintain the structural integrity of the original text. It's the Hebrew structure of the first creation story that reveals the author's emphasis and primary concern.

In the ancient Near East, specific numbers held more weight than their numerical value. We are no different. Some of our numbers take on extra content. When we hear someone mention the number thirteen, usually our first response is, 'unlucky'. Not that we're superstitious, but it's embedded in our culture. The same is true with the number seven. It's our conventional number for luck.

To the people of the ancient Near East, the number seven was also an exceptional digit, but it didn't signify luck; instead, it stood for perfection, completeness and wholeness. Perfection is the point the first creation story is trying to get across. When the ship left the dock, it was perfect.

As I teach the book of Genesis, I tell the students that if this first chapter was a rock and I hit it with a hammer, it would break into seven pieces. If I hit any of those seven pieces with a hammer, they'd also split into groups of seven. In the Hebrew text, the first sentence is made up of seven words. The second sentence is made up of fourteen words (2x7). After the opening verse (1:1), the panorama of creation is displayed in seven paragraphs. Many of the words and phrases in the narrative appear seven times, or in multiples of seven.[4]

The climax of the creation week (day 7) also drives home the point. In the centre of the paragraph are three consecutive phrases, and the word 'seven' appears in each one of them. 'By the seventh day God had finished the work he had been doing; so on the seventh day he rested from all his work. Then God blessed the seventh day and made it holy' (Gen. 2:2–3).

The divine appraisals also highlight the perfection of the created order. The fact that God keeps repeating how good it is, and sums it all up with 'very good', adds weight to the word 'good'. It is God's way of saying, 'When this *Titanic* left the harbour, it was perfect.'

Perfection is what God, through the inspired writer, is trying to convey. There was nothing wrong with creation when it left the pier. This *Titanic* is impeccable. The kingdom of God on earth is without flaw. Nothing can be added to it, or changed, to make it better. It is very good.

Second Creation Story

Now let's wade into a different pool. This one is gritty and dark. The story is told from an earthly perspective. It tells us what happened when the boat left the dock. There is probably no other narrative in the Bible that has triggered our imagination and impacted our theology as has Genesis 2 and 3. God chose Adam to take the helm and steer the ship on its maiden voyage. He trained him. Every evening the Creator and Adam would have a walk around the deck. 'Adam, I'm appointing you to captain this ship. Take inventory of the cargo.'[5] Stay clear of the iceberg.'[6]

Well, we know the tale, don't we? Adam and the first mate run the ship into a wall of ice, and there it still flounders. The ship is afloat, but it's no longer perfect. It's damaged and slowly going down.[7] Many blame God for the damage. 'Why did you make me like this? Why do all these bad things happen?'

What the writer of Genesis wants us to know is that the ship was perfect when it left the shore. This is why we have two creation stories side by side. The boat didn't go down because of internal or external flaws. It's sinking because the captain didn't heed the Creator's manual. He ran the ship into the iceberg, and we're still reeling from the event.

We try to keep the ship afloat in its damaged state, which isn't a bad thing. We want to save the planet. We do what we can to patch the holes, regain purpose, dominion, joy, peace, justice, love, fulfilment, security, but now we do it from a different manual. As pastors, we often preach about what we lost in the second creation story, but what we often overlook is what we gained. We acquired a new set of instructions. It's a new set of rules on how to conduct life. It's called the 'knowledge of good and evil'.[8] The New Testament calls it the 'wisdom of this world'.[9]

> When the woman saw that the fruit of the tree was good for food and pleasing to the eye, and also desirable for gaining wisdom, she took some and ate it. She also gave some to her husband, who was with her, and he ate it. (Gen. 3:6)

Adam and Eve gained wisdom but lost a close relationship with the source of all wisdom. So, branded with the knowledge of good and evil, the couple leave the garden dragging us with them. As time goes on, we realise we'll never get off this boat alive by ourselves, so we reach out to God using the manual handed to us. As generations march across the stage, the image of God becomes distorted; people no longer know what he is like or who he is. He's indistinct; distant. We have faint memories of those evening strolls. They brush our heart like a wisp of air, a primordial echo – a longing. The memory lingers just beyond our reach and comprehension. We don't know who we are because we lost sight of who he is. The image is blurred.[10]

In the first eleven chapters of Genesis, we find humanity going from bad to worse. These are four vivid pictures of a sinking ship: the expulsion from Eden, Cain kills Abel, the flood and the Babel incident. There isn't much love or hope in these early chapters. We're left hanging to the side of the boat waiting to die. It appears that even God finds it disturbing. 'The LORD regretted that he had made human beings on the earth, and his heart was deeply troubled' (Gen. 6:6).

The Promise

So the Creator throws out a lifeline. It's a beacon of hope. It shines across the pages. It comes in the form of a promise, conveyed in words that hold the same creative force as when God said, 'Let there be light.' To grasp the theological significance of what we are reading, we again have to look at the structure. The promise uses the same scaffolding we find in the first creation story; it's the number of perfection. There are seven actions interlaced with the word 'bless'. It's no coincidence. It's intentional.

1. I will make you into a great nation,
2. and I will bless you;
3. I will make your name great,
4. and you will be a blessing.
5. I will bless those who bless you,
6. and whoever curses you I will curse;
7. and all peoples on earth
   will be blessed through you. (Gen. 12:2–3)

Immediately we are drawn back to the created order before the ship hit the iceberg. The promise is a snapshot of the kingdom of God. It comes quietly. It's as small as a mustard seed. It enters our soil unnoticed by everyone except Abraham. God didn't plant the promise on earth for our benefit; he planted it for his glory. The Creator has a vision of what the kingdom should look like, and he's not going to rest until he sees it.[11]

The word 'bless' occurs five times in these seven phrases. In contrast, the word 'curse' appears five times in Genesis 1 – 11.[12] Gordon Wenham suggests this is the writer's way of telling us the promise given to Abraham will negate all the curses that have gone before it.[13] This observation may be overstated, but theologically it captures the fundamental nature and heart of the text. The multiple occurrences of the word 'bless' is making a point. It's a nostalgic nudge towards the Eden we forfeited. Notice, too, the blessing is progressive and heading towards a goal.

1. I will bless you.
2. You will be a blessing.
3. I will bless those who bless you.
4. In you all the families of the earth shall be blessed.

The blessing starts with one individual and ends with all the people of earth. It's a spiritual seed planted in our soil. Its ful-filment will be the manifestation of the kingdom of God on this planet; the good news Jesus proclaimed throughout his ministry.

> Again he said, 'What shall we say the kingdom of God is like, or what parable shall we use to describe it? It is like a mustard seed, which is the smallest of all seeds on earth. Yet when planted, it grows and becomes the largest of all garden plants, with such big branches that the birds can perch in its shade.' (Mark 4:30–32)

Intermission

Well, the stage is now set. We caught a glimpse of the kingdom of God in the first creation story. The second creation story opens the curtain a little bit wider, but the scene is short, and it's filmed in black and white. We can only imagine what the kingdom of God looked like: walking in paradise with a good Father, the Creator of the universe. The sad thing is, this isn't the world we know. By the end of Genesis 11, we are left hang-ing on the side of the sinking ship, treading water, marking time. The world outside of the garden is violent, scary, chaotic, unloving and cursed. The boat has a hole in it, and we're all going down with the ship. Lord, have mercy.

The brilliance of Genesis is that God doesn't leave us dan-gling there, but he doesn't hand us all of the survival notes either. Don't go looking for *Ten Easy Steps to Happy Sailing* in these troubled waters. Those chapters may be on the shelf of our Christian bookshop, but we won't find them in Genesis. Instead, God draws us into a reality show. The strolls through paradise on a balmy evening are over. Now the Almighty invites us to walk in the footsteps of four chosen individuals. Here, life smacks us in the face. It's hard going. The halcyon days are over. Theologically, these patriarchs and their families are heading back to Eden, and God drops us into their world to show us how they did it.

Individually, each story is anchored to the promise God gave Abraham in Genesis 12. Within this promise, there are four major components:

1. Descendants
2. Land
3. Great Name
4. Mediation of blessing to the world.

This sets the stage for the kingdom of God on earth. It shows us what the kingdom is to look like on this planet. Each component is uniquely mirrored in the life of these individuals: Abraham, Isaac, Jacob and Joseph. What we sometimes overlook when reading these stories is the struggle each of them had with particular elements of the promise.

1. Abraham's main obstacle was descendants.
2. Isaac's primary issue was the land.
3. Jacob's key battle centres on the great name.
4. Joseph is the only one who blesses the entire known world.

Can you see the pattern here? The four elements of the promise are displayed in the lives of four individuals over four generations. These are the four corner pieces of the puzzle we are trying to put together regarding the kingdom.

In Genesis 1 – 11, we have four accounts of failure and gloom (Eden, Cain, the flood and the Babel episode). In Genesis 12 – 50, we have four stories of hope. The hope chapters are four times as long as the ones that plunge us into the pit of despair. This pattern is also theologically charged.

As we pick up each of these four corner pieces, they will help us make sense of all the other pieces laid out on the table. It's the starting point. Genesis sets the stage for the greatest show on earth. Love is invading an orphaned planet.

Shaking the Box

When I was growing up, gifts would appear under the Christmas tree a week before the big day. It was fun. My brother and I would look to see whose name was on the package. Then we'd compare the size and check whose gift was larger or weighed more. Of course, we had the rattling session, trying to guess what was inside. We had a good idea, but there was still a question mark about the details. What will it be like to touch it, play with it and use it? How will it fit into our room? What colour is it? However, there was one thing we both knew for sure: if your name was on that package, it was yours.

Then on Christmas Day you'd witness a frenzy of elbows and kneecaps bouncing around the tree as my brother and I leapt from gift to gift, ripping paper, whooping and hollering like mad things let out of a cage. It was an exhibition of glee. Of course, we had no problem knowing which gift to open because we had them all memorised. We knew which ones had our name on them.

This illustration is what it looks like to have biblical hope. When the Bible mentions hope, it isn't talking about wishful thinking for what we don't possess. Hope recognises a gift is yours, even though you haven't opened it yet. You know it's yours because God stamped your name on it. Faith knows one day you will hold it. Faith keeps hope alive. Faith and hope go hand in hand. 'Now faith is confidence in what we hope for and assurance about what we do not see' (Heb. 11:1).

Abraham received his package in Genesis 12. It's the hope for a sinking ship. His name is written all over it. Throughout his life, he will shake the box and imagine what the gift will look like unwrapped. For Abraham, the promise is a legacy stretching far beyond his generation and regional concerns. By faith, he has to hold on to it and interact with it, and dream, and pray about it. Abraham has to rip off the paper, cut the ribbon and open the lid.

The promise recorded in Genesis 12:2–3 requires obedience and faith. Abraham will have to surrender the knowledge of good and evil and follow a new path that will lead humanity back to the perfection of the created order; the manifestation of the kingdom of God on earth. But the moment Abraham tries to open the gift, his hands grow limp. You can hear the gears grinding before he even gets to the starting line. To see the promise fulfilled, he needs children. A great nation requires citizens. God said, 'To your offspring I will give this land' (Gen. 12:7). Abraham doesn't have any offspring, and his wife Sarah is barren.[1] Now, that's a kick in the teeth. What's he to do with that?

So Abraham shakes the package and latches on to his nephew Lot. He apparently thinks, 'Since my wife and I can't have children, Lot must be the descendant God chose for me.' So Abraham takes Lot to Canaan with him.[2] Lot, however, is soon disqualified and eventually sets up camp in Sodom.[3] Again, Abraham is back to square one. So he wisely brings the package before God and gives it another shake.

How am I to open the gift? I don't have any human means to get descendants. Without descendants, I have no one to possess the land. If I have no one to possess the land, then there is no one to confer a great name upon, and no one to bless the world. God, something's just not adding up here.[4]

At this point in the narrative, Abraham is still holding on to the knowledge of good and evil. He can't help it. It's all he knows. He was born with it. Throughout Genesis, God is coaxing the patriarchs to lay down the manual of good and evil and pick up the guidebook of the kingdom. The promise depends on it. The kingdom of God can't grow in soil fertilised with the knowledge of good and evil.

So the Creator gives Abraham another peek into the box. 'This man will not be your heir, but a son who is your own flesh and blood will be your heir' (Gen. 15:4). Whoa! Now that's news. Why didn't God mention this little fact earlier? Why keep it a secret? Where does Sarah, Abraham's wife, fit into this picture, as she's the barren one? Why doesn't God mention her? Curious, isn't it? So, like most husbands, Abraham tells his wife what God revealed to him. Sarah, in turn, picks up her manual of the knowledge of good and evil and tells Abraham to procreate with her servant Hagar. It makes sense. It's logical in light of what God has revealed so far.[5]

We watch Abraham embrace Ishmael, the son born of Hagar. He rationally assumes Ishmael is the chosen one. Why wouldn't he? But, later on in the story, we surprisingly discover this is not to be the case.[6] Ishmael is not God's chosen descendent, but why not? Ishmael came from Abraham's body, didn't he? Sarah is still barren, isn't she? Doesn't the manual of the knowledge of good and evil tell us Ishmael is the only reasonable option?

So again, we find Abraham and Sarah standing before the Creator giving the box a third shake: 'What's exactly in this package?' God gives them another peek and tells them how the ongoing saga is going to play out, 'Your wife Sarah will bear you a son, and you will call him Isaac' (Gen. 17:19).

What? This is the first time God mentions Sarah and her infertility. Does this seem strange to you? Is this poor management? It makes you wonder why God didn't tell Abraham this in the first place. It would have saved Abraham and Sarah years of grief and disappointment. Why didn't God reveal this pertinent bit of information back in Genesis 12? Why did God give a childless couple an impossible promise in the first place, and then drag it out through decades of setback and disappointment? Well, it all has to do with the kingdom of God and how the kingdom works. God is preparing the soil for the growth of his mustard seed.

Faith and the Knowledge of Good and Evil

Have you ever wondered why God is so fixated on faith? Our salvation is by faith. We are healed and see miracles by faith. Hebrews 11:6 tells us we can't possibly please God without it. I often hear people on the street ask: 'Why doesn't God reveal himself so I can see him, feel him or audibly hear his voice? Why can't science prove his existence? Why all the mystery?'

These are the kinds of questions the manual of good and evil prompts us to ask because it makes sense to us. If the one true God exists, why doesn't he make a scene and shout, 'Here I am'? These questions sound logical because we ask them from the deck of a sinking ship, but God is working from a different vantage point.

'For my thoughts are not your thoughts,
    neither are your ways my ways,'

                                    declares the LORD.

'As the heavens are higher than the earth,
    so are my ways higher than your ways
    and my thoughts than your thoughts.' (Isa. 55:8–9)

The Creator is gently guiding the human race to lay down the knowledge of good and evil because it doesn't promote the life of God. In us, it's sense-driven. It relies on what we see, feel, hear and experience in the material world.[7] The chief opposition of faith isn't unbelief; it's what we see with our eyes. It's allowing our physical senses to have the final word regarding reality. We often let what we observe with our eyes dictate the standards and filter of our hearts.[8]

For in this hope we were saved. But hope that is seen is no hope at all. Who hopes for what they already have? But if we hope for what we do not yet have, we wait for it patiently. (Rom. 8:24–5)

So we fix our eyes not on what is seen, but on what is unseen, since what is seen is temporary, but what is unseen is eternal. (2 Cor. 4:18)

Now faith is confidence in what we hope for and assurance about what we do not see. (Heb. 11:1)

By faith we understand that the universe was formed at God's command, so that what is seen was not made out of what was visible. (Heb. 11:3)

Though you have not seen him, you love him; and even though you do not see him now, you believe in him and are filled with an inexpressible and glorious joy. (1 Pet. 1:8)

God is trying to free us from this prison. We've crawled into a little cage, and God is prying it open. He's prompting us to loosen our grip on the manual of good and evil. We can't silence the voice human ears can't hear, or allow what we see with our natural eyes to quench the faith that springs from a heavenly vision.

As soon as Adam and Eve ate from the tree, the text tells us, 'The eyes of both of them were opened, and they realised that they were naked' (Gen. 3:7). This is a poetic way of saying they are now led by what they see. It affects the course of their life. Their behaviour exemplifies it. They take on a human, victim mentality. Now humanity points the finger at everyone but themselves.[9] Our senses and self-preservation drive us. Our soul is curved in on itself (*incurvatus in se*[10]).

We reached for the tree. We took the initiative, and we ate. We still hold the fruit in our hands. It's dripping from our lips. It's stamped into our mind. We hold tightly to the manual: the knowledge of good and evil; the wisdom of this world. We don't realise how far it has affected and permeated us. We conduct our lives from this manual, and the results are apparent: it's chaos.

Fortunately, God will not leave his people broken and damaged this way. So, in his wisdom, he sets kingdom principles in motion. We consciously ate the fruit; now God wants us to spit it out and deliberately lay it down. God's not going to rip the manual out of our hands; instead, he invites us to surrender it. The Almighty puts us in situations that facilitate this surrender.

We reject the manual of the knowledge of good and evil each time we step out in faith. That's why faith is so important to God. 'The righteous will live by faith.'[11] When we act on the word of God, we cast off the lies we've been feeding on. Jesus said, 'The truth will set you free' (John 8:32).

God is always prompting us to step outside the boundaries of our natural senses. Self-preservation is no longer to be the prime motivator of our existence. Each fence we climb over is another step closer to Eden. It's how we gain passage on the life raft. Faith is taking one step further than the road we see. It's reaching one inch beyond what we feel. It's making a declaration that transcends our life experience. Faith is embracing a thought that defies all logic. When Peter stepped out of the boat and walked on water, he willingly laid down the manual of good and evil and followed the king of the kingdom.[12] The mustard seed can't grow in faithless soil.[13]

The road God mapped out for Abraham and Sarah provoked this faith. The revelation regarding the promise unfolds gradually throughout their story. Abraham and Sarah interact with the promise, but only at the level of their understanding. Each step of the journey deepens their trust in what they cannot see. God observes their choices. In Genesis 12, God monitors Abraham. In Genesis 15 and 16, God watches Sarah.[14] In Genesis 17, they both receive the reward. We cannot allow the wisdom of this world to guide us and follow God at the same time.[15] The mustard seed only grows in soil fertilised by faith.

Abraham and Sarah's names were on the package from the beginning. They kept shaking the gift and walking forward. They never gave up. They desperately wanted to open the box that had their name on it. They required a descendant, or the promise would go with them to the grave. God was so impressed by their faith; he eventually stamped their name on the gift itself, not just the packaging. It's a name worthy of the commitment and perseverance they demonstrate.

> No longer will you be called Abram; your name will be Abraham, for I have made you a father of many nations. (Gen. 17:5)[16]

> God also said to Abraham, 'As for Sarai your wife, you are no longer to call her Sarai; her name will be Sarah. I will bless her and will surely give you a son by her. I will bless her so that she will be the mother of nations; kings of peoples will come from her.' (Gen. 17:15–16)

The Finish Line

Now, this would've been an excellent place to end the story, wouldn't it: 'And they both lived happily ever after'? Many people, Christian and otherwise, actually wish the story did end here because what follows offends us. We don't like it. Every parent cringes at the thought of it. It's where people often draw the line and say, 'No!'

> Then God said, 'Take your son, your only son, whom you love – Isaac – and go to the region of Moriah. Sacrifice him there as a burnt offering on a mountain that I will show you.' (Gen. 22:2)

This story is out there. It prises open our little logic box. It smashes all those cherished shards of orthodoxy we guard inside of it. We say: 'Can this be God speaking? It sounds more like the serpent, not our Creator.' But, remember, Abraham is the soil from which the mustard seed of the kingdom is to sprout. Abraham holds the plans of the life raft that will carry humanity back to Genesis 1.

How far will Abraham's faith stretch? How far down the road will he go? If Abraham kills Isaac, it wouldn't just be a case of filicide. To Abraham, his son Isaac is the encapsulation of all his encounters with God. Isaac is the promise personified. All the other options have been exhausted: Isaac is it.

Unlike many of us, Abraham doesn't even question God's command, which is also alarming. He humbly packs the bags, grabs his boy, takes him to the top of the mountain, raises the knife . . . Metaphorically speaking Abraham wasn't just holding a blade in his hand that day; he was clutching the handbook of the kingdom of God. He was raising it above the knowledge of good and evil. Beyond all logic, Abraham rejects the manual handed to him in Eden. He strikes a final death blow to the serpent's lies on how to conduct life in this world. To Abraham, this was the *coup de grâce*.[17] It is the death blow to the manual of the knowledge of good and evil in his life. It's the kind of soil in which God plants the seed of the kingdom.

Can you grasp the faith and trust Abraham displayed here? It is exemplary. This act was about the promise, not Isaac, his son. We focus on the fate of Isaac and let that cloud what God is trying to tell us. God said, 'Take your son, your only son Isaac, whom you love.' We know that Isaac wasn't Abraham's only son. Isaac had a brother called Ishmael. The writer is giving us the parameters of the test. It's not about the brother or the son. It's about the promise, the fate of the promise, the seed of the kingdom, not the future of Isaac as a person.

By faith Abraham, when God tested him, offered Isaac as a sacrifice. He who had embraced the promises was about to sacrifice

his one and only son, even though God had said to him, 'It is
through Isaac that your offspring will be reckoned.' Abraham reasoned that God could even raise the dead, and so in a manner of
speaking he did receive Isaac back from death. (Heb. 11:17–19)

Abraham valued what God told him in the past, but he knows
he can't ignore what God is commanding him in the present,
even though it breaches his theology and offends the logical
mind. So Abraham explores what is and isn't spelt out. He
searches for God in the mystery. Abraham doesn't ignore the
gap that often looms between logic and obedience. Instead,
he rattles the package. The writer of Hebrews elaborates this
when he says, 'Abraham reasoned that God could even raise the
dead.'[18] Here is one of the most significant revelations Abraham
had of God, and it wasn't discovered in the words of the promise, or in the command to offer up his son (which made no
reasonable sense). He finds the revelation in the gap; that silent
space between God's promise and the ludicrous command that
warred against it.[19]

It was the road, the process God led him on, that prompted
Abraham's willingness to sacrifice his son by faith. In many
ways, Abraham had already sacrificed two possible heirs: Lot,
and Ishmael. Through these experiences, Abraham learned
God could be trusted. Now Abraham is asked to make the ultimate sacrifice: Isaac. Each step of the way, God was inviting
Abraham and Sarah to pick up the handbook of the kingdom
and throw the other one down. The New Testament calls this
action the renewing of our mind.[20]

Then he reached out his hand and took the knife to slay his son.
But the angel of the LORD called out to him from heaven, 'Abraham! Abraham!'

'Here I am,' he replied.

'Do not lay a hand on the boy,' he said. 'Do not do anything to him. Now I know that you fear God, because you have not with-held from me your son, your only son.' (Gen. 22:10–12)

Intermission

What drives the Abraham story is the search for an heir. God was plotting Abraham's choices each step of the way. He was stretching him; giving him opportunities to pick up the hand-book of the kingdom and lay down the knowledge of good and evil. It was not a smooth ride, but the repercussions of his obe-dience and faith have changed the world. The mustard seed of the kingdom is now planted in our soil, and it is still growing.

Once Abraham's goal regarding descendants is achieved, he is tested once more in that same arena; he must sacrifice his son Isaac. The theological significance will become more evident as we explore the lives of the other three patriarchs. Abraham's story is the first corner piece to the puzzle we are trying to assemble. It is foundational to our understanding and praxis of God's kingdom.

Passport Denied

Like his father Abraham, Isaac also struggles with the promise, but it isn't with descendants. Abraham had already won that battle. However, there is a déjà vu moment; Isaac's wife is barren, just like Sarah. But in one verse, the crisis is quickly defused. Isaac prays, God answers, and Rebekah carries twins.[1] How easy was that? The author wants us to know that for Isaac and Rebekah, the struggle for descendants is not the issue they will wrestle with regarding the promise. Instead, Isaac's story is about real estate: the promised land itself.

Of the four patriarchs examined in Genesis, Isaac is the only one who wasn't allowed to leave Canaan. Abraham tells his servant to go back to Abraham's hometown and arrange a marriage for Isaac.[2] Abraham wanted Isaac to marry someone from his tribe back in the motherland, not a Canaanite woman. So the servant weighs up the options and asks Abraham what he should do if no one returns with him. Should he take Isaac back there and let him chose his wife? Abraham's response is a quick and adamant, 'No!'[3]

Now, this episode wouldn't be that significant if it was the only time Isaac was coerced to stay in Canaan. Two chapters later, God also commands Isaac not to leave the land promised to him.

> Now there was a famine in the land – besides the previous famine
> in Abraham's time – and Isaac went to Abimelek king of the Phil-
> istines in Gerar. The LORD appeared to Isaac and said, 'Do not
> go down to Egypt; live in the land where I tell you to live. Stay
> in this land for a while, and I will be with you and will bless you.
> For to you and your descendants I will give all these lands and will
> confirm the oath I swore to your father Abraham.' (Gen. 26:1–3)[4]

Here, the writer of Genesis is making a comparison between
Isaac's and Abraham's situations. Abraham survived an earlier
famine by leaving the land and going down to Egypt.[5] Leaving
the land wasn't a problem for Abraham. When famine came,
Abraham packed his bags and off he went. When Isaac faces a
famine just as severe as his father suffered, God personally tells
Isaac, 'Do not go down to Egypt.'

It takes a lot of faith to stay in the land during a famine,
especially when you know there is food over the border. It's just
not logical to hang around and die. The manual of good and
evil says, 'Catch a bus to Cairo and buy a burger, get a pizza,
bring back some bagels, be proactive; do something to save
your family. I mean, the other three patriarchs left the land
because of adverse circumstances and famine; why shouldn't
you?'[6]

At a future date, Jacob and all his sons will journey to Egypt
to escape starvation.[7] God will even appear to Jacob and tell
him, 'Do not be afraid to go down to Egypt, for I will make
you into a great nation there. I will go down to Egypt with you'
(Gen. 46:3–4). It seems as though God and everyone else can
go to Egypt because of various famines, but when Isaac faces a
famine in the promised land, he's commanded by God not to
go there.

So, like his father Abraham, Isaac obeys. What else can he do? He rattles the box under the Christmas tree and decides the only option left to him is to find water and plant a garden. It's a step of faith. Now I am no gardener, but who plants a garden during a famine? God honours the faith of Isaac like he praised the faith of Abraham. 'Isaac planted crops in that land and the same year reaped a hundredfold, because the LORD blessed him. The man became rich, and his wealth continued to grow until he became very wealthy' (Gen. 26:12–13).

God miraculously blesses Isaac for survival in a famine-ridden land, a blessing that was beyond the expectation and experience of the other three patriarchs. It's one of the main reasons Abimelech and Phicol later confess to Isaac, 'We saw clearly that the LORD was with you' (Gen. 26:28).

Isaac obeys God's directive not to leave the land, and he prospers in it. Once Isaac sees the positive result of his obedience, he faces one more trial; like sumo wrestlers, the Philistines attempt to push him over the border. Each time Isaac digs a well to water his crops and growing herds the Philistines come and confiscate it. Abimelech approaches Isaac and tells him to leave the area.[8] On two occasions, the Philistines negate Isaac's claim to the land by filling up his family wells.[9] Fortunately, Isaac's third attempt to stay in the area is successful.[10] By faith, Isaac never surrendered or gave up the right to the land God had promised. Subsequently, Genesis 26 ends with several symbolic claims upon the land: Isaac pitches his tent and builds an altar,[11] he digs another well,[12] and he ratifies a peace agreement between himself and Abimelech.[13]

Isaac was a man of faith. Like his father before him, he too faced impossible, illogical commands in adverse circumstances. Isaac could have ignored the voice of God and followed his family's example: 'Go south, young man, and get a burger or two.' Isaac always had a logical excuse to fall back on: 'Well, my father Abraham did it. If it was alright for him, it must be alright for me.'[14] But Isaac valued the handbook of the kingdom more than the wisdom of this world. By faith, he leaned into the kingdom of God. There you can reap a full harvest during a famine. You can prosper while those around you are struggling to survive.

Intermission

Abraham's struggle regarding the promise centred on progeny; Isaac's battle was real estate. The story of Isaac has to do with roots; how deep will they go? Will he let circumstances rule his judgement? Will he allow the appetites and what he sees with his eyes umpire his life? No! He embraced the handbook of the kingdom and ignored the manual of good and evil, the wisdom of this world. Isaac stood his ground and saw the reward of obedience. His last recorded trial also focused on real estate. The decision to settle in the land was violently challenged, but it drove his roots deeper into Canaan's soil, and God established him there.

Reading the four stories in Genesis 12 – 50 is a pilgrimage. God is taking us somewhere. The stories of Abraham, Isaac, Jacob and Joseph are the four corner pieces to one puzzle. Isaac's foothold in Canaan is the second corner piece. If we read these individual narratives in isolation from each other, we can easily miss the point. So, let's move on to the third corner piece of the puzzle and take a few steps down the road Jacob travelled. His primary battle is on the same playing field but not with the same issues as faced by Abraham and Isaac. Jacob's fight is with himself, but God knows how to woo the human heart.

What's in a Name?

God leads Jacob on a path similar to Abraham and Isaac but, as an individual, Jacob is a bit more complicated than his forefathers. Jacob is a third-generation patriarch. He doesn't have the same fire in his belly as his ancestor Abraham. Jacob will do anything to get the blessing, but not the source of that blessing. He wants the gift but is ambivalent about the giver. This patriarch won't surrender the knowledge of good and evil without a fight. He wants both worlds, but God won't let him go.

Before his mother can slip a diaper on his bottom, Jacob is at odds with his brother.[1] When he comes out of the womb, he's grabbing his older brother's heel.[2] Jacob's parents, recognising the child's disposition, name him accordingly, 'heel catcher'. Within the context of the story, the connotation is not flattering. Jacob is a grabber, a supplanter, as well as a deceiver.[3] Esau's assessment of him confirms this character evaluation. 'Isn't he rightly named Jacob? This is the second time he has taken advantage of me: he took my birthright, and now he's taken my blessing!' (Gen. 27:36).

The New Testament justifiably condemns Esau's lack of moral judgement.[4] Selling his birthright for a bowl of soup is insulting.[5] However, Esau's moral deficiency is no excuse for

Jacob's behaviour. Jacob is always working a scam to get a blessing.[6] He's obsessed with it. The benefits come from God, but God is not the object of his desire. He coerces his brother to sell him the birthright. Jacob deceives his father to get his brother's blessing. After Jacob steals the blessing and Esau uncovers the ruse, Jacob runs for his life outside the boundaries of Canaan.[7]

Jacob begins his career through connivance and fraud. He cheats, deceives, and takes from everyone around him. Subsequently, Jacob runs from Esau, leaves his father,[8] runs from Laban[9] and, metaphorically speaking, he even runs from God. The struggle Jacob has with the promise is his character and the name that accurately describes it. It's Jacob's recurring challenge; his name is anything but great.

God pledged descendants, land, and a great name, but none of it comes naturally.[10] Jacob is yet to climb aboard the life raft. God often meets with Jacob to reaffirm the promise of Genesis 12. He even invades Jacob's dreams, ensuring his protection as Jacob leaves Canaan.[11] Nevertheless, Jacob's relationship with God is conditional. 'Then Jacob made a vow, saying, "If God will be with me and will watch over me on this journey I am taking and will give me food to eat and clothes to wear so that I return safely to my father's household, then the Lord will be my God"' (Gen. 28:20–21).

We can assume from this declaration that Jacob's devotion to God is on hold. If God fails to live up to Jacob's agenda, he won't pledge himself. This non-committal frame of mind underscores the gap between Jacob's spirituality and that of Abraham and Isaac. Jacob needs a change of heart. He's clutching the wrong manual, just like he clutched his brother's heel. The mustard seed of the kingdom can't prosper in this kind of soil. So we find Jacob holding on to the side of the boat furiously treading water, but he's going down with the ship, and the family name is going down with him.

The climax of the story is one of the most dramatic episodes in Genesis, an epic showdown. The setting is the Jabbok River. There, Jacob has a divine wrestling match with an unidentified assailant. Again Jacob is striving for another blessing, and he knows his opponent can grant it. Surprisingly that blessing was a change of character and status. 'Your name will no longer be Jacob, but Israel, because you have struggled with God and with humans and have overcome' (Gen. 32:28). God knew the blessing Jacob needed. Jacob, the heel-grabber, is now Israel.

Name adjustments mark a change of status. That day Jacob's reputation and character were altered before God and humanity. Jacob is now the bearer of the great name Israel. It's still with us today. The nation is called Israel, not Abraham, not Isaac or even Joseph. Jacob is the one who acquired the great name. He wrestled with God's angel and wouldn't let the angel go. Little did he know where the blessing he sought all his life was going to take him.

Proceeding from the Jabbok scene, Jacob remains true to his word and commits himself entirely to the God who walked with him all these years.[12] The Creator proved he was faithful and brought him back home safely.[13] The incident prompts Jacob to build his first altar. He names it *El Elohe Israel* (the mighty God of Israel).[14] The God of his fathers is now his God.

Jacob lays down the knowledge of good and evil and climbs aboard the life raft. His new name will eventually be the declarative title of the great nation promised to Abraham. Nevertheless, even after this victory, Jacob must face another trial. Like his grandfather and father before him, Jacob will be tested. It happened to Abraham regarding descendants.

It challenged Isaac concerning the land. Now it comes knocking on the door of Jacob. It's about his reputation and the great name.

As soon as Jacob receives his new identity, he faces a crisis. Shechem rapes Jacob's daughter, Dinah. Shechem is a citizen of a nearby town also called Shechem.[15] The situation quickly spirals out of control; Jacob's sons take matters into their own hands. They work their scam and ultimately wipe out the whole town.[16] They plunder everything: women, children, fields and cattle.[17] Their vengeance far outweighs the crime, and everyone in the land knows it. When Jacob hears of this, he is fearful of reprisals. 'You have brought trouble on me by making me obnoxious to the Canaanites and Perizzites, the people living in this land. We are few in number, and if they join forces against me and attack me, I and my household will be destroyed' (Gen. 34:30).

What Jacob is saying here harkens back to his life struggle. At Jabbok, his name is elevated, but now it's dishonoured, scandalised and made notorious. His sons discredit him, and the retribution will be hard.

The real test for Jacob, however, is how he responds to this situation. Is he going to fall back on his old ways as Jacob? Is he going to trust in his own wit and ability to connive and then run away; or is he going to put his faith and fate in the hands of God?

Fortunately, he embraces his new identity as Israel. He listens and obeys God's instructions to go to Bethel. He orders everyone to purify themselves and get rid of all the idols and foreign gods they brought with them.[18] Jacob is now fully committed to the one, living God whose blessing he had been seeking all his life. The man who prevails with God is now the man who lets God prevail with him.

The God of Israel guarantees Jacob's safety. The towns Jacob passed by on his way to Bethel are afraid to attack him. God is watching his back.[19] Then the God of Israel reaffirms Jacob's new identity.[20] Israel is living up to his name.

Intermission

The pattern still unfolds. Each of these patriarchal stories builds upon the other. They each follow the model set out in the promise God gave to Abraham. They are the four corner pieces of the puzzle we are putting together. They give us boundaries. They anchor us to God's vision. They mark the path back to Eden. They focus the camera, adjust the view, and set the stage for the greatest show on earth: the kingdom of God manifested on this planet.

We watch Abraham plod through disappointment and frustration, steadily lifting one foot in front of the other despite the obstacles and setbacks. Isaac's roots sink deep into Canaan's soil. Jacob wrestles God to the ground, refusing to let go. Descendants, land and the great name are planted in earth's soil. God passionately watches over the process, as he directs the show. He never relents. The establishment of the kingdom on this planet means more to him than it does to them. However, the story is still incomplete. There is one piece missing. If we drop this one, the whole puzzle falls apart. It's the theological climax of the entire journey. If we lose sight of Joseph, all that preceded will be meaningless and self-serving. We need all four of the corners if we want to put the rest of the puzzle together and see the picture on the box.

A Victim of Blessing

Joseph is a victim of blessing. He doesn't have to connive or wrestle God to the ground to obtain it. His father Jacob has already won that battle. Grace follows this fourth-generation patriarch everywhere he goes, but each time he is sincere and faithful or attempts to be a blessing, he is misunderstood and persecuted. His father favours him, which instigates his brothers' loathing.[1] Then God gives Joseph two prophetic dreams that exacerbate this hatred.[2]

Nobody in the narrative fully understands the implication of these dreams when Joseph first relates them. Joseph's attitude may not be entirely altruistic, but his only offence is revealing them. Joseph didn't interpret the dreams; his family drew their own conclusions. His father and his brothers are the ones who give the dreams a negative slant. To the family, the dreams indicate subservience; they were following the wrong manual. They just didn't get it.

So, clouded by hatred, the brothers abandon Joseph to die in a pit. Later they pull him out and sell him to Ishmaelite traders.[3] The traders drag him down to Egypt and deliver him to Potiphar.[4] As a slave, Joseph settles in admirably. He carries God's blessing with him. His Egyptian master prospers because of it.[5] The presence of Joseph invites God's favour to this foreign neighbour. Things are good until Potiphar's wife tries to seduce him. Joseph runs from her advances; being jilted and rejected by a Jewish slave angers her. She accuses Joseph of rape. That's when the police arrive and drag him off to prison.

Joseph brought the blessing, and he was the blessing. He lived it out. Joseph remained faithful to God and to Potiphar when he refused to bed with Potiphar's wife.[6] As we saw earlier in the Jacob story, obtaining the blessing was not easy, but in the Joseph narrative, we find 'being the blessing' also has its life-altering difficulties.

In prison, God favours Joseph. Everything prospers in his hand. Joseph brings the blessing to those in jail with him. In recognition of this, Joseph is put in charge of all the prisoners.[7] Two years later, he explains Pharaoh's dreams.[8] Pharaoh is impressed, so he elevates Joseph to second in command over Egypt.[9] This is where Joseph peaks. The world comes to Joseph because they have no food, and Joseph gives it to them.[10] Joseph was a blessing to Potiphar, to the prison warden, to Pharaoh, and to the Egyptians and the entire known world.

Again, this seems to be an excellent place to end the story: 'And Joseph lived happily ever after.' However, it wouldn't fit the pattern set by the previous patriarchal narratives. They were all tested. It will be no different for Joseph. His test begins when his brothers travel south for a bite to eat. Joseph knows them, but they don't recognise Joseph. Who would have expected this hated brother would be Pharaoh's second in command?

The remainder of the story focuses on Joseph's turmoil. What is he going to do with his brothers? We watch as he repeatedly wavers between antagonism[11] and mercy.[12] Twice he is so overcome by his own emotions that he has to leave the room. There he weeps alone.[13] Joseph is now confronting the most significant trial of his life. He has to face the murderous brothers who sold him into slavery. The irony is that Joseph is no longer the hapless victim. He now has the authority and position to decide their fate. The test comes down to this one thing: is he going to curse or bless them?

Joseph vacillates before his brothers because he has yet to settle the question within himself. Is he going to continue as a mediator of blessing, or is he going to turn to vengeance? Is he going to hold on to the manual of good and evil, the wisdom of this world, or is he going to pick up the handbook of the kingdom? Fortunately, like his predecessors, Joseph passes the test. He reveals his identity to his brothers, forgives them[14] and resettles his family in Egypt.[15] He provides for all their needs and reassures them of God's purpose.[16] "'You intended to harm me, but God intended it for good to accomplish what is now being done, the saving of many lives. So then, don't be afraid. I will provide for you and your children." And he reassured them and spoke kindly to them' (Gen. 50:20–21).

The climax of the Genesis story is wrapped up in the life of Joseph. The goal of the promise is to bless the planet. This is what the kingdom of God is all about. This is what it's to achieve as it grows and matures. It's God's blessing to the world. Even though the seed is small, the plant will become big enough to hold everyone who will climb aboard its limbs.

Intermission

The structure of Genesis is theologically charged and motivated. As the building goes up, we begin to see the architect's vision. It's a microcosm of God's kingdom reflected in the lives of four individuals. Their history is one story. The primary feature of this chronicle is how the mustard seed of God's kingdom is planted on earth and the way God watches over it. It's all about the promise, not the patriarchs. This is why the story moves through four generations and not just the life of one man and his immediate family.

The author chose to highlight one specific element of the promise in each particular story. The nature and timing of each trial they face enhance that pattern. Genesis tells us that every component of the promise given to Abraham is necessary and of value, but none of them is to stand alone.

Descendants, followers, a large congregation, real estate, legacy, fame, a great name, hierarchical positioning, the desire to be blessed and honoured, can all degenerate into an adolescent, self-absorbed entitlement mentality. If we gravitate towards one or two of the corner pieces unconcerned about the others, the picture on the box becomes distorted. Jesus kept addressing this when he walked the streets of Israel.

1. Descendants

    'Abraham is our father,' they answered.

    'If you were Abraham's children,' said Jesus, 'then you would do what Abraham did.' (John 8:39)

2. Real Estate

    As Jesus was leaving the temple, one of his disciples said to him, 'Look, Teacher! What massive stones! What magnificent buildings!'

    'Do you see all these great buildings?' replied Jesus. 'Not one stone here will be left on another; every one will be thrown down.' (Mark 13:1–2)

3. Great Name

> I say to you that many will come from the east and the west, and will take their places at the feast with Abraham, Isaac and Jacob in the kingdom of heaven. But the subjects of the kingdom will be thrown outside, into the darkness, where there will be weeping and gnashing of teeth. (Matt. 8:11–12)

4. Bless the World

> As you go, proclaim this message: 'The kingdom of heaven has come near.' Heal those who are ill, raise the dead, cleanse those who have leprosy, drive out demons. Freely you have received; freely give. (Matt. 10:7–8)

As ambassadors of the kingdom, we are to be the purveyors of hope.[17] Love is the measure of maturity in the kingdom of God. In the kingdom, we aren't looking for love; we are looking for ways to express it. 'Be the blessing' is the picture on the box of Genesis. It is the heartbeat of God's kingdom. It's what the four corner pieces of our puzzle embrace. We can't lose sight of what this kingdom thing is all about. Our place and function in the kingdom are to invade this planet with the love of God.

PART TWO

**ISRAEL AND THE
KINGDOM**

The Stage

Whenever I teach a class about the kingdom of God, I tell the students to think of it as a movie production. They can relate to that because most of them already have a love relationship with Hollywood. The subject holds their attention and focuses the mind on something familiar. I usually begin the lecture with a question, 'What do we need to make a good movie?'

Some of the bright sparks say, backers, money, cameras, lawyers, contracts, studios, CGI, Dolby sound, and luck. Then, after they exhaust the list, I ask them to narrow it down. 'OK, now pull out the very basics. What are the essential components?'

Surprisingly it usually comes down to the four corner pieces we read about in Genesis. God is way ahead of us here. We need actors (descendants). We require a stage or a setting (land). Of course, there's no story without a script or a hero (the great name and the great nation), and it's all a waste of time without an audience (the world we are to bless). Oh, and one more thing we can't overlook, and that's a good director. God has been directing the show up to this point, and he's going to follow it through until the production covers the entire earth and the heavens above. He is determined.

So are you ready? The stage is set. We have our tickets. We've seen the previews; we've watched the trailers. The door of the cinema is wide open. Let's go in and take our seats. The show is about to begin.

As the lights dim, we slurp our drinks and lift a fist of popcorn. The pages of Genesis have set the scene; now it's time to watch the show. We brace ourselves with anticipation and hope. The curtain goes up. The heavenly music begins as the production title flashes before our eyes: *Israel*.

What? This is where the audience coughs and sputters, spraying white flakes and soda on the various heads in front of them. 'Israel! Why Israel? We don't get it.'

Well, the story is a long one. We yawn our way through Leviticus. I plead with my wife to pull the trigger halfway through the book of Numbers. 'Shoot me now, if I have to read another obscure law or random genealogy to be a good Christian.'

The spicy bits come as Judges hits the stage. We tell our children to close their eyes because of all the murder, rape, violence, debauchery, and spikes pounded into people's heads. This part is classified 'R' or '15'. Israel continually fails as God persistently comes to their rescue. Political factions eventually split the nation.

Throughout their history, we see earthly kings come and go. There are a few stars, but the vast majority are dreadful. They refuse to get on board the life raft. They tread water until the sharks come for a feeding frenzy. At times the entire nation is devoured.

We watch, hoping for better, as the prophets walk on to the stage. Many answer the call but soon regret it.[1] Others run into caves and hide.[2] At least three of them want to die before their time.[3] One walks through the streets of Jerusalem naked for years on end.[4] Another is picked up by his hair and transported to various places on the stage.[5] They run from God.[6] They have visions of doom; the scope is apocalyptic and, at times, global in magnitude.[7] They break down under persecution as Israel's citizens search and destroy.[8] It's not smooth sailing for the kingdom, and Israel is not a straightforward story to tell.

Is this what the Creator envisioned for his great production? If so, then why are the ratings so disparaging? Critics don't like it. Others scratch their heads and wonder what it's all about. Many Christians carry only New Testaments in their bags, purses and pockets; some ignore the Old Testament altogether. Parts of it are embarrassing and morally questionable; just read some of the psalms.[9] We wish the disturbing sections were edited or censored before they hit the main stage. It seems there's a disconnect between the first draft of the kingdom and what we witness on the screen.

The Stage

Is the stage a problem? It is rather small. Globally speaking, Israel/Canaan is minuscule.[10] It's a sliver on any world map. So why would God choose such a small venue for such a significant production? Why didn't God pick a place closer to Abraham's hometown? Why ask him to travel eight to nine hundred miles across dangerous terrain to Canaan?

Well, God had his eye on Canaan for one primary reason: it was choice real estate. Canaan sits at the hub of three continents: Asia, Europe and Africa. The location alone makes it highly visible, which is what you want for any stage. Armies, traders, travellers and commerce between these three landmasses would all have to go through, or near, the boundaries of Canaan. This location is why many of the major roads of the ancient Near East passed through or near its borders: the Way of the Sea,[11] the King's Highway,[12] Via Maris and the Ridge Route. The land of Canaan has been called 'the Sacred Bridge'[13] because it connects these three landmasses. The Bible refers to Jerusalem as the gate to the nations[14] and the belly-button of the world.[15]

Israel's location on the Mediterranean also made it a pivotal point for sea trade. The Jews themselves were not great seafarers, but this would not lessen Israel's geographical impact or detract from the economic possibilities that were afforded by a coastline on or near the Mediterranean Sea.

Intermission

So, for what God was planning, Canaan was a wise choice of real estate. It is small, but not insignificant. The stage was positioned to attract the attention of the known world. There is nothing wrong or lacking in the stage God chose for the production. But what about the audience? Were they the problem?

The Audience

God loves the audience. This is why he's putting on the show. But the audience was a bit unruly and troublesome at times; however, that was expected. They enter the theatre with purses and backpacks full of idols. They carry a lot of baggage with them, in every sense of the word. Sumer, the first known urban civilisation in Mesopotamia, had a patron god for every city.[1] Over two thousand deities knocked on their doors demanding attention. The people of Sumer believed humanity was created to serve and worship these gods slavishly; Enlil, Enki, Ninhursag, An, Nanna, Utu, Inanna, are just a few of the names discovered in the celestial clan.

Egypt also had a glut of deities vying for attention. Anyone who has ever watched *Stargate* on television would know some of them: Hathor, Anubis, Osiris and Ra.[2] The gods are what the ten plagues were about in the book of Exodus. 'I will bring judgment on all the gods of Egypt' (Exod. 12:12). Listed here are a few Egyptian gods the plagues humbled.[3]

- Plague 1: When God turned the Nile into blood, he was demonstrating his power over Khnum, the creator of water and life; Hapi, the Nile god; and Osiris (the Nile was his bloodstream).

- Plague 2: The frog plague struck a blow at Heket, the goddess of fertility, whose symbol was the frog.
- Plague 3: The gnat plague mocked Geb, the god of the earth.
- Plague 4: The fly plague stirred against Kheper, the god of resurrection, whose image was a flying beetle.
- Plague 5: The death of the cattle revealed God's power over Apis, the god of fertility (a sacred bull), and Hathor, the sky goddess, whose symbol was a cow.
- Plague 6: The scourge of boils silenced Sekhmet, the goddess of disease and healing, along with Imhotep, the god of medicine.
- Plague 7: The fiery hail exhibited God's authority over Seth, the god of wind and storm; Shu, the goddess of moisture; Tefnut, the goddess of water and fertility; and Nuit, the god who upholds the sky.
- Plague 8: The locusts pounded against Senehem, who is supposed to protect the Egyptians against pests; and Min, the goddess of fertility and protector of crops.
- Plague 9: The scourge of darkness thwarted the sun gods: Amon-Re, Atum and Horus.
- Plague 10: The death of the firstborn struck a blow against Pharaoh who considered himself a deity. The entire nation suffered with him. The demise of all the firstborn illustrates that Pharaoh is no different than anyone else in Egypt. God was making a statement: 'I'm the true, living God. All the rest are charlatans.'

I know many Christians wince when they read about God hardening the heart of Pharaoh.[4] It especially irks those outside the Calvinist camp. However, the hardening wasn't about human free will or God's sovereignty; it was about power. The Almighty was dealing with Pharaoh as a deity, not as a mortal human being. The hardening of Pharaoh's heart revealed who was boss in Egypt. The imposter gods were being exposed and going down. God is the actual Creator. He holds power and ultimate authority. He carries the sceptre. He wears the crown. Pharaoh's apotheosis looks ridiculous when the eternal God of heaven and earth visits the land of Egypt.

Neutering False Deities

The things God did in the Old Testament weren't just random displays of power. Most of them were explicitly designed to expose and neuter the gods of the ancient Near East, the idols shackling humanity. For example, Ahab and Jezebel promote Baal worship in Israel.[5] Baal was one of the supreme gods of Canaan and Phoenicia. He is often pictured with lightning bolts in his hands because he is a storm/fertility god. Baal is the one you go to when your crops need water, so Elijah comes on the scene and prays for the rain to stop and Baal can do nothing about it.[6] It didn't rain again until Elijah prayed to God three and a half years later. It was a blow against Baal. The storm god was impotent when the real, living God shows his hand. It's also the underlying issue on Mount Carmel. Elijah challenges Israel:

> Get two bulls for us. Let Baal's prophets choose one for them-selves, and let them cut it into pieces and put it on the wood but not set fire to it. I will prepare the other bull and put it on the wood but not set fire to it. Then you call on the name of your god, and I will call on the name of the LORD. The god who answers by fire – he is God. (1 Kgs 18:23–4)

Already we are drawn into the story. This lightning thing was Baal's occupation. It would look bad if he didn't perform.

The suspense builds. It's a showdown. You can hear the music of an old western movie droning in the background as Elijah stands; ready to draw his gun. The camera zooms in on his face. He taunts, relaxed and confident. There's a glint in his eye. Then we get a close-up of his hand. His finger twitches two inches from the holster. He's ready to draw the gun outnumbered by the four hundred and fifty priests of Baal.

Who doesn't love this story? It was a favourite in the hippie church I attended back in Colorado. I think it's what prompted Roger's coin-toss challenge to the Mormons.[7] So let the war of the gods begin. The priests of Baal build their altar and cry out to him half the day. Baal doesn't show up. Elijah gets impatient and mocks them: 'Maybe he's taken the day off or is sitting on a toilet somewhere.'[8]

The absence of Baal and the taunts against him infuriate the priests as they jump around like fleas on a hot brick, shouting into the sky, cutting themselves with knives, and spilling their blood.[9] That's when Elijah takes centre stage and calls out to his God. It is a straightforward, short, dignified prayer, and God dramatically answers it. He throws down fire from heaven and burns up the sacrifice, the water and the stones. All the people witnessing the event fall to the ground on their faces as they acknowledge the existence of the one, true, living God: the God of Israel.[10]

This battle was for the minds and hearts of the people. In one corner we have the lie: Baal, the illusion. In the other corner, we have God, the Creator. The Creator unleashes fire from heaven. Baal, the lord of lightning, doesn't even enter the ring.

The location of this contest is also strategic. Mount Carmel is on the border of Israel and Phoenicia; Phoenicia is Baal's homeland. God spoke loud and clear to both nations that day. Baal is a myth; the God of Elijah is the real, living God of heaven and earth.

These few stories illustrate what God is doing in the Old Testament. He's breaking into a world that no longer knows what he is like or who he is. The audience is distracted. God has to smash through the door to get their attention. It's often a messy business. It's not pleasant or comfortable, but it has to be done.

The Hittites, to the north of Israel (modern-day Turkey), collected gods like Pokémon.[11] Every celestial being was welcomed and embraced. Comparable to lost puppies, these deities were fed, watered and loved in every home. Anatolia, the home of the Hittites, is referred to as 'the land of a thousand gods'.[12] The Babylonians and the Assyrians were no different; they too worshipped countless supernatural beings. All of these civilisations borrowed from each other and renamed the deities in their own vernacular, just like the Greeks and Romans did centuries later.

Idols are Powerless but not Innocent

Now, don't be tempted to think of these gods as harmless, inconsequential diversions like Santa Claus, the Tooth Fairy, or the Easter Bunny. The leverage they wield is much more sinister. These deities fuel all kinds of demonic behaviour. They direct the lifestyle and praxis of the ancient Near East. If you want good crops or successful childbirth, you visit the temple prostitutes.[13] At times the gods require a human sacrifice.

They incorporate magic, witchcraft, necromancy and bestiality.[14] God outlaws these practices because of the damage they do to the people who observe them.[15] This is the audience God wants to reach. It's another reason for locating the stage in the middle of these three continents. During these early years of biblical history, God often displays his power against false deities. It needs to be done, but power, violence and force don't reveal his heart. It demonstrates his existence and ability, but not who God is and what the Almighty is like; only a manifestation of the kingdom of God can do that. Consider the encounter Elijah had with God on Mount Horeb.

> The LORD said, 'Go out and stand on the mountain in the presence of the LORD, for the LORD is about to pass by.' Then a great and powerful wind tore the mountains apart and shattered the rocks before the LORD, but the LORD was not in the wind. After the wind there was an earthquake, but the LORD was not in the earthquake. After the earthquake came a fire, but the LORD was not in the fire. And after the fire came a gentle whisper. (1 Kgs 19:11–12)

God wants to reveal his heart to the world, not just his power. The greatest show on earth was performed on this particular stage, to this specific audience to introduce them to God's whisper: his goodness, his gentleness, his love and kindness. It's powerful enough to change the culture of the ancient world. Lightning gets their attention; love wins their heart.

The Psychic Fair

I have Christian friends who sign up annually for the psychic fair here in Northern Ireland. They don't go there to get their fortunes told, tune into crystals, channel entities, or shuffle tarot cards. They go to minister Jesus Christ in the power and gifts of the Holy Spirit. What better place to meet people who are open and ready to have a divine encounter with

God? My friends pray for the sick, prophesy, and speak the word of God into people's lives; but they also have to make some uncomfortable compromises. They use the vocabulary of a spiritist. Biblical words and phrases such as 'word of wisdom' and 'word of knowledge' are advertised on the booth as 'life readings'. Not every Christian can do this. There's always that niggling suspicion of drifting towards the dark side, especially when you are surrounded by it.

They offer healing prayer like many of the others attending, but my friends pray in the name of Jesus. Instead of charging money like the other participants, they provide their services for free. 'Life readings' and 'healing prayer' are quite attractive to those who are searching. Demons are referred to as 'negative energy' and are dealt with in the name of Jesus.

Well, this is out there. It's on the fringe, and I know many Christians react to it. I am not surprised. Some want to picket the fair and set fire to the booths instead of jumping into the centre of the arena to minister healing, deliverance, faith, hope and love in a language the spiritists can understand. I find it uncomfortable. My friends found it uncomfortable, but they were bold enough to do it.

Jesus told the disciples that the gates of hell would not prevail.[16] We talk about kicking in those gates, but often we're reluctant to step over the threshold once the barrier's down. Our call is not to stand there gaping and wagging the finger. We're supposed to run in and storm the territory; enter the hell people have fallen into and pull them out. Sometimes we give lip service to this idea, but to step up to the mark and do it is not a comfortable, secure or a straightforward exercise.

The real difficulty came when one spiritist asked the group to pray for him. They had no problem with this. They welcomed the opportunity. But after they prayed, the man turned around and said, 'Now, can I pray for you?' Yipes! As I said, it's a messy business. I don't know what I would've done, but they yielded, believing God would protect them. It was a very awkward moment.

The reason I mention this is because the Jewish nation faced similar circumstances, but on a global scale. Stepping on to the stage was like opening a booth in a psychic fair. The audience is polytheistic. Their practices are demonic. The people in the audience do not know what God is like or who he is. God sometimes has to break into their world with plagues and fire from heaven to get their attention. It's a divine shout in the dark.[17] His actions silence the spirits.[18] His interventions preserve humanity, but they don't reveal his heart. Only the kingdom of God can do that.

Intermission

Well, we all know God has more to offer than any idol lurking in the cinema. His kingdom is more attractive than anything these lying deities offer. The influence of God's kingdom is powerful enough to silence every demon that raises its ugly head against it. The audience, therefore, is not the problem when it comes to the success or the failure of the show.

The Actors

The best-selling author Richard Dawkins has quite a large bee buzzing around in his bonnet when it comes to the God of the Old Testament. In his book, *The God Delusion*, he describes the Almighty as the 'most unpleasant character in all fiction.'[1] Of course, Christians react to these sorts of remarks and want to fight God's corner. Just look at some of the Christian book titles on Amazon:

- *Is God a Moral Monster? Making Sense of the Old Testament God*[2]
- *God of Violence Yesterday, God of Love Today? Wrestling Honestly with the Old Testament*[3]
- *God Behaving Badly: Is the God of the Old Testament Angry, Sexist and Racist?*[4]

I would venture to say many of us have been tempted to question God's goodness at one time or another. The Jews in Egypt sure did; just read the book of Exodus. It is rather distressing to see the descendants of Abraham slaving in a foreign land after all that God had promised them in Genesis. When we step into the Hebrew camp, we find the promise all wrinkled up, tattered and stamped with big red letters: Unfulfilled. If we evaluated God's performance up to this point, the negative reviews would be through the floor.

Did the Hebrews have many descendants? Yes, but they were born into slavery. The Egyptian sword was a constant threat; especially when the number of Hebrew children multiplied. The escalation of sons is what brought the Egyptian hammer down on their heads – even baby Moses had to be floated down the Nile to escape Egyptian persecution and paranoia.[5]

Were the Hebrews established in the land God promised them? No, they were captives in Goshen, an area of lower Egypt. The promised land was off-limits to them, and there was little hope of returning there.

Were they a nation of renown? Was their name great? No, they were a subordinate people, beat down, abused and scorned. Israel wasn't a title or a designation attributed to them at this time. They had no authority, resources, security or kudos. They were not a blessing to the world. Life was grim. The promise to Abraham never made it to the finish line.

But then, at Mount Horeb, Moses hears a knock at the door. He answers it, and the caller introduces himself as the God of Abraham, Isaac and Jacob.[6] Now, this introduction would satisfy most people. If we stood before a miraculous flaming bush and saw the angel of God and heard the voice from heaven, I think we would all say, 'Come on in, your word is good enough for me.' But Moses kept God standing at the door and asked him to show his credentials. This kind of chutzpah is what God looks for in a leader.[7]

> Moses said to God, 'Suppose I go to the Israelites and say to them, "The God of your fathers has sent me to you," and they ask me, "What is his name?" Then what shall I tell them?' (Exod. 3:13)

I don't think it would have entered any of our heads to ask that question. Didn't God already identify himself to Moses? 'I am the God of your fathers' (Exod. 3:6). I mean, what more identification do you need: a birth certificate? I'm glad Moses didn't go that far because God doesn't have one, but why ask for his name?

Well, as you know, a name in the ancient Near East describes the character and status of a person. This is why God often changes the names of people in the Bible. What Moses was fishing for here is:

- Who are you going to be for us?
- What is your intention?
- What are you like?
- Can you be trusted?
- Are you good?

Moses asked God this question because, on the 'deity scale', God's success rate was relatively low. However, the Creator is still committed to his people and the establishment of the kingdom on earth, so the Almighty graciously flips open his wallet and shows Moses his badge: 'I am who I am. This is what you are to say to the Israelites: "I am has sent me to you"' (Exod. 3:14).

The name 'I am' is the tetragrammaton YHWH (Yahweh). The meaning of that name is 'I am who I am.' However, in Hebrew, it can also be interpreted, 'I will be who I will be.' Within this name, God is saying, 'Walk with me, and you will see what I am like and what I will do for you.' Then throughout the pages of the Old Testament, we watch the Jewish nation fill in the blanks.

Here is a list of the attributes the Jews eventually attach to that name. These qualities don't originate through study or some academic exercise. The observations are derived from real-life encounters and interactions with God.

- Yahweh Rapha: Yahweh my healer (Exod. 15:26)
- Yahweh Nissa: Yahweh my banner (Exod. 17:15)
- Yahweh Maccaddeshcem: Yahweh my sanctifier (Exod. 31:13)
- Yahweh Shalom: Yahweh my peace (Judg. 6:24)
- Yahweh Roi: Yahweh my shepherd (Ps. 23:1)
- Yahweh Sabbaoth: Yahweh, Lord of Hosts (Ps. 46:7)
- Yahweh Tsidkenu: Yahweh my righteousness (Jer. 23:6)
- Yahweh Shammah: Yahweh is here (Ezek. 48:35)
- Yahweh Jireh: Yahweh will provide (Gen. 22:14)[8]

What's enlightening is that we never hear the Jewish people say things like, 'Yahweh the destroyer of villages', 'Yahweh the punisher', 'Yahweh the angry', or 'Yahweh the unfaithful'. Many of today's critics focus on and write about these fearful acts when they read the Old Testament. What they don't understand is that God had to do these things to preserve and redeem this fallen world. Anger, destruction and punishment are not a reflection of his eternal attributes. Yes, he gets angry at sin. Yes, he destroys villages. Yes, he disciplines the Jewish nation, but that is not what defines him.

The Jews themselves are the ones who experienced all these events at first hand. They are the ones who recorded the stories for us to read. They wrote them down and preserved them for future generations, but they did not attribute them to God's eternal disposition, or his character. They recognised the gulf between what God had to do in a fallen world and who he is.

Establishing God's kingdom on this planet is a messy business, and no one finds the task easy. The generation Moses led through the wilderness was a community of very broken people, and they had some major trust issues.

At first, the actors won't even step on to the stage.[9] They halt at the edge and renege before the curtain goes up.[10] It's a terminal case of mistrust and stage fright.[11] This first generation never does perform. The company hangs about in the dressing-room, grumbling for forty years. It is hard for them to trust any authority after all they suffered. This generation is damaged. They have difficulty believing God or Moses. Their hold on the knowledge of good and evil is white-knuckle tight. Fortunately, the children born in the wilderness don't carry the same baggage. So when the occasion arrives, they step up to perform. They enter the promised land without hesitation. They're eager to jump on stage and are grateful for the opportunity.

These actors are second-generation, wilderness nomads, chosen by God. Their ancestors welcomed God into their history, and God won't let go of them. He is committed. He is good. He is a father. He is a husband.[12] All through the succeeding generations, God proves his faithfulness. He is present. He is active. He disciplines, blesses, corrects, guides, protects and intervenes in ways no other people on earth have ever experienced. The actors God chose for the world premiere are family. They matter to him.[13] God is going to show the world what it's like to be a part of his family. The family is to be the visual representation of the kingdom of God on this earth. Yet, they were the problem. The production floundered because the cast couldn't keep to the script.

Intermission

Today a movie is considered a success if it makes a lot of money. It's a flop or a box-office bomb if it doesn't rake in cash – those involved in the movie-making process like hearing the rattle of coins in the coffers. It makes sense. They invest a lot of time, energy and finance to produce our entertainment, but a film's income is not an issue for many of us. We want to dive into someone else's imagination. I enjoy a movie when I like the actors, the characters and the music. The sound effects also help, along with convincing CGI. The most important thing, though, is the narrative. We are not entertained, enlightened or satisfied if we miss the plot.

Many of us flounder when we step into the world of the Old Testament because we lose sight of the story. It's nebulous. It's not in chronological order. Even when we read it sequentially, we wonder: what's the point? It's lost to us because the actors often forget their lines. It's blurred even more when they ignore the Director and alter the plot. That's when the viewers shake their head and walk away, confused and frustrated. The Director, at times, does the same.[14] It's exasperating trying to keep unruly actors on cue. So we wonder whose story we are reading – is it God's or the Hebrews'?

The difficulty for many of us is that we haven't seen the original script. We have the four corner pieces of the puzzle, but it's difficult assembling the other pieces when the picture on the box is obscured. What was the plot before the actors took it to the stage? What was the screenplay God, the Director, had in mind before the first curtain call?

The Original Script

Have you ever read the Bible in one year? Many do. I have. On the first day, I'm right in there. Life is good. I'm connected. I even cheat and read an extra chapter or two. The Lord congratulates my earnestness. I'm the man: Mr Spiritual walking the planet. However, as the weeks, days and hours go by the enthusiasm wanes, but I hang in there. It's hard work. It's not for the faint-hearted. I don't know if it's made me a better person or not, but by faith and dogged determination, I eventually crawl up to the two hundred and seventy-fourth day and turn the last page of Malachi. I reach a milestone. I have now read the Old Testament from beginning to end. I pat myself on the back.

The following day I welcome Matthew as an old friend. He tells me the story of Jesus. I read the account over and over again because it's repeated four times, but I stay on course. The New Testament is familiar territory. It's the well we dip in for most of our sermons and contemporary holidays. Then, after marking off the twenty-seven books of the New Testament, all heaven watches and cheers me on as I cross the finish line. In slow motion, the instant replay focuses on my lips as I read out the last verse of Revelation. I'm now on my feet shouting and punching the air, 'Yes! Yes! Yes!' I bow as the angels applaud my effort, and it is well, it is well with my soul. Amen.

Now, at this juncture, it's easy to conclude that the script is all about Jesus. We reinforce this with the words Jesus spoke to the Jewish leaders. 'You study the Scriptures diligently because you think that in them you have eternal life. These are the very Scriptures that testify about me' (John 5:39).

We bolster his claim with Luke's narrative on the road to Emmaus. 'And beginning with Moses and all the Prophets, he explained to them what was said in all the Scriptures concerning himself' (Luke 24:27).

Then we wrongly assume the only thing the Jews were meant to do is provide a platform for God's only begotten Son and give us the book that explains him. However, that is not the script.

If the Jesus-filter is the only lens we look through to understand Israel's history and their ancient text, we do them and the Almighty a grave disservice. The script is not all about Jesus and us, or Jesus and them. If the answer to every theological statement, action and historical purpose in Israel's history is Jesus, then there was no answer for the Jewish nation before Jesus was born. We intellectually relegate all those years and multiple generations to the burden of the law and growing anticipation of a Messiah as though the previous generations had nothing more to offer the world in God's great plan.

This one-dimensional approach often blinds us to the bigger picture. It's hard to understand the enthusiasm Jesus had for the kingdom of God if we overlook God's passion for the kingdom in Israel's early history. The kingdom is what the script is all about. Instead of dragging the New Testament into the Old, we need to follow the text from the Old into the New.

An Eight-act Production

The Director handed the actors a script written in heaven. Like a pirate's map, it leads to a treasure. It was the original draft, not the one we see played out through Israel's history. All the Israelites had to do was follow the instructions to get the prize. The kingdom of God manifested within the boundaries of Canaan was to be spectacular, something the world has never before seen or experienced. The title of the script is 'The greatest show on earth'. It's the Director's vision; God's passion, the gospel of the kingdom; the message of Jesus Christ.

Back in Eden, humanity received the manual that leads to death. We hold on to it with both hands and are afraid to loosen our grip – the Director awards Israel a script that leads to life. With cavalier disdain and human fear, they toss it on a bench and walk away. Their story is often our story. Their history is the history of the human race.

The original script is an eight-act play. It is a significant piece of the puzzle. If we don't hold on to this one, the picture on the box will be blurred and incomplete. Each act is necessary to fulfil God's purpose on this planet and in his creation. So, before we dig any deeper, here's a summary of each act.

- Act 1: When the curtain goes up, the Hebrews will march into Canaan and clean up the stage.
- Act 2: The Jews will live by one creed: 'Hear, O Israel: The LORD our God, the LORD is one' (Deut. 6:4).
- Act 3: God will live in the Jewish nation as a good king.
- Act 4: This new society will embrace the Ten Commandments along with all the other righteous laws of God as their constitution.
- Act 5: God will bless Israel, unlike any other nation in the world. It will be the manifestation of the kingdom of God on earth.
- Act 6: The surrounding nations will take notice and say, 'I want som-adat.'

- Act 7: As a nation of priests, Israel will introduce the audience to God: 'Here is how you can get som-adat.'
- Act 8: Then we watch as the kingdom of God grows and extends its branches throughout the entire world.

This show is radical and revolutionary. It is communicated in human language and earthly concepts, but it is a gift from God that will produce otherworldly results. The Creator doesn't want to win the world through violence; he wants to win the world by attraction. It's how he intends the mustard seed to grow and increase. This is what the promise given to Abraham was to accomplish.

God chose the descendants of Abraham to manifest the kingdom on earth. It is their calling. God, the Director of the show, understood his character and glory were best served and displayed through a community, not an individual. He employed individuals – the Bible is full of them – but the only reason God commissioned these people was to keep the actors (the community) in line with the script.

God gave the promise to a particular man and his descendants. He carefully watched over them and directed the family line. God was specific about the DNA of the community. Descendants, land and a great name are necessary components for a vibrant, attractive community in a dark world. The Jewish people were to become a great nation, not only in size but also in character; a culture birthed on earth, energised from heaven to bless the world.

Intermission

The weight of responsibility upon Jewish shoulders is alarming. We watch the Director actively guide and tutor the actors for the big production. God often intervenes to keep the performers alive, steady and on cue. He's also working in the audience, steering them towards salvation.

However, the question is still before us: 'Why does the show often get such poor ratings?' Well, we know there was nothing wrong with the stage. Canaan was a wise choice of real estate to attract the world's attention. We also trust the Director and his management skills. His vision, passion and clarity of thought far exceed that of any actor. On the other hand, we can't possibly fault the audience because they had nothing to do with the show except watch and throw popcorn. The weak link in the chain is the cast, the children of Abraham.

If we've learned anything so far, it's this: the knowledge of good and evil in human hands will never produce the fruit of the kingdom of God on earth. The wisdom of this world may help us navigate this world, but it doesn't have the stamp of heaven upon it, and it will go down with the ship.

A fallen human race is the divine challenge. In love, God is mindful of us, and he is going to work his plan in us and through us. He keeps throwing the ball of the kingdom into our court to see what we will do with it. God knows we will fumble and foul, but the Director keeps picking it up and putting it back into our hands. He has faith in his plan and his method. The Creator entrusts the manifestation of the kingdom into Jewish hands. Later in their history, he assigns it to a small group of disciples. Then he delegates the church to take it forward.

The kingdom of God on this planet has always been a joint operation. God assigned it to the human race when he created us in his image and put us in charge of the garden and its varied inhabitants. Of course, the 'image of God' is wide open to interpretation, and many have tried to pin it down, but from God's perspective, all we can say about the image is this: 'Without it, you create a zoo. With it, you create a friend.'

The garden of Eden was a paradise, but after the couple ate from the tree 'they realised that they were naked' (Gen. 3:7). They knew they had lost something. Paradise was no longer paradise without the friendship of God. An eternal, love relationship with our Creator is the heart of the kingdom. Without it, we may stumble on the fringe and touch the edge of his garment, but we miss the point. The goal of the kingdom is not the place; it's the relationship. Paradise, alone, is not the kingdom. Heaven is not about the place; it's about the relationship. If we sever our relationship with God, the kingdom becomes nebulous and obscure. It's a shell without presence, religion without authenticity.

However, before we get too far ahead of ourselves, let's examine what this eight-act production of the kingdom was supposed to look like at ground level. Let's examine each act and see how God wanted it to play out. What would it look like if the Jews had kept to the original script?

Does God Wear a Watch?

Act 1 of the script introduces us to one of the most disturbing commands in the Bible. No one gets a warm, gushy feeling when they read it. We want it to go away. It just doesn't seem right to march in and wipe the stage clean.

> However, in the cities of the nations the Lord your God is giving you as an inheritance, do not leave alive anything that breathes. Completely destroy them – the Hittites, Amorites, Canaanites, Perizzites, Hivites and Jebusites – as the Lord your God has commanded you. (Deut. 20:16–17)

We call it 'genocide' or 'ethnic cleansing'. The United Nations would never sanction this kind of behaviour, but here we find the living God of love giving the order. It's one of those deeds we can't ignore. If we doubt the goodness of God, we will walk but never run, perform without assurance, speak without conviction, surrender passionless prayers hoping one day our doubts will turn to faith and the virtual will somehow become authentic. If we don't see God's love in the Old Testament, then why assume he's a God of love in the New? The New Testament may declare it with a louder megaphone, but the niggling suspicion we're in a good cop/bad cop scenario isn't peaceable or satisfactory.

Faith in God's love is what motivates us. If we aren't convinced of it, we will waver in our choices, and our morality, because we suspect God is doing the same thing. There's no rest for those who sense the flames of hell licking their toes while the wings of angels brush against their shoulders. Spiritual schizophrenia leaves us divided and insecure. It's just not kingdom, and it sure doesn't sustain or bolster faith.

However, there are things in the Old Testament we can't overlook or pretend aren't there. God is not tame. He is the ultimate authority. We don't question him; he questions us.[1] Just because God does things we wouldn't do if we were in his position, it doesn't mean our moral compass is pointing due north and his is askew. We need to trust, but it also helps to see things from his perspective and not just our own. People often accuse God of all the wrongs in this world.

> Why did he allow this to happen? Why doesn't he step in and make all the bad things go away? Is he just going to sit there in front of his sacred television watching the world's tears flash across the screen and do nothing? Why doesn't he get up and change the channel?

These are some of the heartfelt questions we ask from a sinking ship. From our perspective, God's inactivity reflects a character flaw. We say he's detached, dispassionate and uncaring. This raw and disparaging evaluation is one of the roads numerous people stagger down: 'Give me science without God. Give me evolution. Give me religion. Give me the idols of this world, but not the God of the Old Testament.'

Too many people sink and drown in this pool. For them, the waves are too high. God fell asleep during the commercial, and no one knows when the nap will end. So, what is God doing? Doesn't he want to ease the pain? Why does an all-powerful, good God allow evil to happen in this world?[2] A helpful place to start this inquiry is the second coming; the physical return of Jesus to this planet. Biblically, this is God's ultimate answer to these sorts of questions. The direct rule of Jesus and the establishment of the kingdom is when he makes everything right in the world.[3] As Christians, we wait and ponder. Many think and hope it will happen in their generation. The disappointment and the delay intensify our curiosity.

We put on our watch, grab our day planner, sit down with a calendar, mark our Bible, and predict the day and hour of the Lord's return. Many are fascinated by the coming apocalypse as various wannabe prophets jump in to fuel that glorious and frightful curiosity. They predict all kinds of dates.[4] We can't help ourselves. The fact Jesus tells us no one knows the day or the hour hasn't deterred the forecasters.[5] I hardly ever hear an apology when somebody gets the date wrong; humility is often lost in the process, but is this the way God's timing works?

Is there a red circle around a specific day marking the second coming? Are the angels ticking off the hours waiting to blow the trumpets? Is Michael anticipating the moment Jupiter aligns with Mars to start the final countdown? 'OK, boys, it's a red moon. Saddle up and get out there.'

Some claim the hooves are already thundering across the sky as the four horsemen gallop into earth's history.[6] But does God take such a mechanical, task-orientated, systematic approach when it comes to direct intervention in this world?

When Jesus returns, justice will be universal and irreversible. Every individual will be judged for what they did, or failed to do, in matters of faith and lifestyle.[7] There will be an eternal reckoning. The only one holding it back is God. He waits. He's not ready to pull the plug even though many wish he would do it sooner rather than later. But, what's holding him back? Why the l-o-o-o-ng delay? Consider Peter's take on the subject. It's quite revealing.

> They will say, 'Where is this "coming" he promised? Ever since our ancestors died, everything goes on as it has since the beginning of creation . . . But do not forget this one thing, dear friends: with the Lord a day is like a thousand years, and a thousand years are like a day. The Lord is not slow in keeping his promise, as some understand slowness. Instead, he is patient with you, not wanting anyone to perish, but everyone to come to repentance. (2 Pet. 3:4,8–9)

It all has to do with the way God measures time in the universe and our world. God doesn't wear a watch, and he doesn't mark a calendar. It's one of the reasons we can't predict the date and moment of Christ's return. When it comes to judgement, God determines time by the movement of people, not the hands of a clock.[8] As Peter tells us, the Lord doesn't want anyone to perish. So he patiently waits; it's the divine pause. The return of Christ is yet to happen. The fact that we even know about it reveals the mercy and patience of God towards us.[9]

Here's a scenario to illustrate the point. God sees Aunt Margaret's heart turning towards him, and he knows in about three weeks her nephew Robert will have the opportunity to speak to her about salvation. So God says to himself, 'I can wait three more weeks before I send my Son to earth the second time.' God then watches his servant Susan making preparations to enter China as a missionary. God has set the path, and he knows in three years Susan will follow it, so God says, 'I can wait a few more years.' The Lord sees that the Gentiles are still entering the kingdom. He knows they will eventually present the gospel to the entire world.[10] So God waits. He's patient because he doesn't want anyone to perish. Jesus even tells us the Jews won't see him again until they say, 'Blessed is he who comes in the name of the Lord' (Matt. 23:39).[11]

God holds back until all the aunts have heard, all the nephews have spoken, and all the missionaries have gone out into the world. He delays until every effectual sermon is preached and whoever chooses to come has entered the ark. His chronology is prompted by the hearts of people, not the ticking of a clock. His schedule is interactive and relational.

God will change the channel (the course of events in this world) when the people of earth warrant it. God doesn't order the programme by the cycles of the moon or the number of hours in a day. It doesn't matter to him if he has to wait another thousand years or just a few hours. Specific dates and timetables are irrelevant to love. If there is a chance he can save someone, he will delay the final judgement, even though creation moans under the burden of it.[12]

Love is Patient

I once asked a group of teenagers to write down seven characteristics of love. In this exercise, I was specifically looking for one thing; what will they put at the top of their list? Their answers were reasonably predictable.

- Love is romance.
- Love is a good feeling.
- Love gives presents.
- Love shares.
- Love is acceptance.

These were the kinds of responses you'd expect from young people. Then I asked them the harder question: 'If Jesus was sitting here right now, what do you think he'd put at the top of his page?'

Well, that was a conversation stopper. Some of the students were surprised God even had a list. So I told them, 'In God's catalogue, the number one indicator of love is patience.' They weren't expecting that. I was a bit startled myself when I first discovered it. Would patience be number one on your list? Would it even be in the inventory? It sure wasn't in theirs, and it sure wasn't in mine. Do you remember when Moses asked God to reveal his glory?[1] That was an excellent question, and the answer was a typical God response. It was both unpredictable and enlightening.

> And he passed in front of Moses, proclaiming, 'The LORD, the LORD, the compassionate and gracious God, slow to anger, abounding in love and faithfulness, maintaining love to thousands, and forgiving wickedness, rebellion and sin. Yet he does not leave the guilty unpunished. (Exod. 34:6–7)

Notice how God sandwiches 'patience' between the two 'love' statements. 'Slow to anger' isn't just a primary feature of love; it's an attribute of God's glory. God's patient love displays the glory of God.

In the New Testament, the Apostle Paul wrote one of the treasured, most profound passages on love in the entire Bible. I probably don't need to tell you what was on the top of his list. Read it for yourself: 'Love is patient' (1 Cor. 13:4).

When God doesn't move as fast as we want him to, we say he's disconnected, aloof or doesn't exist. The Bible says it is a revelation of his love and glory. There seems to be this ever-opening chasm between the wisdom of this world and the wisdom of God. Patience is a predominant characteristic of love. God is love. Love is patient. God is patient. We saw how this worked out for the second coming. Now let's see how it translates in one of the other significant judgements recorded in the Bible because these principles and events are closely related to God's command to clear the stage of Canaan.

We often focus on the extent and severity of God's judgements. From the bow of a sinking ship, we fall back on the knowledge of good and evil and assess God's actions from a human point of view.[2] We calculate how it affects us, the earth, and humanity as a whole. No wonder statements like this are often bandied about and quoted: 'My Sunday school teachers had turned Bible narrative into children's fables. They talked about Noah and the ark because the story had animals in it. They failed to mention that this was when God massacred all of humanity.'[3]

'Massacred' is the operative word here. It gets our attention. It's just as emotive as the word 'genocide' or the phrase 'ethnic cleansing'. Do you think Jesus would use words like these to describe his Father's involvement in the world? Scripturally, I believe he'd say, 'No, this is when my Father, in his patient love, intervened to preserve the human race.'

From God's perspective, this is what he was doing during the flood. He didn't massacre humankind. The deluge was God's radical effort to save us. He waited and watched. He had Noah build an ark to give humanity extra time to repent. The ark was more than a life raft; it was another shout in the dark for people to wise up. It was God's last call and attempt to save more than Noah and his family. Did God have a red-letter date marked on the calendar for the deluge? 'Just two years and three months to go till I turn on the tap.' No! He waited and waited, watching humanity go from bad to worse.

The LORD saw how great the wickedness of the human race had become on the earth, and that every inclination of the thoughts of the human heart was only evil all the time. The LORD regretted that he had made human beings on the earth, and his heart was deeply troubled. So the LORD said, 'I will wipe from the face of the earth the human race I have created – and with them the animals, the birds and the creatures that move along the ground – for I regret that I have made them.' (Gen. 6:5–7)

Here we see God wasn't looking at calendars and marking dates; he was observing humanity. The decision to turn on the hose was relational. It had nothing to do with timetables or marking off a task on a to-do list. His patient endurance indicates the depth of God's love. People see it as weakness and moral indifference, but this is not the case. Be grateful God is not quick to act. If he were, we wouldn't be here. God waited until there was only one righteous person left. If he delayed any longer, there would be no one left. The flood is God's radical, last-ditch attempt to save the human race.

Intermission

Is God a moral monster? Is he biting at the bit to destroy and decimate? No! He delays until the spring is stretched as far as it can go without irretrievable damage. He pauses. He wants to save. God steps in to preserve humanity, not massacre it. He changes the channel when every possibility of redemption exhausts itself. People can sit down and flick through the manual of good and evil, and question God's motivation and morality, but he will be true to love even though the world misunderstands him.

After being made alive, he [Jesus] went and made proclamation to the imprisoned spirits – to those who were disobedient long ago when God waited patiently in the days of Noah while the ark was being built. In it only a few people, eight in all, were saved through water. (1 Pet. 3:19–20)

The Culture of Sodom

We have briefly explored two significant judgements in the Bible: the second coming and the deluge. They're both global in scale. No one is left untouched or unaffected. These two events change everything. We want to save the planet; so does God. We do what we can. He does what we can't. He makes hard decisions. He is misunderstood, especially in the Old Testament. People rail against him, but he will take action to preserve love in his creation.

From our perspective, the flood was a mass genocide; from God's perspective, it was an act of commitment and love. The deluge, the second coming and the cleansing of Canaan have nothing to do with ethnicity. It is all about love and morality. God's righteousness is love. God is love. All sin is a transgression of love. The universe is made and sustained by the God of love and was deemed 'very good' because it was functioning in love. Whenever we stray from the Ten Commandments (love God; love our neighbour), we are offending the God of love. We are operating on a rogue wavelength which ends in death.[1]

I brought the second coming and the flood into the discussion because they correlate with God's directive to clear the stage of Canaan. Of course, the world is a much bigger platform than Canaan, and the number of fatalities is extreme and unimaginable, but the motivation prompting God's intervention is the same in all three instances. God doesn't change. He is patient. The Almighty is relational. He's working to preserve, not destroy. He steps in when evil gets out of control and will corrupt whatever comes in contact with it. More than four centuries before God told Joshua to take Canaan, he spoke to Abraham.

> Then the LORD said to him, 'Know for certain that for four hundred years your descendants will be strangers in a country not their own [Egypt] and that they will be enslaved and ill-treated there. But I will punish the nation they serve as slaves, and afterwards they will come out with great possessions. You, however, will go to your ancestors in peace and be buried at a good old age. In the fourth generation your descendants will come back here, for the sin of the Amorites has not yet reached its full measure.' (Gen. 15:13–16)

In this instance, the word 'Amorite' encompasses all the tribes and people's groups of Canaan. They lose the land because of their unrepented sin,[2] not because God randomly chose the Hebrews to claim it. God doesn't immediately pounce upon them. He's not standing on the edge of hell with a cricket bat, itching to whack them in. God waits and observes. He sends Abraham trekking over eight hundred miles from Ur as a witness. Abraham's family prospers in the land. God's blessing is upon him, exhibiting God's goodness. God blesses those who bless Abraham.[3] They can share in the benefits.

Abraham intercedes for Sodom.[4] God delivers Lot, and his family then steps in to stop Sodom's sin from polluting the rest of the land. It has already encompassed Gomorrah and the other cities of the plain and is spreading fast.[5]

In the Genesis story, Melchizedek is an anomaly, but he is also a witness for God.[6] The fact that he is a priest and the king of Salem suggests he has a community behind him with a belief system similar to Abraham's. Both Testaments approve of him.[7]

A word to describe what God is dealing with here is 'culture'. It's difficult to shift and change a culture. It starts moulding a child the minute they're born. When God destroyed Sodom and Gomorrah, he was staving off a contagion, giving the people of Canaan more time to repent and turn to the God of the patriarchs. If he hadn't dealt with Sodom, Canaan would have fallen long before the four-hundred-year prediction.

You may ask, 'But isn't this a date marked on heaven's calendar?' The answer is 'no'. The four-hundred-year prognostication didn't arise out of some celestial board meeting or discussion around the most convenient date to resettle the land. It stemmed from observation. God bases his prediction on the movements of people, not some organisational scheme or programme that takes precedence over the individuals involved. Sodom was gone, but the shadow remained as it slowly crept into the homes of Canaan's population.

Over the next four hundred years, God watches the history unfold. Despite the implanted missionaries, and radical intervention with Sodom and Gomorrah, the population of Canaan and their adopted culture move from bad to worse. After four generations, God takes the descendants of Abraham out of the land and relocates them in Egypt. The people of Canaan were going the way of Sodom, and God wasn't going to let his people be corrupted by them. We saw the same story earlier. God removed Lot and his family from Sodom; now he's distancing Joseph and his family from Sodom's influence.

no one takes it to heart;
the devout are taken away,
and no one understands
that the righteous are taken away
to be spared from evil. (Isa. 57:1)[8]

Although many of the years in Egypt were brutal and gruelling, God was not going to rush his hand regarding the people of Canaan. He delays when there is still a sliver of hope; when that sliver is gone, he acts. God won't clean the stage until the sin of Canaan is all-encompassing and irreversible. He waits till the very last moment; that's when he gets up and changes the channel.

God was patient when it came to the flood. He is patient when it comes to the second coming. He was patient about the stage and the people dwelling there. The citizens of Canaan knew what happened to Sodom and Gomorrah, but it wasn't enough to ward off the evil influence.[9] Four hundred years later, the entire population was engulfed by Sodom. This is the story up to the time of Joshua.

God was protecting his people from the growing influence that swept over Canaan. He took them out of the land to shield them. God is now bringing them back into the neighbourhood to redeem it, but the evil influence is at its peak, and God's people are just as susceptible now as they were during the migration of Joseph. God knows this, so he lays down strict guidelines.

Do not defile yourselves in any of these ways, because this is how the nations that I am going to drive out before you became defiled. Even the land was defiled; so I punished it for its sin, and the land vomited out its inhabitants. But you must keep my decrees and my laws. The native-born and the foreigners residing among you must not do any of these detestable things. (Lev. 18:24–6)

However, in the cities of the nations the LORD your God is giving you as an inheritance, do not leave alive anything that breathes. Completely destroy them. (Deut. 20:16–17)

Genocide, ethnic cleansing, cultural annihilation, population extermination – what words will we use to describe the clearing of the stage? What words could make it more palatable in our present generation? There are none. God doesn't try to make it acceptable in practice or policy. Neither should we. The Jews don't rejoice in it. Judaism doesn't practise it. Today's Christians are often embarrassed by it, and it's not God's heart for the world. To focus on this as the character of God and the expression of his temperament is a gross mistake.

God commanded the cleansing to preserve and implement his witness to the world. He is protecting the show that will save the earth's population. The Almighty is watching the actors' backs. He is breaking into a world that no longer knows what he is like or who he is. God chose a small stage because of what he would have to do to claim it. He was very strict about the boundaries.

You are about to pass through the territory of your relatives the descendants of Esau, who live in Seir. They will be afraid of you, but be very careful. Do not provoke them to war, for I will not give you any of their land. (Deut. 2:4–5)

God wanted to expand the borders, but he had no intention of using force.[10] He was going to plant his people on a small, uncontaminated stage, and the cultural influence of the kingdom of God was to spread by attraction. This is how God wants to expand the kingdom. This is the way he wants to reveal his heart to the world. He is going to use blessing, not violence; a culture born from heaven, not Sodom.[11] This is the motivation driving the first act of the show.

Act 1: When the curtain goes up, the Hebrews will march into Canaan and clean up the stage.

Living the Creed

It's easy to make declarations of belief and intent, but to follow them through without compromise takes it to another level. A good friend of mine in the hippie church I attended once told me that if you want to know a person's doctrine, don't just listen to their words but watch how they live. He was a wise man. I never forgot that.

I was once going through Belfast city centre with my wife and our oldest boy. He had just got back from university, so we decided to go to the city centre and do a bit of Christmas shopping. On the grounds of the City Hall, there was a giant Ferris wheel; it's called the 'Eye'. They tend to pop up in significant locations around the world. Well, we were driving by it looking for a parking space, when my wife said: 'Son, have you ever been on the Eye?'

'No.'

'You should do it while you're home.'

'Maybe.'

'No, you should really do it while it's here in town. It would be fun.'

'I'll see.'

'Ah, come on. You need to ride on it today. You won't always get the chance to see Belfast from that high up.'

'But I don't want to see Belfast from high up.'

'You don't? It would make your holiday. Come on. You have to ride on the Eye while you have the chance; I'll even pay.'

'But I don't want to go on the Eye.'

I dropped out of that conversation. From the very start, I had already sided with my boy. Who wants to go on the Eye? To me, it was a big yawn on the horizon: an expensive way to fall asleep. So, in love, I patiently bit my tongue and kept quiet. You would've been proud of me, but as the conversation went on, my temporary vow of silence started to crumble. I eventually caved in and asked my dear wife the question, 'Love, have you ever been on the Eye?'

Well, that was close to a marriage breaker. Neither of us had ever been on the Eye, and there was no compulsion to climb on board. As a matter of fact, my wife is afraid of heights. I don't know why our boy's participation was so urgent that day. I guess that will be one of life's little mysteries. Nevertheless, my boy didn't waver and kept his feet securely planted on good old terra firma as the big Eye rolled off into the distant past; an opportunity lost to the Porter family.

Just for the record, my wife and I are still together, but I'm continually learning the connection between patience and love. I also respect the correlation between what I say and what I do. I suppose the word we use when they don't match up is 'hypocrisy'. No one likes that word, no matter which side of the fence they're on.

Displacing a Culture

The second act of the script requires the Jewish nation to march into the land and declare, 'Hear, O Israel: The Lord our God, the Lord is one' (Deut. 6:4). This creedal declaration is what defines the Jewish people then and today.[1] It is radical and extreme, especially when you announce it amid a poly-theistic world. It's the banner flying over their booth at the global psychic fair; it's the marker that will shape and influence their culture from the inside out. The Jewish people will stand unique and separate from all the other nations of the world.[2] Can you imagine it? It flies in the face of ancient Near Eastern culture and society. It relegates all those deities, begging for attention, to the rubbish bin. The nations would need a huge fleet of trucks to haul away all the household trash.

Act 2 is a culture changer. Get rid of the idols, and you silence the demons. Silence the demons, and you are open to hearing a different voice. Listening to a different voice will modify your belief system. Alter your belief system, and you will behave differently. Change your traditions, and you change a culture. The culture of Sodom would die. The culture of God's king-dom on earth would become the main attraction and spread throughout the world. But it's one thing to declare it and another thing to live it. Remember, this is God's ideal plan: the original script. It's how he expected the actors to behave on the world stage. His reputation was at stake.

The choice of words in this declaration carries more weight in Hebrew than it does in English. When we say 'hear', we mean to listen with our ears.

- 'Did you hear the news today?'
- 'Can you hear me?'

In Hebrew, it means to 'listen and do'. This declaration of faith calls for action, not study and contemplation. Declare your allegiance to one God. Speak it out. Then live as though you believe it. There is no room for misunderstanding in this pronouncement. It's more than listening to affirmations. It's declaring a lifestyle that is authentic and matches up to the words spoken and heard. The code they are to live by is the first line of the Ten Commandments. It's crucial to the script. It's fundamental in the Old Testament; it is decisive in the New Testament. If the actors on the stage don't live up to it, the entire production flops, and the plot will be lost. The audience will be confused, and later generations will wonder what the show was all about. It is paramount that the actors keep to the script. The second act is crucial to the show's success.

Act 2: The Jews will live by one creed. 'Hear, O Israel: The LORD our God, the LORD is one.' (Deut. 6:4)

God in the Camp

Act 3 focuses on God's living presence in Israel. It is a bumpy ride for both God and the Hebrew nation. To invite the almighty, true and living God, who split the Red Sea, drowned the Egyptian army and orchestrated the ten plagues, to come and live in the middle of your camp is risky on many levels. It's a scary business.

The Hebrew nation at Mount Sinai learned from experience that this venture with God wasn't going to be a smooth ride. They trembled when God revealed himself to Moses on Mount Sinai. They wanted a buffer between them and the Almighty.[1] Very quickly, the Hebrews learned that the presence of God was different from the presence of idols. Idols don't do anything; God does, and he means business.

While Moses was on the mountain receiving the Ten Commandments, the people below were revelling before the golden calf. They strayed from the script before they even got to the stage. The cultural influence of Sodom was already engulfing them.

Moses saw that the people were running wild and that Aaron had let them get out of control and so become a laughing-stock to their enemies. So he stood at the entrance to the camp and said,

'Whoever is for the LORD, come to me.' And all the Levites rallied to him.

Then he said to them, 'This is what the LORD, the God of Israel, says: "Each man strap a sword to his side. Go back and forth through the camp from one end to the other, each killing his brother and friend and neighbour."' The Levites did as Moses commanded, and that day about three thousand of the people died . . . And the LORD struck the people with a plague because of what they did with the calf Aaron had made. (Exod. 32:25–8,35)

This episode also has its cringe factor. There are many more like it in the Bible, especially when it comes to the actors and the stage they perform on. The Director will often take extreme measures to get the show on the road and keep everyone on board with the script. He is not going to let the culture of Sodom get a foothold in his people or the mission. It's all about establishing the kingdom of God on earth. It's the life raft for humanity. It's embedded in the promise given to Abraham. The kingdom of God manifested on the world stage is central to revealing the heart of God to the citizens of this planet.

God promised us there wouldn't be another global flood.[2] Why? Because he knew the infiltration of the kingdom would prevent the world population from going completely rogue. There will always be more than one person who will say 'yes' to God. A Noah sequel won't be necessary. The kingdom will present an alternative culture. All of God's dealings on the stage and with the actors is what's holding back global destruction. God will protect the production anyway he can – no matter how extreme, radical or distasteful it seems to us.

My boy once said, 'Dad, the kingdom of God is the only thing standing between us and the zombie apocalypse!' What could I say? The detail about the zombies may be overstated, but at least he was thinking theologically. That boy will lead someday. I just pray it's in the kingdom and not some zombie survival cult.

So, how is this going to work? We have a holy, living, actively engaged, all-powerful God who will not tolerate idols or sin, moving into a camp of people who are stubborn, unruly, ungrateful and have the sin of the world stamped all over them. In many ways, this doesn't look like a marriage made in heaven, but that's what it is. God proposed on Mount Sinai, and the people accepted.[3] God saw it as a marriage, and so did Israel.[4] This is why God and the prophets shout 'adultery' each time the nation invites an idol into their home.[5]

It was a rocky marriage from the start. If God and the Hebrews came to me for premarital counselling, I would've cautioned against it. It's just not a good match.[6] It's one thing to have a wedding, but then comes the marriage. The golden calf incident took place between the wedding and the honeymoon. They didn't even get to the union. God wants to move into the middle of the camp, but the way things were going, he knew something had to change; for their sake, not his.

> Go up to the land flowing with milk and honey. But I will not go with you, because you are a stiff-necked people and I might destroy you on the way. (Exod. 33:3)

These are not comforting words. It's harsh, but remember what's at stake here. These are the chosen actors. They have to honour the script and take it seriously. But here's the impasse: how can a holy God dwell and travel with an immoral, unfaithful people? The citizens would be damaged. The bride wouldn't survive the honeymoon, let alone the marriage. Even though the Israelites mourned when God said he wouldn't go with them, the statements that he would kill them off increased their trepidation.

It can be dangerous with God in the camp. Many probably sighed with relief when they heard God wasn't going with them.[7] The Israelites knew the perils of hosting the Creator. They were learning how vast the gulf was between religion and presence. An idol stashed in your pocket isn't a threat. A holy, living deity with strong moral values and robust opinions is a different story altogether. You will need a lot of prayers and crash helmets to survive the journey. However, Moses saw the bigger picture.

> He made known his ways to Moses,
> his deeds to the people of Israel. (Ps. 103:7)

The Israelites complained all through the wilderness because they saw only God's deeds, but they never drew close enough to learn God's ways. As a leader Moses wasn't going to drag an empty tent, the tabernacle, through the wilderness. Moses knew God's absence wouldn't work. He recognised the love and patience of God. So he prayed:

> 'If your Presence does not go with us, do not send us up from here. How will anyone know that you are pleased with me and with your people unless you go with us? What else will distinguish me and your people from all the other people on the face of the earth?'
>
> And the LORD said to Moses, 'I will do the very thing you have asked, because I am pleased with you and I know you by name.' (Exod. 33:15–17)

The Hebrews may not have realised it, but this was good news. God desires to be in the centre of the camp, not left behind on some isolated mountaintop. He wants to break into the world and establish the kingdom. He wants to be the centre of everything. It's in the script, but how can God do it? How is this going to pan out? Well, one thing is irrefutable; Moses and the Hebrew nation can't set the terms because they aren't the ones posing the danger. They aren't the threat. If God is going to move into the middle of the camp, he has to legislate the requirements, not the Jews.

They could set up their own religion if God were one of the idols enshrined on the mantelpiece, but this God is real and alive. The Hebrews could issue all the crash helmets and fireproof clothing they want, but that wouldn't stop God from being God. They aren't participating in a simulated religious exercise; this is the genuine article.

So, God writes the contract. He sets the terms. They aren't ideal for him or the Hebrews. There would be a compromise on both sides. The stipulations God set out were never meant to be a permanent fixture, but they were necessary for the initial establishment of the kingdom in that world culture.

Only God can tell the Hebrews how to make the relationship safe. He sets the boundaries and the guidelines that will protect and guide them. It's how deity and humanity, in a fallen world, can step out together.[8] The relationship is utterly unique. God isn't just trying to save the world; he's also protecting the actors. He wants to restore the stage and the planet. God requires the earth to be like heaven.

The boundaries God establishes are physical, relational and religious. Some of the rules are strange and difficult to understand, but that doesn't matter. What matters is that God understands them. What matters is that it is possible to have God in the middle of the camp and not offend him nor die prematurely. The first boundary God introduces is the tabernacle: 'Then let them make a sanctuary for me, and I will dwell among them' (Exod. 25:8).

God goes into great detail regarding its construction.[9] The three sections of the tabernacle protect the people at various stages of the encounter. Israel can enter the outer court. The priests can enter the holy place. The high priest can enter the holy of holies, where the tangible presence of God abides. The closer a person moves towards God, the higher the value of the surroundings and the furniture.[10] This tent is the physical boundary God laid out to keep the people safe while he was in the camp.

The laws regarding the priesthood, the sacrifices and the rituals are the religious boundaries. These include clothing, festivals, what is clean and unclean, offerings, diet, respect for the land, and sacramental proceedings.

The relational boundaries have to do with communal living. They describe how to behave towards your family, your neighbours, guests, resident and transient strangers, how to conduct war and relate to enemies. Of course, there is no dichotomy between the secular and the spiritual in the Bible or the Hebrew nation. Sin is probably the only non-spiritual idea we observe in the Bible. Going to work in the morning and doing a good job was just as spiritual as going to the synagogue and saying a prayer. All of life was before an audience of one: the almighty, living God.

The laws and regulations recorded in the Old Testament aren't meant to burden the Jews but to protect them. They were divine stipulations to keep God in the camp and the people safe as they lived in his presence. God then bends down and confines himself to this little, sequestered space called the 'holy of holies'. He didn't do this with any other nation on earth. The ark of the covenant becomes his earthly throne.[11] He wants to be in the centre of the camp, even though it costs him.

Of course, God is everywhere. Israel knew this.[12] But we're talking about his manifest presence; the place where God reveals himself in tangible ways, such as the fire by day, the cloud by night, the Shekinah glory. Act 3 is foundational. The manifest presence of God among his people is what makes the production authentic, real and challenging. His presence is what brings the blessing. It is central to the kingdom of God.

The culture of the kingdom must not copy the culture it's displacing. Images of God are not allowed on stage.[13] The Hebrews didn't need idols to represent God. His presence was tangibly alive and active in the midst of them. God's living presence was necessary at the time of Moses, evident at the time of Jesus, and is imperative for the church today.

Act 3: God will live in the Jewish nation as a good king.

No Longer Single

Now, as the wedding fades into the past, the marriage begins. The Hebrews leave Sinai behind and settle in the promised land. It's flowing with milk and honey. In due course, the Song of Songs becomes the number one hit in the nation's discography. It's the inspired expression of God's love for Israel.[1] The marriage certificate is sealed safely in the ark of the covenant, and the book of Exodus becomes the notarised chronicle of the ceremony.

Today we have photos to remind us of our wedding day. We pull the album off the shelf, sweep off the dust, turn the pages and reminisce about how happy we once were (and still are). Back then, we had hair, and it wasn't grey. We were wrinkle-free, mobile and obediently fulfilling God's directive in Genesis 1:28.

I married late in life. I had forty-odd years of bachelorhood behind me, and I was set in my ways. Israel was the same. Like every married couple, my wife and I had to make adjustments; so did Israel. Whenever I put on the kettle and pour one cup of tea, my wife says, 'Oh, I see you're in bachelor mode today.' That's when I turn and hand her the cup: 'No. I made this for you, dear.' She isn't that easily fooled, though, and I admit it was a lie. Suffice it to say, I had a lot of changes to make over the years. I think God gave men wives to keep them from going feral. I'm just about domesticated, but now and then I still drift into bachelor mode; so does Israel. For the Hebrews, the day-to-day adjustments of setting up the house and living together with God is no longer a future dream. He's down off the mountain and in the middle of the camp – no more bachelorhood for the people.

Adjustments and Laws

The new society has a lot of adjustments to make. The Hebrews now have to embrace the Ten Commandments along with all the other righteous laws of God. It's a new constitution. It's a new deal. The government of God is upon them and regulated within their borders. This is Act 4.

The history recorded in the Bible confirms God isn't into making laws. God is into freedom.[2] There was only one law in the garden of Eden: 'Don't eat from that tree.' It was a warning to protect us. If we obeyed there would be no need for future legislation, but we couldn't keep our hands off the fruit. We broke the law. Legislation is now required. Circumstances have altered. The new situation requires more robust measures to curtail the encroaching chaos we allowed back into the world. God had to expand one law to ten. He made them easy to remember. You can count them on your thumbs and fingers.

The Ten Commandments are kingdom principles: love God; love your neighbour. Unfortunately, before Moses even stepped off the mountain, the people had already violated laws one, two, three and seven.[3] If they obeyed the ten, that would've been enough. However, in the Old Testament, the Jewish nation ends up with 613 of them.[4]

They moved from one to ten, to 613. Jewish history from Moses to Malachi is approximately one thousand years. For that length of time, 613 laws to govern a nation is quite minimal. I know it's not fair to compare an ancient culture with what we face today, but I do find it interesting how legislation in Western countries escalates. For example, in 2016, the State of California passed 900 new laws.[5] The BBC reports Britain added 3,506 new laws in the year 2010.[6] The continual escalation of lawmaking will likely make us all criminals at some time in our lives, and we won't even know it until we're fined or marched off to jail. God gave Israel only 613 laws for a millennium.[7]

So, let's ask the question. Did God give Israel an unbearable burden when he gave them the law? Many would argue that the number of rules is irrelevant. If you disobey one, you break them all; Eden already explored that scenario. If there is only one law, we would probably violate it. The number is irrelevant.

Perhaps we should address the question another way. Did God give Israel a task he knew was impossible to fulfil? If so, then how would this benefit what he was trying to accomplish? Is it counterproductive to hand the actors a script they couldn't perform? God's reputation was at stake. Why commission entertainers and then withhold the props?

There's no doubt some of us are already reaching for our Christian hat and quoting Paul.[8] I won't refute his take on the law, and I don't intend to preach a different gospel.[9] That would be stupid and dishonouring to Christ. However, to grasp what Paul and Jesus say about the law in the New Testament, we need to appreciate its purpose in its original context. As I pointed out earlier in Chapter 10, instead of dragging the New Testament into the Old, we first need to follow the script from the Old into the New.

God knows we are incapable of keeping any law. He witnessed our failure to obey one, let alone 613 of them. That's why so many of the rules given to Israel deal with sacrifice and offerings. Provision is made for *when* we break one; not *if* we break one. The high priest offers atonement once a year in the holy of holies for the entire nation.[10] There are also various offerings for unintentional sin.[11] In many instances, God even forgives the person who sins intentionally.[12] The point is God knows the actors.

The offerings, rituals and commands were not given to make people good or to produce saints. The law was given to keep God in the camp and the people safe in his presence. It also dispelled the culture of Sodom. It was a buffer between the Jewish nation and the idols of the world. It provided a platform for the kingdom of God on earth. The law doesn't establish the kingdom; the presence of God amid the people is what the kingdom is all about. The pagan nations surrounding Israel had laws; some were good and were similar to the commandments of Israel.[13] However, only the Jews had the tangible presence of God in the camp, and the blessing he bestowed on them. The law was necessary to make this happen.

Act 4: This new society will embrace the Ten Commandments along with all the other righteous laws of God as their constitution.

The Benefits

At this point in the production, I'm sure many of us are wondering if it's worth it. Would I want God to live in the middle of my town? When the Philistines captured the ark of the covenant, they couldn't wait to send it back to Israel. God in their camp almost killed them off.[1] They didn't have the boundaries to protect them.

The Jews often wrote of the times they themselves offended God, and the outcome was extreme. During the first ceremony of the tabernacle, Aaron's sons disobeyed God's directives and were incinerated.[2] Later in Jewish history, Uzzah reaches out his hand to steady the ark of the covenant and is struck dead.[3] At times God judges the whole nation because one person misbehaves.[4] Obedience to the boundaries God set up is what keeps the actors safe while God is in the camp. It also holds back the culture of Sodom and the influence of idols from overwhelming them.

God doesn't want to judge, or hurt people; he wants to bless them. From the very start, Eden was a paradise. God was in the middle of the camp. He would spend time with the couple he created in his image. They could eat from the tree of life any time they desired. From the very beginning, God's heart was to bless the human race, but each time the blessing was bestowed human behaviour deteriorated to a place warranting judgement. Throughout the Old Testament, we witness God's desire to bless, and humanity's incompetence to maintain the privilege. It frustrates us. It exasperates him.

> Rid yourselves of all the offences you have committed, and get a new heart and a new spirit. Why will you die, people of Israel? (Ezek. 18:31)

> As surely as I live, declares the Sovereign LORD, I take no pleasure in the death of the wicked, but rather that they turn from their ways and live. Turn! Turn from your evil ways! Why will you die, people of Israel? (Ezek. 33:11)

> The LORD will rise up as he did at Mount Perazim,
>   he will rouse himself as in the Valley of Gibeon –
> to do his work, his strange work,
>   and perform his task, his alien task. (Isa. 28:21)

God's strange work, his alien task, is when he has to judge his people. No parent likes to discipline their child, but it has to be done to protect the child's future; the community was God's child as much as each individual participating in it.[5]

Act 5 is what God desires for Israel. He wants to pour his blessing upon them.[6] The grace of God is necessary for them to fulfil their purpose on this earth. God is doing everything he possibly can to bring Israel to the place of blessing and then keep them there.[7]

Here is a snapshot of the blessing God wants Israel to experience and demonstrate before the world. It incorporates safety, peace, no fear, no lack, purpose, success, prosperity, perfect health, long life and justice.

1. You will be the leader in world affairs (Deut. 28:1).
2. All urban and rural populations will prosper (Deut. 28:3).
3. All your children, pets and livestock will be safe and multiply (Deut. 7:13–14,24; 28:4–5).
4. Wherever you go and whatever you do, you will be successful (Deut. 28:6).
5. You will dwell in peace, without fear. God will protect you from all enemies. He's watching your back (Exod. 23:22; 26:6–8; Deut. 28:7).
6. Everything you plant, and everything you do will prosper. No one will go hungry (Deut. 28:8–9).
7. You will be established and defined as God's holy people. The nations will stand in awe (Deut. 28:9–10).
8. Your prosperity will exponentially escalate (Deut. 28:11).
9. You will be debt-free and stay debt-free. You will be the lender. Everything you touch will turn to gold. Even the weather will work for you; not against you (Deut. 28:12).
10. You will be leaders, always on the top, not the bottom (Deut. 28:13).
11. No one in your land will be poor or homeless (Deut. 15:4).
12. There will be no sickness or disease within your borders (Exod. 15:26; 23:25–6; Deut. 7:15).

Is this a prosperity gospel? No. It's the gospel of the kingdom.[8] By Act 5, we should see Israel on a clean stage, declaring and serving the one true, living God, embracing his constitution and welcoming him into the neighbourhood. Then God can outrageously pour his blessing upon them as his holy people. Israel will then stand out unlike any other nation in the world. They will be great. Their name will be renowned. God will be able to display his heart for the human race. The world will see his character and goodness. This is attractive. It's a contagious allurement. It's the kingdom of God manifested on earth as it is in heaven. God reveals himself through his family; a community reconnected and in right relationship with their heavenly Father. The world then watches on as love invades an orphaned planet; it's the greatest show on earth.

Act 5: God will bless Israel, unlike any other nation in the world. It will be the manifestation of the kingdom of God on earth.

Som-adat

The fun part of the script comes when the surrounding nations take notice of Israel and stand in awe of God's goodness. Orphans are attracted to a just, fair, loving family living under the blessing of a good, kind parent. This is what Act 6 is all about. It's what God had in mind when he told Abraham, 'In you all the families of the earth shall be blessed' (Gen. 12:3, NKJV).

Being a channel of God's blessing in this world is Israel's assignment. Get in the blessing; stay in the blessing. Then the world will see the goodness of our heavenly Father. News will travel fast. When merchants, armies and travellers pass by or through Israel and witness the blessing of God upon the people, they will point and say, 'I want som-adat.' They will then report to others what they had witnessed in Israel.[1]

Why do they want som-adat? They want som-adat because that is what they have been searching for all their lives. The blessing of God is what the world was chasing and hoping to get from their idols. The child sacrifice, the temple prostitutes, the bestiality, witchcraft and occult practices the idols demanded of them didn't bring the goods. The audience suffered from illness and disease. Their spells didn't bring the remedy. They were fearful and superstitious because they didn't have a deity as faithful and consistent to watch their back. The idols of the ancient Near East weren't known for their love.

We witnessed what some of the blessings of God looked like in the life of the patriarchs. This is where the rubber meets the road. It's a microcosm of Israel in 3-D. Abraham and Sarah have a miracle child. Isaac reaps a full crop during a severe famine. Jacob is protected and receives a great name. Everything thrown at Joseph turns to good as he becomes the head and not the tail.[2] We caught a glimpse of the blessing in each life. Now we find the same grace brought together and multiplied in the nation. The laws kept the idols and the culture of Sodom outside the border. The blessing wasn't just what God bestowed, but it was God himself.

We find Israel's experience often expressed through poetry and song. The psalms speak of the joy they experienced in the presence of God.

You make known to me the path of life;
    you will fill me with joy in your presence,
    with eternal pleasures at your right hand. (Ps. 16:11)
How precious to me are your thoughts, God!
    How vast is the sum of them!
Were I to count them,
    they would outnumber the grains of sand –
    when I awake, I am still with you. (Ps. 139:17–18)
One thing I ask from the LORD,
    this only do I seek:
that I may dwell in the house of the LORD
    all the days of my life,
to gaze on the beauty of the LORD
    and to seek him in his temple. (Ps. 27:4)

I will say of the LORD, 'He is my refuge and my fortress,
my God, in whom I trust.'
Surely he will save you
from the fowler's snare
and from the deadly pestilence. (Ps. 91:2–3)

Israel's list goes on and on. Is it worth having the Almighty in the centre of the camp? You decide. We all have to choose. It's his kingdom. It's his show. It's counter-cultural. There is no other show on earth like it.

Act 6: The surrounding nations will take notice and say, 'I want som-adat.'

A Nation of Priests

After fulfilling a course of study, attending many interviews, and serving as an associate pastor in Glasgow, Scotland, I was officially ordained an elder in the Church of the Nazarene. Immediately, the district superintendent wanted to slap a clerical collar on me. You know, one of those white rectangles fastened under the chin of priests and clergy. I don't know if it was a vestige of hippie nonconformity, but I couldn't do it. However, I do understand and respect my colleagues who sport one.

During my twenty-two years of service as a pastor, I never owned, borrowed or wore a collar. I did give in and wear a suit and tie for a few years, but it was never comfortable or conducive to survival. I mean, if the apocalypse hit on Sunday morning, how far would I get wearing a suit and tie? If anything, I should at least be allowed to wear shoes I can run in.

Here's the strange thing though: God wanted everyone in Israel to wear a clerical collar. He didn't just call specific individuals to the priesthood, he summoned them all. The entire population, as one body, was officially chosen to wear a collar. 'You will be for me a kingdom of priests and a holy nation' (Exod. 19:6).

I don't know if this sends a shudder down your spine; it sure does mine. I find it hard to imagine. Have you ever been in a room full of clergy? Can you envisage a herd of priests stomping around in the grocery store, or stampeding through the shopping mall?

So what is God saying here? He had already appointed a small priesthood to serve the community. The priests he chose were to wear different clothes and follow specific laws. God wasn't as strict with the rest of the population.[1] So what does this verse in Exodus mean? If everyone becomes a shepherd, then where's the flock? It appears God had something else in mind when he called Israel to be a nation of priests.

What is the primary function of a priest? Fundamentally, a priest takes a human hand and places it in the palm of God: 'God, this is the Queen of Sheba. Queen, this is the true, living God.' The formal introduction is the theme of Act 7. When the nations of the world come to Israel announcing, 'I want som-adat', Israel will take hold of their hand and place it in the palm of God and declare, 'This is who you need to know if you want som-adat.'

The nation, as a community, is the witness. The citizens living in the kingdom of God is the attraction. They aren't just to give a message; they are the message. Together, they stand as a living endorsement of God's goodness.

At this point in the production, Israel should be ushering people to their seats and handing out tickets to those who are pushing to get in the door. Jesus tells us 'the good news of the kingdom of God is being preached [revealed], and everyone is forcing their way into it' (Luke 16:16).

God is in the middle of the camp. The people are embracing the culture of the kingdom. The blessing of God is upon them.

your kingdom come,

your will be done,

on earth as it is in heaven. (Matt. 6:10)

God was setting Israel up to reach the world – not just the borders of Canaan. It's similar to what John Wesley said regarding the mission: 'I look upon all the world as my parish.'[2]

Israel is a nation of priests called to reach the inhabitants of the world. The audience is Israel's flock. Israel is the gateway, the fountain of love and hope. This is how the love of God is going to invade an orphaned planet. It's through a community living in and manifesting the kingdom of God.

Act 7: As a nation of priests, Israel will introduce the audience to God. 'Here is how you can get som-adat.'

Always Room for More

Have you ever thought what this world would be like if Adam and Eve had behaved themselves? What if they had ignored the serpent and reached for the tree of life instead of latching on to the knowledge of good and evil? If we had a chance, I think all of us would like to jump aboard a time machine and whisk ourselves back to that shocking moment. I'd take a gun and an axe with me. You know; shoot the serpent and chop down the tree before the picnic begins. If they had only known what we know now, things would be so different.

According to Genesis, eating from the wrong tree is what brought death into the world.[1] It's all we know. It's embedded in our history. Life is temporary; enjoy it while you can. Life is hard, and then you die. What staggers me is that no one is comfortable with this situation. Almost every religion speaks of an after-life that reaches beyond the grave. Why is that? Why do we even think this way if death is the natural order of things? If we were born to live, die and disappear, then why do we claw for more hours, and desire unending moments? The majority of humanity doesn't want to cease. Why is that?

In the garden, Adam was never told to eat from the tree of life. The serpent didn't tempt Adam and Eve with life. Why?

Humanity was created for it. We already had it. The image and breath of God in us shouts, 'Life, life, eternal life.'[2] Some philosophers and scientists consider death to be a friend; the human majority and the Bible label it an enemy.[3] It was not God's ultimate plan, nature or desire.[4]

But, let's imagine we succeeded. We were able to talk H.G. Wells out of his time machine and travel back to the beginning.[5] We just put the serpent down and axed his favourite hangout – yee-haw! But what would this earth be like if no one ever died? We would have a problem. For some countries, it's already a grave concern. From 1979 to 2015, China passed a one child per family law. The reason was overpopulation. Even with the spectre of death, the earth can only support so many individuals. Can you imagine what it would be like if no one ever died? How many cars would be on the road? How much food would we need? How many would be sharing a house with us?[6] It is unthinkable and unworkable, especially when God tells us from the very start to have babies and fill the earth.

If no one died, this planet would fill up exponentially quickly. Longevity would be a curse for future generations. However, God had a much bigger plan. We see it when we look at the sky at night. We dream about it. We write about it. We fantasise, but we don't get it. The garden of Eden was a special place. It would soon fill up with people. What were the occupants supposed to do? They were supposed to go outside the garden and plant new gardens; take what God showed them in Eden and terraform the planet. They were to leave Eden with God's blessing, not under the dark cloud that followed them. Spread your wings and fly. Fill the earth, but then what? Then look up.

Why did God create billions of stars, planets and galaxies? There were more than Abraham could number.[7] There are so many we can't even count them with our high-powered, orbiting telescopes. From the start, God was providing unlimited space. Astronomers watch as new planets are born.[8] Science tells us the galaxies are still expanding and growing.[9] Why? One genuine possibility is that it's increasing for us, but we just haven't kept up with it.

'Fill the garden.'

'OK, then what?'

'Fill the earth.'

'OK, then what?'

'Fill the sky.'

'OK, then what?'

'Don't worry. My universe has no limit. I will always make room for you.'

This scenario could have been our story if we had chosen to eat from the tree of life. Living forever was no problem, but since we got the knowledge of good and evil, we spend all our time on war, weapons and sustenance. We can hardly reach the limits of our solar system, let alone explore the galaxy and beyond. Our wrong choice in Eden has constrained us. It has preoccupied us with survival and the search for happiness. We wouldn't have had to spend so much money and effort searching for security and fulfilment if we had eaten from the right tree and ignored the serpent.

This brings us to Act 8. God wants the kingdom to spread exponentially in the same way he desired humanity to increase in his creation. It is a step-by-step process. God could've created us all at once and put us on a planet big enough to sustain us but, instead, he created us one at a time. He blessed us with the creative force of procreation and commissioned us with the task of expansion. It is also the way God works when it comes to the kingdom. He starts with a small mustard seed and plants it in our soil. He calls one man and makes a nation. He takes one country and watches the kingdom spread throughout the earth. Act 8 was to witness the kingdom of God stretching across the continents and islands of this planet.

In Act 8, the audience is supposed to stand up and shout acclamations of praise and worship. The critics are to reward the production with a five-star rating, provoking the world to gaze in awe at the goodness of God. The standing ovation was to echo around the planet and beyond, as the actors receive their Oscars and thank the Director for his creativity, love and patience to make it happen. This is nothing less than the kingdom of God on earth as it is in heaven.

Intermission

The plan is a good one. This is the original script as it was supposed to play out. It's what God had in mind before the screenplay left the drawing board. The kingdom of God displayed through its citizens was to reveal God's heart and character to an orphaned planet. It was a shout to the world: 'You have a good Father, and you are so, so loved.' Then the world was to reject their false gods and renounce the influence of the serpent. Lay down the knowledge of good and evil, and pick up the handbook of the one and only true God.

The sad part is, it never happened. There were a few stars in the show and a few glorious moments,[10] but a majority of the actors through multiple generations messed it up. At times they crumpled the script, chucked it over their shoulder and walked off. Their improvisation was terrible. People still read the story up to Malachi and wonder: 'What is God like? Who is he? What is this Israel thing all about?'

Here's a challenge that would probably benefit all of us. The next time we decide to read through the Bible in one year, let's try to understand it from God's perspective. Let's pray and consciously scan the pages with this overarching question in mind: 'Father, what do you get out of it?' Amen.

Act 8: Then we watch as the kingdom of God grows and extends its branches throughout the entire world.

Street Cred

A film director is the creative force that steers the production. They are responsible for the script and the film. They carry the vision and guide the actors towards its fulfilment. It's not an easy task, especially when performers flounder and exhaust their passion.

All directors have their way of handling awkward people and situations. Whether strict, flexible or accommodating, they have to inspire and keep the actors on board. This is often the case with Israel. Sometimes mortals question God's people-skills, but he is passionate about the final product because his reputation is at stake.

But is God really bothered about what people think of him? Many would say he is above such petty concerns. I mean, he is God, isn't he? Would we care what people thought of us if we held the fate of the universe in our hand? Ultimate power brings its own kudos. Who needs a good reputation if you are called God, and your last name is Almighty?

Perhaps the best way to explore this issue is to step on to one of the sets and watch God in action, especially when the actors stray from the script. For example, after the golden calf scene, God tells Moses to stand aside because he's going to judge the perpetrators. Instead, Moses jumps into the middle of the arena and pleads with God.

> 'Lord,' he said, 'why should your anger burn against your people, whom you brought out of Egypt with great power and a mighty hand? Why should the Egyptians say, "It was with evil intent that he brought them out, to kill them in the mountains and to wipe them off the face of the earth"? Turn from your fierce anger; relent and do not bring disaster on your people.' (Exod. 32:11–12)

The main thrust of this prayer is God's reputation.

> Yes, Lord, they are your people. Yes, Lord, they ran after other gods. Yes, Lord, your judgements are valid and right. Yes, Lord, this is justice, but what will the Egyptians think? How will they interpret your behaviour? They won't understand. They will say you are evil and not good. What you do here right now will not be quickly forgotten. I know the Egyptians. They raised me. If you judge your people at this time, your name will be slandered. They won't forget it. Once posted on their Facebook page, it will never go away.

So, is this a good prayer? Is God at all concerned about what the Egyptians think of him? He already blasted their gods out of the water, killed their first-born and wiped out their army. 'Wise up, Moses. What planet do you inhabit?' But as always, God will be God. He's not like us. What he does next is quite astonishing. 'Then the Lord relented and did not bring on his people the disaster he had threatened' (Exod. 32:14).

Why does God change his mind? Because his reputation is at stake. Surprisingly, God is concerned about what the Egyptians think of him. This story and the motivation behind it are deeply embedded in Old Testament theology; we can't get away from it. Three times in the book of Ezekiel, God reminds the Jewish nation why he withheld his judgement against them.

1. God withholds judgement in Egypt.

> So I said I would pour out my wrath on them and spend my anger against them in Egypt. But for the sake of my name, I brought them out of Egypt. I did it to keep my name from being profaned in the eyes of the nations among whom they lived and in whose sight I had revealed myself to the Israelites. (Ezek. 20:8–9)

2. God withholds judgement in the wilderness.

> So I said I would pour out my wrath on them and destroy them in the wilderness. But for the sake of my name I did what would keep it from being profaned in the eyes of the nations in whose sight I had brought them out. (Ezek. 20:13–14)

3. God withholds judgement in later generations.

> So I said I would pour out my wrath on them and spend my anger against them [children born] in the wilderness. But I withheld my hand, and for the sake of my name I did what would keep it from being profaned in the eyes of the nations in whose sight I had brought them out. (Ezek. 20:21–2)

Does God value his reputation above his righteousness and divine justice? In these few instances, he does. God says the same thing in the book of Isaiah.

> For my own name's sake I delay my wrath;
>> for the sake of my praise [my reputation] I hold it back from
>> you,
> so as not to destroy you completely. (Isa. 48:9)

It appears God often has the audience in mind as he guides his people. We emphasise God's mercy over judgement, but a factor we often overlook is the motivation behind it. The decisions on the set are determined by what the audience will think of him as a director. In his wisdom and all-embracing love, God never loses sight of the audience.

The Ten Commandments

Consider the Ten Commandments. They're not just a list of rules to promote ethical behaviour; it's a handbook protecting God's reputation in this world.[1] The first two commands separate God from all the other gods the nations worshipped. 'I am the only God, so don't be tempted to make a pantheon of my attributes and project them on to idols.'[2]

God doesn't want confusion. He won't tolerate any usurper god grabbing the attention.

I am the LORD; that is my name!
   I will not yield my glory to another
   or my praise to idols. (Isa. 42:8)

The third commandment is even more direct. 'You shall not misuse the name of the LORD your God, for the LORD will not hold anyone guiltless who misuses his name' (Exod. 20:7).

I often ask my class what this means. Usually, the first response is, 'Don't use the name of God, or Jesus Christ, as a swear word.' This is the answer we'd probably get from most people on the street. Keep the divine name out of exclamatory expletives. The Jews are so paranoid and respectful of it they won't even pronounce his name in sermons or godly conversation.

I know when I became a Christian one of the first things I had to change was my language. I never used the name of God or Jesus as a swear word, but I still had a vast arsenal of ribald obscenities. My four years in the Navy armed me well. I could melt the ears off any respectable person who stepped into my line of fire. However, when I met Jesus, I knew it was time to modify the vocabulary. Who wants to get the 'censor bleep' when you talk to a pastor, or join the prayer meeting, or share your faith story in front of a congregation?[3] I'm sure most Christians have had to renounce a few colourful adjectives along the way. People of faith don't want offensive words to leak out of their mouth.

'You shall not misuse the name of the LORD your God' is a significant part of the script, but what does God mean by that? I believe wholesome language is essential, but to say, 'I don't swear anymore; I keep the third commandment' may not be what the Director had in mind. This ordinance goes much deeper than the cessation of celestial obscenities.

So let's say Ernie Schwartz opens a kosher bakery in Jerusalem. After a few years, his reputation spreads: 'If you want a good bagel, go to Ernie's.' Then one day the neighbours notice a delivery man from Ashdod dropping off a tub of pig fat. People begin to riot and picket the shop: 'You say you are kosher and then cook your bagels in pig fat?'[4]

This is what it means to take the Lord's name in vain. It's pledging allegiance to God while carrying idols in your pocket. It's worshipping God in the tabernacle and then hosting a seance in your home. It's declaring your allegiance to Christ while getting drunk at the pub. It's saying you're a Christian in the morning then snorting cocaine with your mistress at night. 'Cigarettes and Whiskey and Wild, Wild Women' isn't quite what God had in mind for his disciples.[5] It dishonours his name and reputation among the audience he's trying to reach. When we pronounce our allegiance to God and cultivate a lifestyle that ignores the things he stands for, we break the third commandment.

The other seven commands reveal the virtues God esteems. He values work and rest, human life, fidelity, respect of property, justice, love, faithfulness in the family, honesty, peace, and goodwill between neighbours.[6] If Israel disregards these, God is not honoured. The audience is confused. No one will see the kingdom of God manifested on the stage of Israel. The production staggers and falls.

The Prayers of Israel

If you want to know a person's theology, listen to their prayers. The petitions of ancient Israel are quite revealing. God's reputation is the primary concern, and the saints recognise Israel's responsibility to guard it. This awareness far outweighed their personal agenda or self-proclaimed interests. Listen to some of their prayers and the passion that drives them.

Although our sins testify against us,
    do something, LORD, for the sake of your name.
For we have often rebelled;
    we have sinned against you. (Jer. 14:7)
We acknowledge our wickedness, LORD,
    and the guilt of our ancestors;
    we have indeed sinned against you.
For the sake of your name do not despise us;
    do not dishonour your glorious throne.
Remember your covenant with us
    and do not break it. (Jer. 14:20–21)

Now, our God, hear the prayers and petitions of your servant.
For your sake, Lord, look with favour on your desolate sanctuary.
(Dan. 9:17)

He guides me along the right paths
    for his name's sake. (Ps. 23:3)
For the sake of your name, LORD,
    forgive my iniquity, though it is great. (Ps. 25:11)
Help us, God our Saviour,
    for the glory of your name;
deliver us and forgive our sins
    for your name's sake.
Why should the nations say,
    'Where is their God?' (Ps. 79:9–10)

God's reputation in the world is what motivates these prayers
and statements. God should save his people, forgive their sin,
and restore them for only one reason – to protect his street cred
in the audience, among the nations of the world.

Intermission

God is very protective when it comes to his reputation. He
doesn't want to be misrepresented or misunderstood. He
knows he is good. He knows love is driving his motivation.
All of heaven is acutely aware of this, but the citizens of earth
have a hard time perceiving it. If people have misguided ideas
about God's character and identity, they won't turn to him,
trust him or value his kingdom. So God moves in surprising
ways to accommodate our fallen perception.

Fire the Boss

There are multiple factors why a movie flops at the box office. Sometimes it has to do with the release date. If you launch your film the day a significant franchise hits the cinemas, the franchise usually wins out. It doesn't mean your movie is terrible, but the competition is extreme. Another reason a film fails is the foreign market. How will a distant audience respond to the script? Then there is casting; will the actors relate to each other on the set? Is there chemistry between them on the big screen? These things aren't easy to predict.

Now we know God's timing is impeccable. We also realise no other script on this planet can match the scope of God's vision and resources. So, what went wrong in the first production? It all came down to one thing: casting. Abraham was an excellent choice, along with a few others, but most of the descendants just couldn't act.[1]

From the start, we witness Israel's propensity to distance themselves from the Director. The first auditions scared them to death. They pleaded with Moses: 'Speak to us yourself and we will listen. But do not let God speak to us or we will die' (Exod. 20:19).

The pattern of separation escalates when they ask for a more approachable director: 'Now appoint a king to lead us, such as all the other nations have' (1 Sam. 8:5).

God knew where this request was going: 'Listen to all that the people are saying to you; it is not you they have rejected, but they have rejected me as their king' (1 Sam. 8:7).

Sacking the Director was a big deal. Jesus refers to it in the parable about the talents: 'But his citizens hated him and sent a delegation after him, saying, "We don't want this man to be our king"' (Luke 19:14).

The actors were trying to rewrite the script. The whole purpose of the show is to introduce the audience to something different: an alternative culture, a separate kingdom, and the one and only true God. Take him out of the equation, and the show falls apart. God didn't want Israel to be like all the other nations.

So what is a director to do when the cast rebels? How many script changes can a production sustain without morphing into some other entity? No one wants their vision to become Frankenstein's monster, and neither does God. The Director often lifted the script off the floor and put it back into the actor's hands.[2] One generation would refer to it; the next generation would throw it out of the window. There was no consistency. The manifestation of the kingdom of God didn't have a chance.

Act 1 was about cleaning the stage. Unfortunately, the Hebrews never finished the job. Early on, God warned the actors that cohabiting with the Canaanites would be their downfall.[3] It wasn't long before the culture of Sodom engulfed them. Now, instead of being a counter-cultural witness to the world, they became the world. The Jewish nation celebrated the foreign gods they were supposed to displace. Instead of destroying them, they invited them into their homes and introduced them to their children. Their practices were abominable and demonic. The actors became worse than the audience they were sent to rescue.

This is what the Sovereign LORD says: this is Jerusalem, which I have set in the centre of the nations, with countries all around her. Yet in her wickedness she has rebelled against my laws and decrees more than the nations and countries around her. She has rejected my laws and has not followed my decrees. (Ezek. 5:5–6)

You not only followed their ways and copied their detestable practices, but in all your ways you soon became more depraved than they. As surely as I live, declares the Sovereign LORD, your sister Sodom and her daughters never did what you and your daughters have done. (Ezek. 16:47–8)

But the people did not listen. Manasseh led them astray, so that they did more evil than the nations the LORD had destroyed before the Israelites. (2 Kgs 21:9)

So what was God to do? The working conditions were impossible. The Director's reputation was at stake.

Intermission

God always has a plan, and it's a good one – even when things go wrong. He doesn't ordain or force people to disobey.[4] However, when our desires pull us away, God has tactics to drag us back, hopefully not kicking and screaming.

One of these strategies is embedded in the contract God made with Israel on Mount Sinai. Unlike the contractual regulations we find in contemporary law, this one is progressively redemptive and effective. God employs it to protect his reputation in the world. For us, it is one of the pieces to the puzzle we're assembling. God often utilised it to keep the show on the road.

The Morality Clause

I don't know if Hollywood celebrities make us feel better about ourselves, but we sure love to hear and read about them. We fill our magazine shelves and libraries with their stories. They often top the headlines, especially when a scandal hits the news. We feed upon their escapades. It's candyfloss or cotton candy to the brain when we want to escape our own world for five minutes. Some of it is silly; some of it is quite serious.

Way back in 1921, Fatty Arbuckle was accused of rape and murder.[1] At the time he was one of the highest-paid actors of silent films. The scandal was notorious. Three times he faced a judge for this crime. The media were on it day and night. The first two trials ended in confusion. The jury couldn't decide if Arbuckle was guilty or innocent. The third time he was acquitted. However, the seeds of doubt were sown. His career floundered as the studio tried to distance itself from him and his alleged misbehaviour.

This case instigated what lawyers now call the 'morality clause'. It's in almost every contract drawn up today between celebrities and their employers. Studios demand it. Actors have to sign it. It's a guard protecting the employer's reputation. It says that if the actor's private and public life brings disrepute, contempt or public ridicule to the studio or the company, the producer has the legal right to fire them.

God, of course, is way ahead of Fatty Arbuckle and the legal community when it comes to a morality clause. He embedded it in the covenant. You'd be surprised how many times God implements it when the actors cavort and dance with their idols. Most of us have read the clause without much thought or concern, probably because it's buried in the book of Leviticus. Reading a legal contract with all the fine print is hard work and not that inspiring, especially when the contract is a few thousand years old and doesn't even mention our name.

For God, the morality clause was damage control. If the blessing kept coming to Israel when the actors were serving other gods, the audience wouldn't know where the blessing originated: 'Is Baal doing all these good things, or is it Asherah? Maybe it's a unique assemblage? Perhaps we should add Yahweh to our list of deities?' Of course, this isn't acceptable. It's not in the script and never will be. The Director made that clear from the very start.[2] So, God needed to do something, but what?

How can God reveal himself as a good father abounding in love and mercy if he continually has to discipline his wayward children on the world stage? It's the Director's dilemma. The audience isn't used to a living God who does things. God wants to bless, not punish. He wants to reveal his righteousness to the audience. He wants to show them what love is. The audience needed to recognise him as a good parent, not a cantankerous old bully.

So, in God's wisdom, the morality clause is the solution. It's the balance between judgement and mercy, between correction and reputation. There are five segments to the morality clause listed in the Levitical contract. Each one can last more than a generation. It is a slow-burning, gradual, redemptive process. God hoped the Israelites would turn to him after Phase 1. He never wanted to evoke Phase 5.

Phase 1

> But if you will not listen to me and carry out all these commands, and if you reject my decrees and abhor my laws and fail to carry out all my commands and so violate my covenant, then I will do this to you: I will bring on you sudden terror, wasting diseases and fever that will destroy your sight and sap your strength. You will plant seed in vain, because your enemies will eat it. I will set my face against you so that you will be defeated by your enemies; those who hate you will rule over you, and you will flee even when no one is pursuing you. (Lev. 26:14–17)

Here, God begins to withdraw his protection and favour. He slowly retracts the blessing. Why does he do this in five separate phases? Because it gives the actors time to go home and rethink their lives. He wants them to know the blessing was from him, his presence among them, and not from the idols lurking in their cupboards – to reconsider where grace originated.

God is patient. Phase 1 comes upon a generation. God waits and watches: 'Are they going to notice how things have changed without my blessing? Will you return to me?' However, if they continue to live in breach of contract, God will execute Phase 2 of the morality clause.

Phase 2

> If after all this you will not listen to me, I will punish you for your sins seven times over. I will break down your stubborn pride and

make the sky above you like iron and the ground beneath you like bronze. Your strength will be spent in vain, because your soil will not yield its crops, nor will the trees of your land yield their fruit. (Lev. 26:18–20)

Drought and famine, hunger and thirst – primary sustenance disappears. If this doesn't get a person's attention, I don't know what will. So, again, God watches and waits: 'Will they come to their senses and return to me who brings the blessing?' If there is no movement in his direction, then God implements Phase 3.

Phase 3

If you remain hostile towards me and refuse to listen to me, I will multiply your afflictions seven times over, as your sins deserve. I will send wild animals against you, and they will rob you of your children, destroy your cattle and make you so few in number that your roads will be deserted. (Lev. 26:21–2)

In ancient Israel there were all kinds of wild animals you'd want to avoid: lions, bears, crocodiles, cheetahs, leopards, jackals and poisonous snakes. So God withdraws his protection from the general population. The animals are hungry. The drought of Phase 2 forces them to hunt in more populated areas. Once again, God watches and waits: 'When will you rethink your lives, and return to me?' If the people stubbornly ignore God's voice a third time, then brace yourself, it's going to get worse.

Phase 4

If in spite of these things you do not accept my correction but continue to be hostile towards me, I myself will be hostile towards you and will afflict you for your sins seven times over. And I will bring the sword on you to avenge the breaking of the covenant. When you withdraw into your cities, I will send a plague among you, and you will be given into enemy hands. When I cut off your supply of bread, ten women will be able to bake your bread in one oven, and they will dole out the bread by weight. You will eat, but you will not be satisfied. (Lev. 26:23–6)

Here everything escalates. Enemies transgress Israel's borders. Townsfolk hear the rattling swords in the streets. There's no let-up on the famine. The repercussions are severe. People are dying. A pandemic sweeps through the population leaving a trail of corpses. Fear and panic rule the streets. The penultimate phase is upon them. Sometimes we don't know the blessing we have till we lose it.

You may have noticed the reoccurring statement 'seven times over'. This legal clause is a poetic way of telling us each phase of the operation will be complete. Each stage will escalate and add to the severity of the previous one. It's God's way of saying, 'This is no half-hearted campaign: turn or burn.'

So again God waits. Up to this point, more than one generation has been affected. With each phase, the volume is turned up on the divine megaphone, 'Wake up people. I am your God. You're witnessing what life is like without me. Pay attention. Return to me, and I will restore everything.'

Remember the parable of the prodigal son?[3] The young lad takes his father's money and heads off to uni. There he wastes himself on drugs, drink and unscrupulous women. Eventually, he is spent, hungry and broke as he bends down and chews on what the pigs left behind. Often, this is what it takes to get our attention. Some people just need a gentle whisper, others need a club over the head. I fell in the second category. It's what it took for me when I was lost on drugs and isolated from any viable community. I love the way Jesus describes the healing process:

So he got up and went to his father.

But while he was still a long way off, his father saw him and was filled with compassion for him; he ran to his son, threw his arms round him and kissed him.

The son said to him, 'Father, I have sinned against heaven and against you. I am no longer worthy to be called your son.'

But the father said to his servants, 'Quick! Bring the best robe and put it on him. Put a ring on his finger and sandals on his feet. Bring the fattened calf and kill it. Let's have a feast and celebrate. For this son of mine was dead and is alive again; he was lost and is found.' So they began to celebrate. (Luke 15:20–24)

The morality clause stimulates this response. Yes, it's a hard lesson: 'Come to your senses and repent. I will be there for you. I want to rejoice over you, not weep. Let me throw the party. Make room for my blessing.'

The morality clause is a shout in the dark: 'Turn away from all that pig slop your idols are feeding you.' It's the last-ditch attempt to preserve the Director's reputation, and if all else fails, God the Director will shut the whole thing down. If the actors still trample on the Ten Commandments and continue to ignore the script, God has only one option left to preserve his reputation in the world – cancel the show.

Phase 5

I will scatter you among the nations and will draw out my sword and pursue you. Your land will be laid waste, and your cities will lie in ruins. (Lev. 26:33)

The four phases wash over Israel like the waves of an ocean. The fifth wave is the tsunami. Here we witness God sadly drawing the curtain. He puts the padlock on the door. The ticket stand has a sign hanging in the window: Out of Business. The stage is now empty and desolate. The aroma of popcorn no longer wafts into the street. No audience will warm the seats again. No ushers or nation of priests will be there to introduce God to the audience.

Heaven will look on and witness the extreme loss of potential. What could have been if only the actors had followed the script? It would have been the manifestation of the kingdom of God on earth. Alas, God's chief witness to the world is gone up in smoke.

Intermission

Now, this is what God's morality clause looks like on paper. It's in the contract God made with the Hebrews. The Jews are legally bound to it. The morality clause reveals God's ways in the world, but the world is not held to the same degree of accountability. The Jews signed the contract at Mount Sinai; the rest of the world wasn't invited.

It's a great blessing and a daunting responsibility to represent the almighty God before the nations of the world. The Jewish people found this out the hard way. The morality clause could have easily been dismissed or overlooked like the fine print in any contract, but God is very serious about it. His reputation in the world depends on the Jewish nation adhering to the script. Israel may not have expected God to enforce the morality clause, and I'm sure they were quite surprised at how many times he did. So, let's explore how this works out in Jewish history. It is a pivotal piece to the puzzle we are putting together. From the manger to the cross, the morality clause even shadows the mission and the ministry of Jesus.

The Legal Team

God is never one-dimensional. All his films are in 3-D. He knew the actors had eyes to see but couldn't see, and ears to hear but couldn't hear. So whenever he invokes the morality clause, he also sends in the legal team to back it up. The Bible calls them prophets. They arrive with the script in one hand and the contract clutched in the other. The prophets point to the fine print and instruct the actors. The passion for God's vision burns in their heart as they distribute 3-D glasses to the nation. The Director is doing everything possible to keep the show on the road. It is his primary witness to the world.

Now we know the prophets had direct encounters with God, but you don't have to be a spiritual giant or a legal genius to see the next wave looming on the horizon. If you are unrepentant in Phase 3, then brace yourself, Phase 4 is on the way. It will happen if you defiantly reject the script and ignore the contract. If the news reporter says wild animals are crouching in the back garden, it's time to look up, watch and pray: 'Lord, is this Phase 3? If so, then I should warn the people because Phase 4 is just around the corner.'

Samuel, who was both a prophet and a judge, anointed the first king of the monarchy and established the school of the prophets. Both of these institutions arose in one generation. At first, God sent prophets to the royal court of Israel's kings. Usually, if the king honoured the contract, so did the people.[1] When the kings stopped listening to the prophets, God would send the prophets out among the general population. Two of the biggest stars were Elijah and Elisha.[2] The other prophets have a book named after them.[3] They each appear during one of the five phases. Some come early on. Others, such as Jeremiah and Ezekiel, witness the tsunami. The process is brutal, humbling, and redemptive. God will do whatever it takes to manifest the kingdom on this planet. It's his primary witness to the world.

First Tsunami

The Jewish nation splits after the death of Solomon.[4] The northern kingdom keeps the name, Israel. The southern kingdom takes the name of its largest tribe: Judah. As soon as they draw the demarcation line Israel goes apostate.

Judah, in the south, gets the better end of the deal because they have Jerusalem. They have the temple, the ark of the covenant, the priesthood, and the descendants of King David ruling in the royal court. Judah had continuity. They hold the heart of the nation: Jerusalem. It is a loss to them when the ten tribes of the northern kingdom break away, but it is still business as usual.

The northern kingdom, on the other hand, loses everything: no temple, no priesthood, no royal line of David, no continuity. For Israel, it's not business as usual. It's a major crisis. So they immediately set up two religious centres focusing on the golden calf: one at Dan and the other at Bethel.[5] They take up where the golden calf incident at Mount Sinai left off. For the next two hundred years or so, they slip into the black hole of idolatry. Every single king of the north was an idolater, and the people followed like sheep without a true shepherd.

During this history, God invokes the morality clause. The northern kingdom reels as the blessing of God exits the border. God sends in the legal team. Elijah comes on the scene with power and calls down fire from heaven. He shows the people Yahweh is alive and well and he alone is the one true God. Then Elisha arrives. He comes with a double portion of the miraculous and reminds the people what God is like and how good he is.

Later, Amos comes up from Judah and warns the northern tribes what will happen if they don't repent. His message is direct and harsh. The people don't respond, so God takes a different approach. He sends a prophet from their own borders: Hosea. His message is emotive and tender, expressing the love and mercy of God. The Director is using every means possible to get the production back on track, but the actors are on strike and refuse to budge. So, in anger and sorrow, God sends the tsunami. The nation stands between the fourth and fifth phases of the morality clause and ignores all the warnings just like the early Canaanites did.[6]

To further protect his reputation, God doesn't clear the stage with his own hand because the audience wouldn't understand the motivation and justice prompting the action. The audience isn't aware of the generations when God had patiently tried to shake and woo the people back to himself. So he hires a third party to enforce the contract. The Assyrians come in and wipe the stage clean.[7] God lets them do what Isaiah calls God's 'strange work', his 'alien task'.[8] It's the thing God didn't want to do, but he had no other option. His reputation in the world depended on it. In 722 BCE the northern kingdom of Israel ceases to exist.

The citizens are exiled and assimilated into the audience they were supposed to reach with the kingdom of God.

Second Tsunami (Averted)

Judah had a longer history than Israel, as it wasn't as spiritually dark. Unlike Israel, Judah had a few good kings who were true to Yahweh, but the bad kings opened the doors to idolatry and they were hard to close. Judgement was creeping up on them. After Assyria took Israel, it wanted to get its hands on Judah.[9] This was serious and scary. The Assyrians ruled and conquered by fear. Leaders were skinned alive and left hanging on trophy walls. They would decapitate portions of the population leaving large mounds of heads in the city streets. Others were burned alive. Soldiers would have their hands and feet or their ears and nose sliced off. Many were impaled on stakes and set aflame. When the Assyrians knocked on your door, you knew you were about to enter your worst nightmare.

Judah is now in the fourth phase of the morality clause, and King Hezekiah is trembling in the palace. The first thing Hezekiah does is try to appease the Assyrians with money. He gives them all the silver and gold in the temple and the royal palace.[10] He didn't want to be skinned alive, and he knew Judah's army was no match against the Assyrian war machine.

However, Hezekiah was a good king. He was faithful during his reign, pushing against idolatry, but the sabres were still rattling at his gate. So he humbles himself before God. The prophet Isaiah and the priests join him.[11] This is the kind of response God was looking for, and he welcomes it with open arms. He embraces the nation like the father embraced the prodigal son. God pours out his favour. His intervention is quick and dramatic.

> That night the angel of the LORD went out and put to death a hundred and eighty-five thousand in the Assyrian camp. When the people got up the next morning – there were all the dead bodies! So Sennacherib king of Assyria broke camp and withdrew. He returned to Nineveh and stayed there. (2 Kgs 19:35–6)[12]

You can imagine the sigh of relief that echoed through the streets and valleys of Judah that day. The tsunami had loomed on the horizon, but now the waters are stilled. Judah repents. They turn to God, and he spares them. He would have saved Israel in the north if they'd only come to their senses like Judah.

Third Tsunami

Unfortunately though, Judah's resolve flitters away like a moth attracted to another flame. The culture of Sodom knocks at the door and Judah runs to open it. The southern kingdom defiantly tosses the script on the ground as the tsunami races towards them a second time.

Approximately one hundred years after Hezekiah's change of heart, the southern kingdom again stands in breach of contract. This time hardly anyone goes home to rethink their lives. They ignore the cue card embossed with the word 'repent'. God sends his star prophets to warn the nation. He chooses Jeremiah to walk the streets of Jerusalem weeping as he calls the people back to the one true God.

God commissions Ezekiel from among the captives in Babylon.[13] However, Judah, as a whole, stubbornly rejects the prophets and their message. The idols were like magical puppies jumping on their laps to be petted, and the people loved it. So, as the citizens of the south ignore the signs of the times, the tsunami rushes to their shore. It isn't wise to ignore the Director's voice, especially after you sign the contract at Mount Sinai. So, in 586 bce, God invokes Phase 5 without reprieve.

Nebuchadnezzar and the Babylonians come in and do God's strange work for him. King Zedekiah, the last reigning monarch of the Jews, along with the remaining population, goes into exile.[14] Through this history, we watch the visible representation of the kingdom of God shrink before the eyes of the world. When Israel was taken captive, Judah still occupied the southern half of the stage. A sliver of hope remained for the kingdom of God. Now, Nebuchadnezzar is allowed to remove that sliver. He wipes the stage clean. The promised land lies fallow.[15]

To protect his reputation, the Director had to shut the entire production down. His witness to the world never made it past Act 2. It couldn't blossom in the soil where it was planted. The culture of Sodom spoiled the garden. The weeds of Canaan grew quicker than the seed of the kingdom. The shadow of idolatry engulfed the stage, and no one could see beyond it. The mustard seed was supposed to grow and cover the continents. It was the planet's life raft. So, what does the Director do after he cancels the show? He salvages what can be retrieved and starts again.[16]

Intermission

I often tell my students that if you want to understand the New Testament, you need to know the one that came before it. It's not an easy task, but the journey is well worth the prayer and effort. You may be surprised how many times God had to activate the morality clause in Jewish history, and even more amazed how it landed on the shores of the New Testament.

Snake Water

If a show flops in Hollywood, the director will probably go home, read the negative reviews, break the third commandment like a sailor, and cry into their beer. God, on the other hand, is tenacious. He doesn't flinch or back down. The greatest show on earth is going to hit the main screens of the world no matter what. For God, the contract isn't hidden in some little safety box stashed in the holy of holies; it's written on his heart, and he won't let go of it. The Director won't stand idly by and watch the actors march off the stage; instead, he packs his bags and goes with them. The prophet Ezekiel tells the story.

> In my thirtieth year, in the fourth month on the fifth day, while I was among the exiles by the River Kebar, the heavens were opened and I saw visions of God. (Ezek. 1:1)

Wow! What an introduction. What drama. The first verse sets the scene. We quickly find ourselves sucked into a psychedelic explosion of wonder and amazement. Ezekiel is sitting by the waterside and observes something stirring in the distance. It looks like a little tornado, and it's rushing towards him. The closer it gets, the more explicit the image becomes. The description is strange and otherworldly: wheels spinning in wheels, faces flashing on various beasts, exotic noises, vivid colours of light, and shimmering rainbows.

Some say Ezekiel had a close encounter with an alien space-ship.[1] Others say he was mentally deranged or on some hallucinogenic mind trip.[2] However, this is not the theology of the prophet or his book. We can't project the current, Western culture upon the message of Ezekiel without losing its significance. Ezekiel's divine encounters and prophetic words are far more insightful and rewarding than these other empty speculations. The theology behind this vision is that God has abandoned the temple. He has left the holy of holies and Jerusalem behind and has come to dwell with the exiles in Babylon. God wants to get the show back on the road, so he arrives to support the remnant, those who survived the tsunami.

The actors temporarily left in Jerusalem were oblivious to what was happening behind the scenes. They didn't even notice God packing his bag and heading for the door. The religious system surrounding the temple was enough for those who stayed in Jerusalem; God's presence was irrelevant to them. It didn't faze them that the God of Israel went AWOL. They loved the religion but not his presence. So they wrote their own script. It read like this.

1. We are okay. We are still here in Jerusalem.[3]
2. Those taken to Babylon are the villains. God fired them, but we still have our jobs.
3. The exiles won't be returning, so let's divide up their land.[4]
4. We still have our old-time religion and our idols to nourish and entertain us. It's party time!

How wrong and deluded can people be? To disengage a relationship with the one true living God and then focus on the structure is like severing your one link to reality. It's like dragging an empty tent through the wilderness, thinking that can sustain you. Even Moses understood an empty tabernacle is just a religious shell.[5] Here's how the prophet Jeremiah describes the situation.

'Has a nation ever changed its gods?
    (Yet they are not gods at all.)
But my people have exchanged their glorious God
    for worthless idols.
Be appalled at this, you heavens,
    and shudder with great horror,'

declares the LORD.

'My people have committed two sins:
They have forsaken me,
    the spring of living water,
and have dug their own cisterns,
    broken cisterns that cannot hold water.' (Jer. 2:11–13)

Living water, in the Bible, speaks of movement, as water in a stream or a river; water that is fresh and not stagnant. The idols were stagnant; God was alive and real. Cisterns are the underground receptacles that hold stagnant water for future use.

Broken Cisterns

In my hippie days, I rented an old farmhouse in Kansas. The rent was ten dollars a month. It was cheap because no one in their right mind would live there. In 1973 I wasn't in my right mind. I had just returned from Vietnam, and I had wasted myself on drugs. I found it hard being around people, so I isolated myself in the middle of rural America; this was before I downsized to a tepee.

The house had no plumbing or heating, but it had an old cistern and a hand pump to bring the water up. When I first moved in, I opened the top of the reservoir to see what was down there. It was a massive, cement-lined cavern, about 20 feet deep and 10 feet wide. It held water, but there were cracks in the lining, and it had dead snakes floating in it. I just ignored the snakes and used the water for baths. I found an old, 10-gallon milk can in the barn. I used it for drinking water. I could fill it up in the nearby town of Roxbury for twenty-five cents.

A bath back then was a big event. The whole operation took more than three hours because I'd have to cut wood, light the cook stove, fill up three metal buckets from the cistern, set the snake water on the burner and wait for it to heat up. I found an old tin tub in the yard. It was about 4 feet long and 2 feet wide. I could bend my knees and sit in it.

When everything was ready, I'd set the tub in front of the oven, pour in the water, and open the oven door to keep myself warm. At that time, I thought it was a cool thing to do. I was taking a bath Wild West-style. It was just like the old cowboy movies I used to watch as a kid. I found an old Stetson hat in the attic and sometimes wore it to make the experience more authentic. However, forty baths or so later, I noticed snake scales in the bucket. The water level was going down, and I had done nothing to replenish it. I could take a bath like the Wild West, but I didn't know how to keep the system going.

Those old pioneers knew a lot of tricks for survival; I didn't. They had the brains; I had the hat. So what else could a drugged-up hippie do? I tied an old sock on the end of the spout to filter them: no more snake scales, just dirty socks. Problem solved.

Winters in Kansas can be ruthless. One day during a blizzard, I ran out of drinking water. Outside was icy with about three feet of snow. My truck didn't start, but it wouldn't have moved anyway. So, desperate times call for extreme measures. I didn't want to die of thirst, so what would a person do in the old West? Easy; they would melt some snow, but I never thought of that. Instead, I boiled some of the snake water, hoping that would remove the impurities. As the old saying goes, 'Bottoms up.'

I don't know if changing the sock on the spout would've helped, but I didn't think of that either. I just filled a bucket with snake water, trusting it would boil before I dehydrated or decomposed. It was a long wait for the boil. My lips were dry, and my tongue felt like someone was dragging it through the desert tied to the back of a horse. At last, a couple of hours later, it was ready to drink. I dipped my cup and took a sip. Have you ever drunk boiled snake water? I tell you, it would gag a maggot. I spat it out and thought, 'No way can a person drink this rancid stuff.' It almost put me off taking a bath in it.

But the pioneer spirit was upon me. If I wanted to live, I had to face the elements like a fully-fledged adult. So I grabbed my 10-gallon milk can, put on my Stetson, and trudged through the snowy blizzard to get water. The journey into Roxbury was arduous. It was even worse coming back. Ten gallons of water weighs about eighty pounds. It was awkward and cumbersome. I eventually made it home and had a drink of the living water. It saved my life. I now understand heaven's dismay and alarm when someone chooses stagnant, old snake water stored in a broken cistern over fresh, living water.

God left the temple in Jerusalem because he wasn't going to share his glory with dead snakes. If the actors are stubborn enough to let all those idols into the temple like serpents in a cracked cistern, the living God was not going to hang around. God didn't want to leave. He desired to stay in the middle of the camp, but as he said to Ezekiel, 'Son of man, do you see what they are doing – the utterly detestable things the Israelites are doing here, things that will drive me far from my sanctuary?' (Ezek. 8:6).

God Exits the Temple

Fortunately for us, and them, God is love. Love is patient. God is patient. God doesn't just disappear from the temple in a puff of smoke; instead, he slowly withdraws. Each step could take more than a generation. He does it this way for the same reason he invokes the morality clause in five long phases. 'Will people come to their senses and realise that I am the blessing?' The kingdom of God is his presence in the middle of the camp. So, as God leaves, the blessings go with him. God gave Ezekiel a vision of his reluctant departure.

The first movement: 'Then the glory of the Lord rose from above the cherubim and moved to the threshold of the temple.' (Ezek. 10:4)

The second movement: 'Then the glory of the Lord departed from over the threshold of the temple and stopped above the cherubim. While I watched, the cherubim spread their wings and rose from the ground, and as they went, the wheels went with them. They stopped at the entrance of the east gate of the Lord's house, and the glory of the God of Israel was above them.' (Ezek. 10:18–19)

The third movement: 'The glory of the Lord went up from within the city and stopped above the mountain east of it.' (Ezek. 11:23)

With each movement, God waits. 'Will they go home and rethink their lives? Will they even notice I'm gone?' God wanted the people and the priests to ask the question: 'Where is the LORD?'[6]

Intermission

In 1925 H.G. Wells published a perceptive story called 'The Pearl of Love'. A prince builds a mausoleum for his dead princess, but over time he values the beauty of the tomb more than his lost love. This poignant tale parallels the history of ancient Israel. The temple routines and the religious system became so entrenched in Jewish culture the people no longer required God's direct influence to guide them. They had the institution. They could turn the wheels without God, and the wheels did turn, but dragging around an empty tent is like holding a bucket of dead snake water. It may help with a bath now and then, but you will eventually die of thirst.

26

Religion or Presence

I confess there were moments in my life when I valued religion over God's presence; it was so subtle I didn't even realise it. Once I was praying with five pastor friends at a Christian retreat centre in Oban, Scotland. For two days, we fasted and prayed from morning to night. One of my pastor friends said, 'Let's pray through the book of Isaiah.' We jumped on it. Each of us would take a turn reading a chapter out loud. Then we would all pray what God revealed to us. For over eight hours, our prayers marched through the entire sixty-six chapters. It was a marvellous exercise: spiritually insightful and rewarding. One of the pastors said, 'I never knew how concerned God was about justice until I prayed through the book of Isaiah with you guys.'

A few months later, I was praying with four friends in Belfast. We were in the church building walking up and down the aisles crying out to God. After about an hour, the Lord stopped me in mid-sentence. He didn't speak audibly, but I sure heard him in my heart and mind: 'You love to pray more than you love me.'

I was shocked. I stopped right there; I confessed it to my friends, went down on my knees and asked God to forgive me. I never forgot that moment. I had made prayer into a religious exercise. It looked so righteous and holy, but in God's eyes, I had latched on to the religion but let go of him. I didn't value his presence. I never thought of asking the question, 'Where is God in all of this?'[1]

My attitude towards prayer and other religious disciplines has changed since that moment. If God isn't in it, I don't want it. The relationship and the presence of the Holy Spirit are what I value more than definite answers to various requests. I no longer read the Bible just to get information or direction. I now read it to encounter God. I pray to meet God. It's the presence of the Lord that gives meaning and life to everything we do. The kingdom of God is about connection and a living relationship with God, not religion. Religion without presence is an empty tent.

Once I was sitting at my desk, working on a sermon, when the presence of God came upon me. He was calling me to spend time with him. In the back of my mind, I foolishly thought, 'When I finish this I'll be right with you.' Ten minutes later, I left the keyboard and started to pray, but the presence of the Holy Spirit wasn't there like before. Then God spoke directly to my heart. 'You always want me on your time, but you never come to me on my time.'

It was different circumstances but the same issue. I repented. Again I had elevated religion and ministry over presence. Ministry is essential, but like Jesus said, 'The poor you will always have with you, but you will not always have me' (Matt. 26:11). I'm learning presence means more than preparing a good sermon, singing songs, reading the Bible or running to the mission field. Without him, we're just dragging around the empty tent. For the Jewish nation, reality doesn't hit home until they face the consequence of their actions. Then comes the remorse, the tears, despair and beating of the chest.

- What have we done?
- What have we lost?
- What could have been?

In gradual steps, God leaves the temple, but where does he go? Well, we come back full circle to Ezekiel 1. God went to the exiles in Babylon. He stayed with them, protecting them, ministering to them. His dealings instigate a change of heart. He inspires hope.

> 'This is what the Sovereign LORD says: although I sent them far away among the nations and scattered them among the countries, yet for a little while I have been a sanctuary for them in the countries where they have gone.'
>
> Therefore say: 'This is what the Sovereign LORD says: I will gather you from the nations and bring you back from the countries where you have been scattered, and I will give you back the land of Israel again.'
>
> They will return to it and remove all its vile images and detestable idols. I will give them an undivided heart and put a new spirit in them; I will remove from them their heart of stone and give them a heart of flesh. Then they will follow my decrees and be careful to keep my laws. They will be my people, and I will be their God. (Ezek. 11:16–20)

Seventy years later, we find the actors returning to the stage.[2] The box office is open again for business. The storm is over. Ezra and Nehemiah lead the charge as the prophets Malachi, Haggai and Zechariah motivate and encourage the surviving actors to stay on script. The performers have been retrained and recommissioned. They still have their quirks, insecurities and impulsiveness, but the one thing they repented of was idolatry. They came to their senses in Babylon, and that issue doesn't arise again.

Fourth Tsunami

When we enter the doors of the New Testament, we find the nation of Israel once more standing between the fourth and fifth phases of the morality clause. The Romans have invaded the stage, and the Israelites are subject to them. One more time, God faithfully sends the prophets. Some people return to God and repent through the ministry and message of John the Baptist. Many follow Jesus, but the Jewish leaders reject and instigate his crucifixion. Like the prophets of old, Jesus warns them.

> The days will come upon you when your enemies will build an embankment against you and encircle you and hem you in on every side. They will dash you to the ground, you and the children within your walls. They will not leave one stone on another, because you did not recognise the time of God's coming to you. (Luke 19:43–4)

This is the fourth time in Jewish history that the Director had to invoke Phase 5 of the morality clause. The people of Israel no longer worship idols, but their leaders, priests and king still reject his presence. God stands right in front of them face to face, eye to eye, and they shout, 'We don't want this man to be our king' (Luke 19:14). Like Jacob, they want the blessing but not the source of the blessing. They hold tight to the religion, but they don't value or recognise the presence of God when he comes back to the temple. The kingdom of God cannot grow in this soil. It's too hard. So, once again, God closes the door and cancels the show.

In the year 70 CE, after a 140-day siege, Jerusalem falls. The Romans, under Titus with thirty thousand troops, batter the gates of Jerusalem and destroy everything. They ransack the temple and rip off the gold. Hundreds of thousands die. Tens of thousands more go into exile.[3] They are taken as slaves to work on the Colosseum and the Forum of Peace in Rome. The remaining population is dispersed throughout the empire. The tsunami hits hard, as the nation reels and collapses before their eyes. If they hadn't rejected Jesus, we'd be reading a different story today.

However, God never gives up. The show must go on. Around 1880 Jews were encouraged to resettle the land once again. They reclaim and buy back the stage. The world gasps as Israel declares its independence in 1948. The United Nations recognises the statehood of Israel on the world map. We again hear the echo of Isaiah's prophesy:

Who has ever heard of such things?
  Who has ever seen things like this?
Can a country be born in a day
  or a nation be brought forth in a moment?
Yet no sooner is Zion in labour
  than she gives birth to her children. (Isa. 66:8)

The Jews are back on the stage. The Director hasn't given up hope in spite of the actors' chequered history. God is good. God is love. God is patient. God is God, and he does what he wants. The Director has a method and a script. God is continually breaking into this world to reveal what he is like and who he is. It's hard for us to keep up with him. He is full of surprises, and he is persistent. The Jews are on the stage right now, today. How long will they remain? That is yet to be seen. All we can do is watch and pray. It seems God has a few more performances up his sleeve.

Intermission

The gospel of the kingdom is the greatest show on earth, but as yet, we haven't seen its best production.[4] We catch small glimpses and highlights here and there, but it still plays out like an old, 1950s, low-budget B-movie; the one you had to sit through before the main feature. It seems heaven and earth just haven't been that compatible, but the story isn't over yet, and it appears more days are on the horizon.

The Director is radical and innovative. Sometimes all a production needs is a new face to revive interest. In Bethlehem, we watch the Creator of the universe clothe himself with humanity. This is our introduction to the star of the show. However, it might surprise us how we have boxed and packaged him with our slogans and religious catch-phrases over the centuries. We tend to shrink him down to poster size and radio soundbites. It's how we introduce him to the audience and often how we reintroduce him to ourselves in our creeds, songs, hymns and various mission statements. Our packaging, however, is a problem, especially if we want to see how the pieces of the puzzle fit together. When it comes to the kingdom of God, we know Jesus is the star of the show but, like Abraham, it is good to rattle the box now and then because there is always more than meets the eye.

PART THREE

JESUS AND THE
KINGDOM

Jesus is Reality

Many of my friends, and those who came to Christ during the Jesus Movement years, were looking for something genuine and legitimate. Drugs never took us where our hearts wanted to go. The society we grew up in didn't do it either. The word 'plastic' was often bandied about when something lacked the essence of authenticity. When we touched something authentic, we'd say it was 'real'. For me, the reality of Jesus is irrefutable. He is real. However, the longer I walk the path, the more I realise he is 'more real' than I imagined. Jesus is the source and sustainer of reality itself. Jesus is reality!

Now I know this may be a weird way to describe the Son of God, but it's no stranger than many of the other words the Bible uses to express who he is and what he does. When the Bible starts using words like 'bread', 'door', 'truth', 'life', 'way', 'word', 'lamb', 'lion', and 'branch' to describe someone, you begin to realise human language can't fully explain or define him.

Over the past forty years, I've come to understand you can't restrict Jesus to the inspired words on a page.[1] He is more than the source of divine ethics in this fallen world. Christ is more significant than a saviour, a prince of peace, Messiah, prophet, priest or king. The role he plays in and beyond our brief history far surpasses any human concept of mediator, intercessor, advocate, counsellor or shepherd.

Jesus is more than a solution to a problem or the answer to our many questions. He is more than a corrector of wrongs or the remedy for sin. To call him 'Lord' is honourable, yet insufficient. He far exceeds all these concepts, titles and descriptions. If true worship in spirit and truth depends on a full revelation of who Jesus is, we will always be dependent on the Holy Spirit to enlighten us further.[2]

To say Jesus is reality is not hyperbole. We often find the writers of the New Testament struggling to articulate the magnificence of Christ. Even though the cross is the central tenet of our theology and encounter with the Almighty, the cross is not what fully defines the Son of God. Jesus transcends our need to be rescued.

I find it fascinating how many of the New Testament writers describe Jesus Christ. Forget any preliminary explanations or build-up to their proclamation. The moment ink touches the page, they've already dived into the mind and heart of God. All the reader can do is try to keep up and grasp the revelation. To the intellect, it's audacious. To the open heart, it resonates with authenticity. It's real, even though it overwhelms us.

Consider the first paragraph in the book of Hebrews. Imagine the reaction of those who have never heard of Jesus and are reading this for the very first time.

In the past God spoke to our ancestors through the prophets at many times and in various ways, but in these last days he has spoken to us by his Son, whom he appointed heir of all things, and through whom also he made the universe. The Son is the radiance of God's glory and the exact representation of his being, sustaining all things by his powerful word. After he had provided purification for sins, he sat down at the right hand of the Majesty in heaven. So he became as much superior to the angels as the name he has inherited is superior to theirs. (Heb. 1:1–4)

This paragraph is shocking. It takes us far beyond any regional, or even global, Messiah remit. Jesus not only saved us, but he also made the universe. He not only created the world, but he is the glue holding it all together. His living word is still alive and actively sustaining everything we know to be, or exist. Everything we see, touch, hear, smell and experience is because of him. He is holding time and space in sync. The mind boggles.

Intermission

Of course, the writer of Hebrews was not alone in his appraisal of Jesus. We find these concepts and this kind of language throughout the New Testament. It is alarming and quite astonishing. Read the first few paragraphs of John's Gospel; notice how the revelation of Christ overwhelms the Apostle Paul. Paul moves from disbelief to divine encounter, then to awe and wonder.

I often pray, 'Lord, overwhelm me with the same revelation these early writers had of you. Help me to see what they saw and to worship you with the same, informed passion.'

Gleeful Revelation

As a pastor in Belfast, I often played badminton with the children attending our youth club. One evening a 9-year-old girl mastered the serve and won the point. She had tried many evenings without success. This time, however, I witnessed an explosion of joy. She dropped her racket, clenched her fist and frantically waved her arms up and down, jumping where she stood with a grin bigger than her face. I only have one word to describe it. It was pure, unbridled glee.

I went home that evening thinking and praying about how so many of us have lost this attitude. Glee is not just for children who experience something for the first time. It is a human expression. It's even for grown-ups. It can be embarrassing, but to be overcome with pure joy and liberating glee is the kind of response God desires when his children encounter the king and the kingdom of God. Perhaps this is what prompted Jesus when he said, 'Truly I tell you, anyone who will not receive the kingdom of God like a little child will never enter it' (Mark 10:15).[1]

When a heart is overwhelmed by joy, glee will find its expression. It may not look the same for each person, but it will leak out somewhere. The Apostle Paul leaked joy and glee when he wrote the letter to the church in Ephesus. Unfortunately, our

English versions tend to tame and control it; not for doctrinal reasons or subterfuge, it's just that glee isn't always that easy to translate.

In the Greek New Testament, the opening verses of Ephesians (1:3–14) flow as one long, complex sentence. The words spill over each other like water surging over the Niagara Falls. The excitement of what he's saying left little room for refined punctuation. It is more important to Paul that this revelation is communicated rather than grammatically polished. In his way, Paul was clenching his fist, frantically waving his arms up and down, with a grin bigger than his face. He was overcome with the awe and wonder of Jesus as his expression of joy and glee gushed and cascaded over the page.

This one long run-on sentence is a theological explosion of wonder and joy. What Paul is communicating here is that, in Christ, we have every spiritual blessing – every one. The benefits are authentic and real. There's nothing more he could give us. He has already provided it because it is himself. It's not something he dumps on us. In him, we have every blessing. It's him. We have him as he has us, but Paul is just warming up here.

In verse four, we are told that before God declared 'let there be light', we were in his heart and mind. We are not some afterthought on day six. We are not created for adversity. We are not part of some divine experiment gone wrong. We were not conceived for failure and then redemption. We were created for his praise and glory. The apostle is very excited about this as the revelation continues to gallop across the page.

However, Paul does not ignore our fallen-ness or our need of a saviour, but notice the words he uses to describe our redemption. It stems from 'the riches of God's grace that he lavished on us' (vv. 7–8). It sounds like God couldn't wait to bless us because we were in his heart and mind before he created the heavens and the earth. Within the divine wisdom and under-standing, God reveals his Son. Jesus was, before all things. The Son became a human being (fully God, fully human). Jesus will have a human face for the rest of his existence throughout eternity. He died for us. He rose from the dead.

To reveal Jesus this way pleased God. It was wise. He under-stood what he was doing and his intention for doing it. He fully embraced living out the whole process. It will eternally bless him.[2] Heaven will always stand in awe and worship. Jesus will continue to hold all things together by his word because he is now intricately committed to his creation. Eternity has invested in space and time, and the cord will not break. The Messiah's story is written down here on earth; the story that was in God's heart before the world began.

Jesus took our humanity to heaven and sat down next to the Father. When the Father looks at his Son, he will see a human face staring back at him. When the angels worship, they will gaze upon a human face. When we meet him, the face we see will be fully human, yet fully divine, and the time is coming when everything will be the way God planned it before the creation of the world.

No wonder Paul was stumbling over his words. It's awesome, more than our finite minds can grasp. One day heaven and earth will be unified.[3] We will have heaven on earth because the presence and the love of God will define it – in, through and by Jesus Christ, who is our reality. He is the star of the show.

Paul's mind and heart must have been exploding at this point, just like those of the brothers and sisters in Ephesus who were reading and listening to his declaration. Today, we still wrestle with these statements. The thoughts are too big. The scope reaches further than our minds can comprehend, and here, twelve verses later, the sentence ends. The Holy Spirit of God seals us; God in us, us in Christ, heaven and earth brought together.

Paul is telling us in the first sentence of this letter that history, stretching from eternity back into eternity, is all about Jesus Christ. There is no thought significant enough to explain him. Language will always fail us. Feelings of awe and wonder probably communicate more to us than our feeble attempts to mentally grasp all he is, what he has done, what he is doing and going to do. Jesus is our reality.

Now, Paul knew he had just overwhelmed himself and the readers in Ephesus. He recognised no one could comprehend who Jesus is and what he means to us without a revelation from God. It takes more than reading the words on a page or quoting them as proof texts, so Paul interrupts the letter with a prayer. The essence of Paul's prayer is this: 'Jesus, open their eyes and heart to grasp what I just said. Give them a revelation of who you are and who you are for us.'[4]

What Does Revelation Look Like?

Helen Keller and her lifelong friend and teacher Anne Sullivan were remarkable women.[5] Helen couldn't see or hear. She was lost in a dark, silent cave and had no concept of language. She had no way of communicating with the world around her. Patiently, her teacher, Anne, would use sign language to spell words into Helen's hand while Helen touched the object Anne was spelling. After many fights, much frustration and angst, there was a moment of epiphany. Anne was at the pump, spelling w-a-t-e-r into Helen's palm while holding Helen's other hand in the stream that came from the spout. For some reason, at that moment, Helen grasped what this was all about.

It was as though someone reached into her heart and turned the switch on.

She started to comprehend that these finger movements weren't just random exercises, but there was a meaning behind them. It was intentional. They were words. There was language to describe the world around her. Then with glee, Helen runs around to the various objects in the garden signalling for her teacher to spell them into her hand.

Before that moment, Helen felt only the touch of Anne's fingers, but when Helen realised the significance of that touch, everything changed. This is what revelation is. This is what revelation does. This awakening is what revelation looks like when someone finally gets it. Revelation is when the lights come on for the first time. It happened to Paul, and now in Ephesians, he's praying this would happen to us. If we don't grasp the magnitude of Christ, the king, it is hard to get excited about him and his kingdom.

The Divine Voice

Like the writers of Hebrews and Ephesians, the Apostle John also had a revelation of Christ that went far beyond any concept of messiahship. Paul, in Ephesians, let the revelation pour out on to the page as an overflow of his heart. The writer of Hebrews was more restrained but no less astonishing. Each of them had their specific purpose for writing, but they each introduced their message with the magnificence and glory of the Son of God. John does the same. He pulls the string of his bow and releases God's arrow in the first three words: 'In the beginning'.

Immediately he hits the target and sets the tone of his proclamation. We can't escape it. We are instantly drawn into one of the most dynamic chapters of the Bible: the creation story of Genesis. It reverberates throughout the book of John. It's the template John follows to communicate the wonder of Christ.

In the beginning God created the heavens and the earth. (Gen. 1:1)

In the beginning was the Word, and the Word was with God, and the Word was God. He was with God in the beginning. Through him all things were made; without him nothing was made that has been made. (John 1:1–3)

The book of John is an echo of Genesis, but John adapts the message to declare the divinity of Jesus. Open any significant commentary on the book of John, and you will find a discussion surrounding the Greek word *logos*. The English translation of *logos* is 'word'. It's a term pregnant with meaning. Greek philosophers and academics today have a lot to say about it. However, we can't discard the context John chose to explain his revelation of the pre-existing Son.

In the creation story of Genesis 1, God speaks and things appear. It's the dynamism of his words that bring everything into being. Since this is the context in which John couches his gospel, we can't help but draw a connection between God's creative utterances in Genesis and John's claim. The Son was present before the Father said, 'Let there be light.' How was the Son there? He was the Word. Remember, God only took on human form when Jesus was born to Mary in Bethlehem. Before this event, Jesus was Son, and God was Father, but in what way we can't even speculate. All we have are a few hints found in the Bible. In our stumbling, we continue to search for the means to communicate a revelation that should leave us speechless.

Perhaps we can say it like this, 'Before the Son of God became a man, he was the Father's voice, but he is also so much more. He too is God. He is the creator and the sustainer of reality.' This is where John is taking us. John continues to use the creation story the same way Anne Sullivan spelt words into Helen Keller's palm. He's hoping we begin to see what he knows and understands of Jesus.

Genesis describes the creation of visible light (1:3–4); John depicts Jesus as the light of humanity (1:4–5). Genesis calls the sun the greater light and the moon, the lesser light (1:16). John uses the same imagery, introducing Jesus as the greater light and John the Baptist, the lesser light (1:6–9).

The fact that Jesus performs seven miraculous signs throughout John's Gospel mirrors the seven days of creation in Genesis.[1] Another consideration is that John's is the only gospel to record Jesus breathing on the disciples to receive the Holy Spirit, which is reminiscent of God breathing life into Adam.[2] John wants us to know that when Jesus stepped into creation, the impact was just as dramatic as when 'Let there be light' reverberated throughout the primal darkness. This is what John is trying to communicate.

Did Jesus stop being the *Logos*, the dynamic of creation, when he took on our humanity and ascended back into heaven? No! Christ, the Word, is still holding the universe together, but it's not just the word spoken by the Father, Christ *is* the Word. Jesus himself is what stops reality from unravelling.[3]

God cannot lie because everything he says comes into being.[4] God is the Word. The Word is God. God cannot deny who he is: 'I AM WHO I AM' (Exod. 3:14). The dynamic of the Father's declarations is the Son of God. The Son is the voice of the Father. He comes from the Father; he is eternal. He is God. John keeps drawing us back to this in his gospel.[5] The Father, Son and Holy Spirit set the parameters of our reality. The Holy Spirit is the Spirit of Christ.[6]

All the promises spoken by God stand forever because the voice, the dynamic of those promises, is the divine presence. When God answers a prayer, it's not because he pushed the 'yes' button on some heavenly computer. It's because of his presence, the living Word; his Son is actively bringing it to pass in and through the Holy Spirit.[7] When we declare God's word and the promises, we are participating in the living Word. God loves this. He invites this. It's relational. It's kingdom. We are not working through some legal, biblical clause in a contract; God is the promise. God is the answer to our prayers. Evoking a divine promise is not some magical incantation; it's calling God himself, his presence, to create intentionally and act on our behalf.

This Jesus is the king of the kingdom. He whole-heartedly invests in creation for all eternity. He is relationally connected with us forever. The Word of God is upon the throne of heaven working for us in close relationship with us. He is always drawing us into himself and is actively and dynamically alive in us.

Intermission

In the next chapter, we are going to row the boat into deeper waters. It is worth the journey. It's another piece to the puzzle. We have to know the king if we want to understand, recognise and participate fully in the kingdom.

Wisdom is a Person

Orphaned humanity often asks the same questions.

- Who am I?
- Where do I belong?
- What is this all about?

The ancient cultures surrounding Israel were the same. They also wanted answers to these questions; answers they could relate to in everyday life. So they each developed their own story of origin. To many of us, they appear bizarre and mythical, but philosophically, they are quite similar. There is a thread that ties most, if not all, of them together. It's one of the biggest fears these ancient people faced. It was a monster in their eyes, and that monster was called 'chaos'. I suppose if we were to encapsulate all our current fears into one word, we probably couldn't come up with a term more embracing or emotionally charged.

In these ancient narratives, chaos was in the beginning, and nothing survives in the midst of chaos. It's the enemy of life. Chaos is often described as a serpent, a dragon or even a large body of water. In their mind, no one could tame or control these creatures or live long on the waves of an ocean.

Archaeologists discovered one of these creation stories in Heliopolis, an ancient city of Egypt. It describes how the Egyptian creator god (Atum) lived inside the god of chaos (Nun). Nun is a chaotic mass of water undulating in and out of itself. As the story goes, Atum climbs out of this watery mass onto a piece of dry land he created. The Egyptians called this ground *benben*; it's shaped like a pyramid. Then Atum establishes the world.

We find the same kind of idea in the Canaanite myths. They tell us, in the beginning, Baal defeats the chaos god, Yam. Yam was the sea serpent that ruled over the oceans. This thread is also present in *Enuma Elish*, the creation myth of Babylon. In their story, the chief god (Marduk) grabs hold of the chaos serpent (Tiamat) and cuts her in half. Her upper torso becomes the heavens, and her lower half becomes the earth.

In these few examples, chaos is portrayed as the enemy of life. It's the unpredictable force that needs a divine hand to subdue it. To the ancient mind, the dry ground was stable, sturdy and predictable. We can live on dry land. We drown and die in the chaotic waves of an ocean. However, chaos wasn't just a concept in the ancient Near East; it was also an entity, an anomaly that was and is contrary to life – a god in the form of water or a serpent.

Chaos is Satan

Surprisingly, we find the same ideas percolating in the creation story of Genesis. The earth is a watery mass. It's formless, empty and chaotic.[1] God separates the waters. The upper level he calls the sky.[2] God then speaks, and dry land appears.[3] Genesis doesn't attribute personalities to the natural elements like these other creation stories, but the entity of chaos is still present. It's the serpent hanging about in the tree of the knowledge of good and evil.[4] The ancient people familiar with this biblical text would have understood this. They wouldn't need anyone to explain that the serpent represents chaos. It's embedded in their culture. The serpent is there trying to unravel the 'very good' creation. It is the anomaly, the enemy of life.[5]

The serpent is the voice and the door to chaos. When that door opens, chaos can reassert itself. It breaches the divine boundaries that promote life. History displays our various attempts to close that door. We now live in a chaotic world, and the disorder affects all of creation, not just humanity.[6]

The book of Revelation also builds upon these first images of chaos. John doesn't leave this enemy-of-life any room to hide. In one sentence, he rips off the mask and exposes the fiend to everyone reading the disclosure: chaos is the great dragon, the ancient serpent, the devil, he is Satan himself.[7] John, then, describes the end of chaos and his influence. 'And the devil, who deceived them, was thrown into the lake of burning sulphur, where the beast and the false prophet had been thrown. They will be tormented day and night for ever and ever' (Rev. 20:10).[8]

'For ever' sounds final, but John drives the message home in the next chapter. 'Then I saw "a new heaven and a new earth," for the first heaven and the first earth had passed away, and there was no longer any sea' (Rev. 21:1).

I used to wonder why God gave John this information. What about the trees and plants? Why not tell us about the fate of our pets? Instead, he focuses our attention on the sea – it's gone. My good friend Ivan loves to sail. For obvious reasons, he doesn't like the last part of this verse. He can't imagine the attraction of a new earth without a sea. Where will he launch his boat? However, that's not the point. John's not giving us a geography lesson of the new earth; he's explaining the theology that sustains it. He's telling us that this new earth will not end up like our present existence.

God isn't anxious about large bodies of water. That's where he put the fish and tells us it was a good thing to do.[9] I think we can also assume John isn't interested in after-life boating excursions or the celestial fishing environment. In this little, six-word phrase John is telling us there will be no place for chaos to lift its head again. There will be no chaotic anomaly or events. There will be no reason to fear what's lurking around the corner. Chaos will no longer be part of our existence or reality. The culmination of God's kingdom will be a 'chaos-free zone' for all eternity. Not only is the anomaly locked away forever and ever, but the door of entry is gone.[10] It's not just boarded up or secured with a big key; it's eradicated. It has disappeared.[11]

Wisdom and Chaos

But what about now? Creation is still groaning. We know the impact of natural disasters. We also observe and experience chaos throughout our world and local events. Chaos is seeping through the cracks and doors all around our cities, towns and homes. So what is God's immediate answer? How do we survive in such a chaotic world? How do the king and the kingdom of God fit into this picture?

Well, at first, God's answer to chaos may sound strange and cryptic, but it made perfect sense to the people of this ancient world. It rises to the surface throughout the Bible, especially when the Bible talks about the created order. God's answer to chaos is wisdom.

A gentle answer turns away wrath
   but a harsh word stirs up anger. (Prov. 15:1)

This is a wise saying. It's good counsel. These words have probably saved many relationships and prolonged people's lives. I'd often quote the Bible's wisdom to my teenage boys. Each Saturday around noon I'd fling open their bedroom door, open wide the curtains and shout,

> As a door turns on its hinges,
>> so a sluggard turns on his bed. (Prov. 26:14)

Then I'd stand there wisely smiling. For some reason, this exacerbated the chaos I was hoping to deflect. I've learned over the years that the wisdom holding back chaos transcends pithy quotes, emotional intelligence, social skills or knowing what to do with all the facts. The chaos in this world has an entity behind it, but so does wisdom. The wisdom that restrains chaos is also an entity.

Wisdom and the Almighty

The literature of ancient Israel often personified wisdom.[12] Wisdom was present at creation, guiding, organising, giving meaning and purpose, pushing back and taming chaos. In the Old Testament, the Hebrew word for wisdom is *chokmah*. Grammatically the word is feminine, so wisdom's personification in the ancient text is also female. In the Old Testament, wisdom is a lady.[13]

> She is a tree of life to those who take hold of her;
>> those who hold her fast will be blessed. (Prov. 3:18)

Chaos hangs its hat on the forbidden tree; wisdom hangs her hat on the tree of life. Further on in Proverbs, wisdom speaks in the first person, testifying who she is and her activities, especially when it comes to the subjection of chaos.

> The LORD brought me forth as the first of his works,
>> before his deeds of old;
> I was formed long ages ago,
>> at the very beginning, when the world came to be.
> When there were no watery depths, I was given birth,
>> when there were no springs overflowing with water;
> before the mountains were settled in place,
>> before the hills, I was given birth,
> before he made the world or its fields
>> or any of the dust of the earth.
> I was there when he set the heavens in place,
>> when he marked out the horizon on the face of the deep,
> when he established the clouds above
>> and fixed securely the fountains of the deep,
> when he gave the sea its boundary
>> so that the waters would not overstep his command,
> and when he marked out the foundations of the earth.
>> (Prov. 8:22–9)

Wisdom was dancing with God, marking out boundaries; they were bringing order out of chaos. The plan was developed and executed with, and by, wisdom. Wisdom's relationship with the Creator was full of wonder, joy and life. If wisdom's voice were heard, it would be a song. If wisdom's creativity were mapped, it would be a waltz. If we caught a glimpse of wisdom at work, she would have a smile bigger than her face. Glee was all over her and her relationship with the Almighty.

Then I was constantly at his side.

I was filled with delight day after day,

    rejoicing always in his presence,

rejoicing in his whole world

    and delighting in the human race. (Prov. 8:30–31)

Jesus is Wisdom

In the Old Testament, the personification of wisdom is a colourful linguistic tool. It was God's way of spelling words into the palm of Israel. The revelation, however, came in the face of Jesus Christ. Like Helen Keller, the New Testament writers had an epiphany: Jesus is the wisdom of God.

Jesus was there at creation, rejoicing, bringing order out of chaos, and delighting in us. God created us in the divine image. Wisdom is personified poetically in the Old Testament; historically recognised in the New Testament. Understanding this helps us to grasp the wonder of Christ's sovereignty and the dynamics of his kingdom. He is the star of the show.

Earlier, we explored how the Jewish readers of John's Gospel would interpret the Greek word *logos*. To the Jews, it was God's creative word and voice at creation. But those familiar with Hellenistic/Greek culture wouldn't stop there. Within the philosophies and theology of ancient Greece, *logos* became one of those magnetic words attracting all kinds of meaning and definition. If we could pick up the word *logos* and tip it like a salt shaker, two main concepts would keep falling on to our plate: wisdom and reality.[14]

John deliberately used the word *logos* as a two-edged sword. The Jews would make the connection with God's creative utterances in Genesis. The Greeks would consider the wisdom displayed in the created order. In John, both ideas encapsulate the person of Christ. Both the wisdom that was with God at creation and the divine utterances are made flesh.[15] Jesus Christ is wisdom.

The Apostle Paul also draws from this well. In the middle of a long discourse describing two kinds of wisdom, Paul tells us the wisdom of this world is detached from God's direct influence, presence and the person who is wisdom itself: Jesus Christ.[16]

> Jews demand signs and Greeks look for wisdom, but we preach Christ crucified: a stumbling-block to Jews and foolishness to Gentiles, but to those whom God has called, both Jews and Greeks, Christ the power of God and the wisdom of God. (1 Cor. 1:22–4)

The wisdom from God cannot be separated from his active presence in our lives. 'It is because of him that you are in Christ Jesus, who has become for us wisdom from God – that is, our righteousness, holiness and redemption' (1 Cor. 1:30).

Chaos thought it had won when the body of Jesus was taken down and put in the tomb, but wisdom's plan was so deep chaos couldn't comprehend it. We can hardly get our heads around it.

> We do, however, speak a message of wisdom among the mature, but not the wisdom of this age or of the rulers of this age, who are coming to nothing. No, we declare God's wisdom, a mystery [secret] that has been hidden and that God destined for our glory before time began. None of the rulers of this age understood it, for if they had, they would not have crucified the Lord of glory. (1 Cor. 2:6–8)

If we were all to sit in a room and write up an ideal strategy to save the world from chaos, I guarantee that no one would suggest doing what God did on the cross. When Jesus, God's wisdom, rose from the dead holding the keys of death and hell, pouring out grace and forgiveness with the gift of the Holy Spirit, chaos knew it chose poorly. In the presence of wisdom, chaos always chooses poorly.[17]

Paul received the revelation. He understood that wisdom is a person. That person is Christ. The wisdom of this world, all the bright ideas detached from the person of wisdom, is foolishness in the eyes of God.[18] The wisdom that keeps chaos at bay is the Son of God.[19] When we have him, we have the power and the insight to manifest the kingdom of God creatively on this chaotic planet. We have the mind of Christ.[20]

Jesus often displayed his power over chaos. He sleeps through a storm on the sea. It's no threat to him.[21] He commands the wind over the turbulent sea to be still, and it obeys him.[22] He even walks on water.[23] Chaos is under his feet.[24] The demons of Gadarene ask permission to enter the pigs and immediately run into the sea. The Jews of this period would understand the significance; the demons run home scared with their tails between their legs. Wisdom spoke, and chaos fled for cover. The life of Jesus is a living illustration of wisdom's power and authority over chaos. It is not without significance that John's first recorded miracle is Jesus turning water (by implication chaos) into wine.[25]

Intermission

Jesus is the creative heartbeat of everything that exists. He holds all things together. His powerful word prevents creation from unravelling. He is the Word. He is wisdom personified – his presence and power silence chaos. His plan transpired before the Father said, 'Let there be light.' The execution of that plan is impeccable. The human drama unfolds in him. He is our reality. Jesus is not creation; he is the creator and sustainer of it, but this didn't prevent him from being born as a human being, and remaining divinely human for all eternity. Jesus will one day bring heaven and earth together.[26] This is the goal.

Perhaps you've noticed a recurring pattern in the drama. We see it all through the Bible. God comes to Adam and Eve in the garden. God is with Abraham in Canaan. God meets with Abraham's descendants in Egypt. God marries them on the foothills of Mount Sinai. He steps down from Sinai and travels through the wilderness with the Hebrew nation. He confines himself to the holy of holies so that he can stay in the centre of their camp. He comes to them in Babylon. He brings them home to Jerusalem. This pattern will escalate when we step into the New Testament. From Genesis to Revelation, there is one inescapable fact we can't ignore: God wants to live with us!

God's not trying to get us into heaven; he's bringing heaven to earth. We aren't going up; heaven is coming down. We are created in his image to thrive on earth. Jesus comes to this planet clothed as a citizen of earth. This is why Jesus will remain fully God and fully human for eternity. Earth is his eternal home. This planet is the final destination. Heaven is already packing its bags and sending the cases on ahead. The new address is the kingdom of God on earth. Jesus is more than a saviour. He's the spearhead of an invasion, an invasion of love. Love invades an orphaned planet and love will win the day.

The Soundtrack of Heaven

As we follow Jesus through the pages of the New Testament, we enter a different world. The territory is familiar, but the horizon has changed. During the four-hundred-year span between Malachi and Matthew, new factions have evolved with their own religious and political ideologies. In some ways, we can compare the situation to the denominationalism we find in today's church. Israel is one nation serving one God, but there are many traditions splashing about in the pool. The more prominent groups are the Pharisees, Sadducees, Samaritans, Herodians and Zealots.[1]

We also find significant shifts in the political arena. The East no longer controls the world. Assyria, Babylon and Persia left their mark, but their ship has sailed. Greece and Rome from the West are the primary movers in the New Testament story. Rome conquers the Greek Empire, but the shadow of Hellenism remains. Greek thought fights for the Jewish mind, while the forces of Rome demand their allegiance. Here is where the Director gets bold and radical. 'But when the set time had fully come, God sent his Son, born of a woman, born under the law' (Gal. 4:4).

We watch as the camera focuses its lens on Bethlehem. We know the story well; maybe too well. We often spotlight

Golgotha and the empty tomb and presume this was the principal reason Jesus came to the planet. We declare it as gospel, but Jesus doesn't do this. Of all the actors in the New Testament, no one held tighter to the original script than Jesus. No one spoke more of the kingdom of God than Jesus Christ. No one demonstrated it more than Jesus. No one exhibited God's character, morality and blessing like the Son of the living God. Jesus came with one message: the good news for the world is the kingdom of God manifested on this planet. The show must go on – even if it kills him.

The Director's Cut

Do you remember when the first video shop opened in your neighbourhood? I remember it well. The thought that you could watch a film anytime you wanted was marvellous. Of course, this happened way back before the dinosaurs, or at least before personal computers, cell phones, CDs, DVDs and the internet. Can you imagine how backward and boring life must have been?

The films were on tape, but none of us could afford the player. New tech was expensive, and no one could predict which format was going to win the day. At that time the battle was between Betamax and VHS. One of them was going to become the standard, but nobody knew which one. Fortunately, the video shop rented the player with the movie.

So six of us got together for our first-ever movie night. It was exciting. We each picked out a film and ordered pizza, but we were still on a learning curve. How can you watch six movies in one evening? Duh! After the second film, I went to bed. Oh well, so much for movie night.

The choices were few when it came to movies back then. The only video available was the theatrical version. That's the one shown in the cinema. Today we almost have as many film versions as we do the Bible. There's the extended version, the editor's cut, the limited edition, 3D, Blu-ray, the remastered version and the special edition. The list goes on, but the one I'm most interested in is the director's cut.

The theatrical version is the film edited by the studio; the motivation is commercial. The director's cut, on the other hand, is how the director wants the story to be portrayed and understood. The two versions don't usually contradict each other or chronicle a different tale, but they each have their particular viewpoint and nuance.

When it comes to the life of Jesus, we favour the theatrical version because it's so familiar. Theologians explain it, pastors preach it and teachers clarify it. The theatrical release is so well-established we hardly ever think to question it. We decode everything that transpired before Jesus came on the scene from a New Testament perspective. In the theatrical version, the Old Testament becomes a relic of illustrative stories or the prophetic pot we dip into when we need to confirm the lordship of Jesus as the Messiah.

The Director's cut doesn't follow this format. Instead, it interprets the New Testament as a page of a long-running script. Jesus will always be the star of the show, but he is only on the stage for thirty-something years. His scene arrives on cue. The Director's cut doesn't reinterpret the message of the Old Testament; it leads on from it.

In the Director's cut, the goal of the production is the same as it was from the beginning; Israel is called to manifest the kingdom of God on earth (the four corner pieces of the puzzle and the eight-act play). The Director (God) hasn't changed his mind about this, or the plan regarding the show. The script is the same in Matthew, Mark, Luke and John, as in the pages of Genesis to Malachi.

Jesus steps on to the same stage Abraham and the patriarchs prepared back in Genesis. Moses instructed the actors to perform on this stage. It's where Joshua settled the Hebrews. It's the same place the kings and prophets of old acted out their drama. Jesus now arrives on this same platform, and he's holding the original script in his hand. The plan hasn't changed. Israel is called to manifest the kingdom of God on earth; the show must go on. Jesus didn't come to start a new religion; he came to reboot the kingdom. He came to get the show back on the road. God is packing his bags and preparing the earth for the big move.

The Soundtrack

It's fascinating how the birth of one child shook the world. The ripples started before his parents lifted him from the manger. At the age of two, Jesus was taken into Egypt because he was a threat to King Herod.[2] During his lifetime he was a threat to the Jewish leaders.[3] His impact eventually reshaped the Roman Empire.[4] Why is that? Power, influence and authority. At various times and locations, many thought Jesus would endanger their jurisdiction, and no one who had a taste of power and control wanted to relinquish it. Jesus was a destabiliser of the status quo.[5]

With any kingdom, the issue is: who's in charge? It was considered treasonous and heretical to declare, 'Jesus is Lord' with Rome breathing down your neck. There was only one ruling authority in that empire, and he went by the name of Caesar. To say 'Jesus is Lord' was intolerable.

King Herod held on to power like a psycho-dictator. He wasn't going to let anyone get between him and his authority to rule. Out of paranoia, Herod had already killed off his favourite wife, his mother-in-law and three of his sons because of real or imagined plots against his throne. Caesar Augustus said it was safer to be Herod's pig than his son.[6] No wonder all Jerusalem was disturbed when the Magi rode into town and asked King Herod, 'Where is the one who has been born king of the Jews?' (Matt. 2:2). If you wanted to wave a red flag in front of a mad bull, this was it. Humanity, power and authority are often a strange mix, especially when we let that power and authority define us. Herod had no qualms when it came to slaughtering the children of Bethlehem.[7] Once you choose a path and start pulling the trigger, it doesn't matter how big or small the target.

If the four gospels had a soundtrack, the authority of Jesus would be the recurring theme. It's the 'royal motif': King Jesus, the name above all names. No wonder the political and religious leaders of Israel were afraid of him and his growing influence. He captured the hearts of the people. He triggered their imagination and implanted the hope of unrealised possibilities. He introduced an alternative culture born from heaven. It was bursting the old wineskins.[8] Authorities at times resorted to violence and execution to patch the holes. It was the only way they knew to protect their cherished realm and sovereignty, but it was unworkable. Martyrs make very poor patches. They exacerbate the tear, especially when the first victim opens his eyes, stands up, and walks out of the grave they put him in.

This 'royal motif' followed Jesus all his life. It's the music driving the production. Whenever the cameras focus on Jesus, the 'royal motif' starts to play in all its various arrangements. What makes the score so interesting, though, is the accompaniment. There is another composition playing in the background.

It begins so quietly you hardly hear it at first. Early on through the four gospels, it builds as it blends with the 'royal motif' and crescendos at the end. This other orchestration is the 'suffering servant song'.[9]

Two different melodies skilfully set the tone of the gospel story. Many of the early and later Jews tried to separate them: 'The Messiah is to rule as a king, not die on a cross.' The Christians, however, had ears to hear. For them the accompaniment wasn't intrusive, it was a new song. It was mysterious and attractive. They could hear a tonal depth that earlier generations tuned out. It was binaural, progressive and otherworldly. The two strains dance around each other as King Jesus rides through Jerusalem's gates on a donkey.[10] The songs merge discordantly, vying for attention as the Master Rabbi[11] bends to wash the disciple's feet.[12]

The two strains are enigmatic and dissonant until the camera focuses its lens on Golgotha. The crucifixion is where the lyrical genius of heaven culminates. That Passover night, requiem and majesty blended into one song. The harmony was something never heard before in Israel. The king of the universe dies as a suffering servant. 'Pilate had a notice prepared and fastened to the cross. It read: JESUS OF NAZARETH, THE KING OF THE JEWS' (John 19:19).

Now, this is probably the only soundtrack we know. It's biblical, historical and irrefutable. The Son takes on our humanity. He lives his life as a servant. The Son of God surrenders to death and conquers it. Jesus now reigns as king, and someday he will return as earth's only reigning monarch. We sing the song. We tell the story. We recite the creed. We listen to the arrangement and rejoice.

Intermission

This is the theatrical version, but how does the story of Jesus fit into the original script? What about Israel? What about the kingdom of God? How does the story develop in the Director's cut?

32

Earworms and Mind-loops

Ever get a catchy tune stuck in your head? You know: a song that just won't quit but keeps repeating itself over and over, and over again. It's not a rare condition or a mental illness, but it sure is annoying. You wish you could rip the tune from your mind, break the vinyl, delete the MP3, erase the tape; anything to get your brain back. Psychiatrists have a phrase for it; it's called 'involuntary musical imagery'. The popular term is 'earworms'. Have you ever had one? I get them now and then. My worst bout was with that old song called 'Puppy Love'.

One summer, I was working for a landscaper. We put in patios, removed old paving-stones, built fences and did a lot of shovelling. It was backbreaking. There were five of us on the team, and one of the co-workers was a giant. He was 6 foot 5 inches tall and built like a brick wall. He'd pass us carrying two large paving-stones while the rest of us struggled with one. It was manly men doing manly things, but some were manlier than others. So for days I had this earworm thingy coming and going in my head. I'd be humming it to myself, and at times I'd let rip and sing the chorus out loud.

This earworm didn't do much for my street cred, but the song hijacked my brain, and I couldn't shake it off. After a few days, the giant came over to me and said, 'Richard, will you quit singing that silly song. I wake up humming it in the morning, and I can't get it out of my head.' That's when I realised earworms were contagious. I told my friend it was the 'Puppy Love' curse and, hopefully, someday we'll both recover. For a while, though, we were an outstanding duet.

Well, I no longer suffer from the 'Puppy Love' curse. That earworm has been spat on, put down and eradicated. It will never rise again. Can I boast? Not really. Earworms come in many forms and disguises, and I'm not immune. They even transcend the lyrics and the melodies that convey them. I suppose a more general term would be 'mind-loops'.

Anything that triggers a loop can kidnap our brain. It could be ideas, world-views, doctrines or any other kind of cerebral positioning that stops us from hearing other voices. Sometimes this is a good thing. It often protects us from lies and deception. Many hang their hat in this room because it's safe and comfortable, but it doesn't always promote spiritual growth and understanding. It can lock us in a narrow place, forbidding future exploration. The real hazard regarding mind-loops is that we rarely recognise them, especially when it comes to Jesus and his approach to the kingdom of God.

The Jesus-earworm is often triggered when we think of mission. We say the only reason Jesus came to earth was to destroy the works of the devil,[1] fulfil the law,[2] reveal the Father,[3] and die for our sin.[4] Some of us don't question or examine this premise because it's ingrained in our psyche, and it's in the Bible. We erect barriers to protect it. We defend it as the original plan and primary purpose of God in Jesus Christ. We hold it up as sound doctrine and safeguard it from unwelcome guests. To query it leads to the dark side, if not heresy. This mind-loop can become so loud, precious and theologically entrenched that we often miss the other biblical conversations going on in the background. We can even tune out and reinterpret the voice of Jesus.[5]

The theatrical version of the gospel story often elevates the 'suffering servant song' above the 'royal motif'. For us, this is customary. It's our mind-loop. Salvation is what affects us now, so we focus on it. It's what brought redemption to the Gentiles. It's what saved me.

The theatrical version doesn't ignore the 'royal motif', but it frequently projects it into the future when Jesus returns to establish the kingdom. It overlooks the possibility that Jesus actually came to fulfil the Jewish expectation in his lifetime. We jack up the volume of the suffering servant and drown out many of the subtleties the 'royal motif' is communicating. It's an earworm. It blocks out the Director's voice regarding the role of Jesus as he steps on to the stage. We shake our heads and question the Jewish expectation along with their theology.

- Why do the Jews always expect a king to come and set things right?
- Why didn't they receive Jesus as a suffering servant?
- Why are they still asking about the kingdom instead of the salvation of their souls?
- Why bring politics and national interest into a religious conversation?

Our mind-loop has blocked out their voice. We don't understand it. Since we don't understand it, we disdain it. We rejoice in the 'suffering servant song' and accuse those who don't elevate it above the 'royal motif' as being spiritually blind.

Oh, those poor Pharisees and Sadducees who study the Scripture night and day and expect a reigning, messianic monarch to take the literal throne of David and elevate the Jewish nation in the world. How sightless can they be? Poor things, why aren't they as enlightened and as spiritual as we Christians are?

But have you ever considered they might be right, and perhaps we got it wrong? We probably never asked this question because we're stuck in a mind-loop. Maybe we need to pay closer attention to their voice. If we want to understand the kingdom of God and how it relates to Jesus, and his passion for it, we have to hear the voice of the Director, not just our chosen theologians.

Spoiler Alert

Any of us who have ever read a film magazine or a movie review will often come across the word 'spoiler'. It's like one of those red or yellow caution signs we encounter on the road. The word warns us that, in the next few paragraphs, plot details will be exposed. For many of us, we don't want the story all spelt out before we see the film. I like a bit of mystery and surprise. If I read the spoiler, I'd probably not bother watching the movie because it is – spoiled.

My wife is just the opposite. She will read the last two pages of a novel first, or read the spoiler and benefit from it. We are very different in that way. However, I'm going to pretend you are like my wife and want to know the plot before the curtain goes up. You can skip the spoiler if you wish to, but it may be beneficial to hear a few of the main points before we unpack them. You know; unhinge a few mind-loops.

1. At the outset, Jesus is sent to minister to the Jewish nation, not to the world. He stepped on to the stage like a prophet of old, and he had the same remit as Hosea, Jeremiah and Isaiah. The main concern wasn't to die for the sin of the world but to get Israel back on the script; to manifest the kingdom of God on earth.

2. Personal salvation is not the chief appeal of the original script. It's a mind-loop we need to break. Our salvation is essential, and it is crucial, but it is not the primary plot line. Jesus came to get the show back on the road.

3. The 'royal motif' and the 'suffering servant song' are both pencilled into the script, but they didn't have to appear in the order history records them. If the Jewish leaders and the nation had recognised Jesus and repented, Jesus would have reigned as king in their generation. The kingdom would have been established on the world stage two thousand years ago. The kingdom was always the Director's goal. Jesus is the star of the show, but the kingdom of God is the production.

4. We can hardly speculate how the 'suffering servant song' would've entered the soundtrack if the Jews had repented and received Jesus as their king and messiah. Historically it didn't happen that way, but the script was open to the edit.

5. The life of Jesus is a continuation of the Old Testament story, which explains why the kingdom of God is the gospel of Jesus. The Apostle Paul also proclaims the gospel, but his primary emphasis is on the king who died on a cross and rose from the dead.

> By this gospel you are saved, if you hold firmly to the word I preached to you. Otherwise, you have believed in vain.
>
> For what I received I passed on to you as of first importance: that Christ died for our sins according to the Scriptures, that he was buried, that he was raised on the third day according to the Scriptures. (1 Cor. 15:2–4)

Paul's gospel focuses on what Jesus did and how this relates to us as individuals. The gospel of Jesus focuses on the community and what it means to the world. They are both one and the same gospel, but the general tendency today is to highlight Paul's gospel emphasis over the one Jesus proclaimed. We need to hold both accounts in tension, or we'll lose something in the telling and in the application. We can't promote one aspect of the gospel above the other.

Intermission

Now I admit this spoiler is a bit radical but please don't put this book down yet. The Bible has many voices. Some we listen to and cherish; others we tend to ignore or deem as unimportant. To break a few of our mind-loops, we need to give some of these overlooked voices another chance to speak. Perhaps they have more to say than we previously realised.

The Gospel of Jesus

Jesus preached one gospel. He announced one gospel. He taught and trained the disciples to proclaim and exhibit one gospel: the gospel of the kingdom of God. It's his mind-loop. It is his primary concern. He is passionate about it because his Father, the Director of the show, is passionate about it.

> Very truly I tell you, the Son can do nothing by himself; he can do only what he sees his Father doing, because whatever the Father does the Son also does. (John 5:19)

> My teaching is not my own. It comes from the one who sent me. (John 7:16)

> I must proclaim the good news of the kingdom of God to the other towns also, because that is why I was sent. (Luke 4:43)

Everything Jesus did was a demonstration of the kingdom. Whenever Jesus mentions the word 'gospel', the kingdom of God is attached to it.

> Jesus went throughout Galilee, teaching in their synagogues, proclaiming the good news of the kingdom, and healing every disease and illness among the people. (Matt. 4:23)

Jesus went into Galilee, proclaiming the good news of God. 'The time has come,' he said. 'The kingdom of God has come near. Repent and believe the good news!' (Mark 1:14–15)

After this, Jesus travelled about from one town and village to another, proclaiming the good news of the kingdom of God. (Luke 8:1)

The Law and the Prophets were proclaimed until John. Since that time, the good news of the kingdom of God is being preached, and everyone is forcing their way into it. (Luke 16:16)

If Jesus had worn a sandwich board through the streets of Jerusalem, it would have read, 'Fulfil Your Destiny – the Show Must Go On'. If he handed out a tract, emblazoned on the front would be 'The Gospel of the Kingdom'. The disciples of Jesus were commanded to proclaim and demonstrate the same message.

These twelve Jesus sent out with the following instructions: 'Do not go among the Gentiles or enter any town of the Samaritans. Go rather to the lost sheep of Israel. As you go, proclaim this message: "The kingdom of heaven has come near." Heal those who are ill, raise the dead, cleanse those who have leprosy, drive out demons. Freely you have received; freely give.' (Matt. 10:5–8)

Now some of us may be asking, 'Yes, but isn't this before the cross/resurrection event? Didn't the gospel change for Jesus after he died for the sin of the world and rose from the dead?' Well, surprisingly enough, it didn't. When Jesus rose from the dead, he spent the next forty days talking about the thing closest to his heart.

> After his suffering, he presented himself to them and gave many
> convincing proofs that he was alive. He appeared to them over a pe-
> riod of forty days and spoke about the kingdom of God. (Acts 1:3)

The apostles were so caught up in his fervour that the last question they ever ask of Jesus is, 'Lord, are you at this time going
to restore the kingdom to Israel?' (Acts 1:6).

John 3

I would guess almost every Christian has quoted from John 3
at one time or another. On the internet, John 3:16 probably
gets more hits than any other verse in the Bible. But a close
second would also stem from that initial chat Jesus had with
Nicodemus. I see it written on church noticeboards all through
Northern Ireland: 'You must be born again' (John 3:7).

This one verse has become the badge of evangelicalism. The
focus is on personal salvation – our ticket to heaven. However,
it's another one of those mind-loops, and it's hard to break. It
tends to drown out the main thrust of the conversation. The
concern of Jesus wasn't getting Nicodemus into heaven but
ushering Nicodemus (and the Jewish leaders) into the kingdom
of God on earth at that moment in time: 'Come on, dude. Let's
get the show back on the road.'

> Jesus replied, 'Very truly I tell you, no one can see the kingdom
> of God unless they are born again' . . . Jesus answered, 'Very truly
> I tell you, no one can enter the kingdom of God unless they are
> born of water and the Spirit.' (John 3:3,5)

We often equate the kingdom of God with heaven, which is
another mind-loop we need to break. Jesus tells Nicodemus
that the kingdom is here on earth, right now.

I have spoken to you [plural – the Jewish leaders] of earthly things [being born again to enter the kingdom here on earth] and you [plural] do not believe; how then will you [plural] believe if I speak of heavenly things? (John 3:12)

Personal salvation is a critical matter for every human being on this planet, but we can't let that conversation drown out the main concern and goal of the Son of God.

Intermission

Jesus instructed his disciples to preach, 'The kingdom of God is near.' He didn't push the message, 'You must be saved.' Of course, it's part of the package, but his emphasis was on the kingdom, not personal salvation. Jesus came to give the Jews another chance to fulfil their mission.[1] The witness God desires in this world is a community of faithful believers, not just specific individuals. God often sent individuals because they are easier to work with than a large body of people. However, the individuals all had one goal and purpose: to inspire the community to fulfil its calling before God and the world, to get the show back on the road!

Guardians of the Kingdom

For a bit of mindless fun and humour, I enjoy the *Guardians of the Galaxy* movies. A genetically engineered racoon, a plant creature called Groot, a two-legged humanoid energised by 1980s music, and a few other alien species, join together to save the galaxy from annihilation. They have vision and purpose. Although this is full-blown, childlike fiction, it does make you wonder why we often think so small. Not to despise the day of little things, but I'll never be satisfied, just working to stay alive, raising a family and watching TV.[1]

Probably the closest we get to saving the galaxy is living for and within the kingdom of God. It's the only kingdom that will remain when all the others fade away. In the Old Testament, the guardians were the prophets; they were the guardians of the kingdom. Their vision wasn't confined to Israel; it was for the entire planet. If Israel got its act together, much of the world would follow. Isn't this what Jesus was referring to when he said, 'You are the salt of the earth' (Matt. 5:13)? Isn't this what he declared when he affirmed the Jewish nation? 'You are the light of the world' (Matt. 5:14). Here, Jesus is quoting the prophet Isaiah.

> I will also make you a light for the Gentiles,
>> that my salvation may reach to the ends of the earth.
>> (Isa. 49:6)

In the theatrical version, we often apply these verses to ourselves and tune out what the original audience heard. The Director's cut, on the other hand, understands these are statements about Israel's destiny and purpose regarding the kingdom. 'Neither do people light a lamp and put it under a bowl. Instead, they put it on its stand, and it gives light to everyone in the house' (Matt. 5:15).

It's a call to pick up the script: 'Don't forget who you are. Manifest the kingdom of God on the stage of Israel. Be a light to the world. Don't hide your light under a basket.'

Jesus the Prophet

In the Old Testament, when kings went off script, the prophets were there beckoning them to pick it up again. When the kings refused to listen, the prophets would turn to the general population, hoping to start a people movement. When the people refused to hear, the prophets were hunted down and silenced. Jesus came to Israel with the same mantle and remit as the prophets of old; he even shared the same fate.

Moses predicted that someday God would send Israel another prophet like himself.[2] This is special. Peter, in the New Testament, tells us that the prophet Moses predicted is Jesus.[3] The actors on the stage recognise Jesus as a prophet of God.[4] Jesus even refers to himself as a prophet.[5]

John the Baptist: a Prophet like Elijah

The close connection between John the Baptist and the prophet Elijah also enhances the prophetic role of Jesus. We may not fully grasp what Jesus is saying when he announces the relationship between John the Baptist and Elijah, but the Jewish audience wouldn't have missed it.[6] If John the Baptist was a prophet like Elijah, then Jesus was a prophet like Elisha. The mission of Elijah and Elisha is interconnected, just like the ministry of John the Baptist and Jesus complement each other.

When I teach the prophets course, I love it when we get to the section on Elijah and Elisha.[7] Their story and testimony are so vivid and dramatic the studio would classify it an action/thriller in any cinema. Three times Elijah calls down fire from heaven.[8] He raises a widow's son back to life, and miraculously parts the Jordan River.[9] At the end of his life, he's taken up to heaven in a chariot of fire – wild stuff.[10] Today, he would be a superhero: a guardian of the kingdom.

Elisha asks for a double portion of Elijah's anointing and receives it.[11] He then performs twice as many miraculous signs as Elijah.[12] Elijah comes to reveal God to Israel; Elisha comes to show Israel God's character. Even their names speak of this: Elijah (Yahweh is God), Elisha (God is salvation). It shouldn't surprise us that the name of Jesus means, 'God saves.'

The Gospel of Matthew specifically draws our attention to Elijah and his relationship to John the Baptist.

1. John the Baptist and Elijah wear the same style of untrendy clothes.[13]
2. They each have a stand-off with political powers. Elijah challenges Ahab and Jezebel.[14] John the Baptist challenges Herod and Herodias.[15]
3. They each anoint their successor at the Jordan River. The Spirit comes upon Elisha when the cloak of Elijah falls from the sky.[16] The Holy Spirit descends upon Jesus at his baptism.[17]

Jesus: a Prophet like Elisha

Do you remember when John the Baptist was in prison? He had a lot of questions going through his mind. He was probably thinking, 'Why am I in prison? The Messiah is supposed to set the prisoner free. He is the king. If he is king, then should I even be here? Have I been backing the wrong horse?' So he asks the question, 'Are you the one who is to come, or should we expect someone else?' (Matt. 11:3). John wouldn't have asked this if he was expecting a suffering servant.

Jesus hardly ever gave a direct answer to a question. His goal wasn't to impart knowledge but to open our spiritual eyes and ears. His responses are often directed to the question that should have been asked. His answer to John may seem a bit cryptic to us, but that doesn't mean it was obscure to John or the people of his day. So, instead of answering John's inquiry with a direct yes or no, Jesus gives John an inventory of Elisha's ministry and applies it to himself.

Jesus replied, 'Go back and report to John what you hear and see: the blind receive sight, the lame walk, those who have leprosy are cleansed, the deaf hear, the dead are raised, and the good news is proclaimed to the poor.' (Matt. 11:4–5)

Elisha also restored sight to the blind,[18] healed lepers,[19] raised the dead,[20] and preached good news to the poor.[21] In his way, Jesus was telling John, 'You aren't backing the wrong horse.'

You are Elijah to this generation as I am Elisha. Our ministries balance each other just as the two prophets, Elisha and Elijah, complement each other. Don't worry. We're on the same page. I am the Messiah.

There are other connections between Jesus and Elisha the Jewish audience would easily have recognised. For example, Elisha raises a widow's son back to life in the village of Shunem.[22] This village is a quarter mile down the road from Nain where Jesus also raises a widow's son to life.[23] The Jews who witnessed this understood the connection.

> They were all filled with awe and praised God. 'A great prophet has appeared among us,' they said. 'God has come to help his people.' (Luke 7:16)

Probably one of the most obvious links between Jesus and Elisha is the way John the gospel writer tells some of his stories. We see it in the report of the loaves and fishes.[24] Elisha and Jesus both feed a large crowd with just a few barley loaves. The episode in John was written to mirror the event written about Elisha.

> A man came from Baal Shalishah, bringing the man of God twenty loaves of barley bread baked from the first ripe corn, along with some ears of new corn. 'Give it to the people to eat,' Elisha said.
>
> 'How can I set this before a hundred men?' his servant asked.
>
> But Elisha answered, 'Give it to the people to eat. For this is what the LORD says: "They will eat and have some left over."' Then he set it before them, and they ate and had some left over, according to the word of the LORD. (2 Kgs 4:42–4)

> 'Here is a boy with five small barley loaves and two small fish, but how far will they go among so many?'
>
> Jesus said, 'Make the people sit down.' There was plenty of grass in that place, and they sat down (about five thousand men were there). Jesus then took the loaves, gave thanks, and distributed to

those who were seated as much as they wanted. He did the same with the fish.

When they had all had enough to eat, he said to his disciples, 'Gather the pieces that are left over. Let nothing be wasted.' So they gathered them and filled twelve baskets with the pieces of the five barley loaves left over by those who had eaten.

After the people saw the sign Jesus performed, they began to say, 'Surely this is the Prophet who is to come into the world.' (John 6:9–14)

There's no doubt Jesus was considered a prophet like the prophets of the Old Testament. However, when we look at the theatrical version, we tend to acknowledge the prophetic statements and actions of Jesus, but we don't take the prophetic charge far enough. There are two reasons for this. One, we let the 'suffering servant song' drown out the other biblical voices. Two, we project the New Testament into the Old instead of reading both testaments as a linear story. The task of the prophets was to reintroduce the actors to the script and inspire them to take it seriously, to usher in the kingdom.

These guardians of the kingdom often surrendered their lives, hoping to see the messianic king. After Jesus was rejected by the Jewish elite, he tells the disciples, 'Truly I tell you, many prophets and righteous people longed to see what you see but did not see it, and to hear what you hear but did not hear it' (Matt. 13:17). What they wanted to hear and see was the establishment of God's kingdom on earth. The Jewish nation carried that same messianic expectation when Jesus walked their streets, but they didn't take it forward.

Conversely, the Director's cut not only recognises the prophetic role of Jesus, but it also values and understands what that prophetic role was trying to achieve. God sent prophets when Israel was in breach of contract. Like the prophets of old, Jesus arrives on the scene when Israel stands between the fourth and fifth phase of the morality clause. Rome is oppressing the people, and things are hard. If Israel doesn't repent and get back on script, Phase 5 is just around the corner. The crisis is real, and God doesn't want to scatter them again. So this time the Director doesn't just send in a prophet like John the Baptist, he also sends his son – the star of the show. The audience wasn't the only one that needed to see the kingdom of God; so did the actors.

There is a very emotive passage in one of the parables of Jesus. Here he traces the prophetic office from the Old Testament up to his current position. Jesus recognises the continuity of his mission as a prophet and how it ties in with the original script and goal of the Director.

> At harvest time he sent a servant [a prophet] to the tenants [the Jews] so they would give him some of the fruit of the vineyard [manifest the kingdom]. But the tenants beat him and sent him away empty-handed. He sent another servant, but that one also they beat and treated shamefully and sent away empty-handed. He sent still a third, and they wounded him and threw him out.
>
> Then the owner of the vineyard said, 'What shall I do? I will send my son, whom I love; perhaps they will respect him.' (Luke 20:10–13)

Oh, the patience and tenacity of God. The world can't comprehend the depth of love and grace displayed in the face of Jesus Christ. When God gave his Son, he gave us everything.[25] 'Surely they will respect him.'

Intermission

The desire of the Father was that the world would receive his Son, not reject and kill him. The fate of this planet lies in the balance. Kingdoms have come and gone as generations slip away without a witness. Some may have seen a sandwich board or two or got a glimpse of God in creation, but up to this point, a sustained witness of the kingdom of God has yet to be seen on earth.

God chose to manifest the kingdom through the children of Abraham, and he keeps pushing, nourishing, guiding, warning, blessing and wooing to make it happen. He never gives up. Now God comes and walks on this ancient stage as a human being. He arrives on cue. Jesus comes as a royal priest wearing the mantle of a prophet. He carries their passion: 'Get the show on the road; manifest the kingdom of God on earth.'

When Jesus teaches on prayer, the first request is to welcome the kingdom.[26] When Jesus talks about our human needs, he tells us to seek first the kingdom and his righteousness.[27] Almost all the parables are related to the kingdom.[28] The Sermon on the Mount is all about the kingdom and how to live in it.[29] For Jesus, the good news for the world is the manifest presence of the kingdom of God on earth. This is his message. This is the goal, just like his predecessors before him. His objective never wavered or changed, even after the cross/resurrection event.

> I must proclaim the good news of the kingdom of God to the other towns also, because that is why I was sent. (Luke 4:43)

Rob the Devil

We live in a cul-de-sac. It's called time and space. It's as big as the universe, and the clock is always ticking. If we speed through the intergalactic frontier and bump against the outermost wall of our existence, probably the other side is what we call eternity. As far as we know, eternity is not bound by time or space. This is one of those metaphysical conundrums scientists, philosophers and theologians often try to comprehend.[1]

God was standing on the threshold of eternity when he called time and space into existence. Do you ever wonder why God put us here and not there? Of course, neither realm is stagnant, but in one there is always a beginning and an end; in the other, time as we know it is irrelevant. Eternity is probably God himself. Who has the words or the mind to describe God? It's like a goldfish trying to understand and explain the world outside the bowl.

We know from the Bible that God is eternal, but things are obviously moving forward in heaven. There is movement between heaven and earth. The Son of God came from eternity. He was born into space and time and returned to heaven, fully God and fully human. From our limited understanding, we believe Satan and the angels were created in eternity, not in space and time.[2] Some angels have fallen from heaven and landed on this planet. We call them demons and fallen angels.[3] Good angels come to earth to further God's purpose.

Time and space comprise eternity's cul-de-sac to work redemptive change. Time and space force growth and development. They give us room to learn, make mistakes and overcome. They put mettle in our heart and soul. They force advancement, progression and maturity.

No one is born into this world fully equipped and developed. No one on this side of the divide has a super divine microchip of eternal knowledge planted in their brain. We learn by a process in time and space. We develop through the choices we make and our actions. When Jesus entered our playground, he played by the rules of time and space, not eternity. It's evident. Jesus didn't come to earth the same way he left it. He arrives as a seed in a mother's womb. Jesus grows. He develops and matures from a baby lying in a manger; he needed the occasional diaper change. He had to be fed, burped and loved like every other human being born on this planet. His wisdom and authority developed through experience, guidance and obedience.

Jesus and Authority

In any kingdom, 'authority' is the operative word. It may surprise us, but Jesus didn't come to earth with ultimate power, and he wasn't born with a royal sceptre in his hand. The Apostle Paul tells us that when God took on humanity, he laid down his divine privileges.[4]

Jesus didn't bring his supreme authority into the world with him. He moved in the authority that God the Father bestowed on him. Jesus grew in prestige and power in and by the Holy

Spirit. It was a process. Of course, the Magi and first-century prophets spoke of his destiny, pedigree and DNA, but it was yet unrealised potential. Like every other human being, Jesus also had to go through the human process of growth in a fallen world. He learned what it was like to take orders. Jesus subjected himself to his parents and his heavenly Father.[5] He paid his taxes.[6] Obedience wasn't comfortable, convenient or enjoyable. Gethsemane is where we witness first-hand the humanity of Jesus emptied of divine privilege.

Jesus didn't arrive on this earth with a full deposit of heavenly wisdom either. It developed with the choices he made throughout his life.

> Then he went down to Nazareth with them and was obedient to them. But his mother treasured all these things in her heart. And Jesus grew in wisdom and stature, and in favour with God and man. (Luke 2:51–2)

Even though Jesus is the personification of wisdom, it was wise for him to grow and walk in wisdom like every other human being born into this world. His sinless life would've been pretentious if he held on to the divine advantage.[7] 'Son though he was, he learned obedience from what he suffered' (Heb. 5:8).

Jesus acquired his knowledge and privilege like any other human being. The same applies to his ability and authority to rule. Majesty is in his DNA as the Son of God, but when God chose to clothe himself with humanity (fully God and fully human), it wasn't just the outer shell of a body he put on, it was the whole package along with the environmental laws of our existence. He participated in everything that makes us human, but without the sin. So how did Jesus receive his authority as a human being? How did he walk in it? Where did it take him regarding the kingdom of God and the divine remit? Well, it started at the Jordan River, the beginning of his public ministry.

Into the Dark

> At that time Jesus came from Nazareth in Galilee and was baptised by John in the Jordan. Just as Jesus was coming up out of the water, he saw heaven being torn open and the Spirit descending on him like a dove. And a voice came from heaven: 'You are my Son, whom I love; with you I am well pleased.' (Mark 1:9–11)

Here are two witnesses commissioning Jesus: John the Baptist on earth and the voice of God from heaven.[8] It's his ordination service. I remember the night I was ordained an elder in the Church of the Nazarene. After all the study, work, prayer and service, it was an honour to be affirmed by God through the church. I had the call from God, and the recognition on earth to preach, teach and pastor a congregation. It was one of those, 'It is well; it is well with my soul' moments. Everything was right with God and the world. However, the only audible voice I heard that evening was the general superintendent and the elders who stood with me, but I was ready to change the world anyway. Yee-haw! It was celebration time.

However, it would have been a different story if we had seen the Holy Spirit descend through the ceiling like a dove from heaven and heard the audible voice of God speak his pleasure and blessing over me. I'd have been shocked, overwhelmed and humbled, but I'd also have thought, 'Forget about changing the world. I have to dream bigger – *Guardians of the Galaxy* move over. I'm coming through. Praise his holy name.'

Now when Jesus saw and heard all of these things at his ordination service, you'd think he'd jump right in there and start saving the world. I mean: 'Preach it, brother. You have the green light. You've got the anointing. Get out there and heal the sick, raise the dead, travel the land doing good deeds, and throw a party. This is definitely a double yee-haw moment.' But amazingly enough, right after God affirms and anoints Jesus in the Holy Spirit, that same Holy Spirit drives him from the crowd into the wilderness to be tempted by the devil. It was not a time for celebration, and it sure wasn't a picnic.

For forty days, Jesus had to be on guard against wild animals and dark spiritual forces. The Holy Spirit didn't even give him time to pack a bag or gather a food parcel. There was no nourishment or the relief of earthly comforts. What is this? Is this the way a loving, heavenly Father acts? One minute he's blessing and affirming his child; the next moment he throws him to the lions to see how he gets on. The wisdom of this world would say this is bonkers, but God does not think like the world, and we can thank God for that.

The first thing the devil does when Jesus is tired and hungry is to tempt him with his current bodily needs. 'Your father didn't pack you lunch, but you can eat right now here in the wilderness; that is if what he said about you is true.'

'If you are the Son of God, tell these stones to become bread.'
   Jesus answered, 'It is written: "Man shall not live on bread alone, but on every word that comes from the mouth of God."' (Matt. 4:3–4)

The response of Jesus was like a punch in the jaw. The devil is bleeding now. He's not used to humanity standing against him. It wasn't that often people wielded such spiritual weapons activated by faith. So the devil tries another tactic.

> Then the devil took him to the holy city and set him on the highest point of the temple. 'If you are the Son of God,' he said, 'throw yourself down. For it is written:
>
> "He will command his angels concerning you,
>> and they will lift you up in their hands,
>
> so that you will not strike your foot against a stone."'
>
> Jesus answered him, 'It is also written: "Do not put the Lord your God to the test."' (Matt. 4:5–7)

Whack! The devil takes a right hook to the eye. Now he's bleeding from the mouth and the face. Things aren't looking good, but the devil's proud. He doesn't like defeat. He knows there's more at stake here than just a few blows in the face from the Son of God.

> Again, the devil took him to a very high mountain and showed him all the kingdoms of the world and their splendour. 'All this I will give you,' he said, 'if you will bow down and worship me.'
>
> Jesus said to him, 'Away from me, Satan! For it is written: "Worship the Lord your God, and serve him only."'
>
> Then the devil left him, and angels came and attended him. (Matt. 4:8–11)

Slam! The devil slithers away like a legless serpent, beaten and bruised. His plan has failed. He wanted the Son of God to obey and worship him, but it's all turned around. Jesus is now the one in charge. He commands the devil to leave, and the devil goes. Satan may have tricked and overcome the first Adam, but not the second one.[9] Humanity has now wounded the serpent's head.[10] The devil could tempt Jesus with the kingdoms of this world because he knew Jesus didn't have them; Satan controlled them. In more than one place, the New Testament tells us this world is in the hands of the devil; he's even called the ruler[11] and the god of this world.[12]

If Jesus possessed all the kingdoms of the world, the temptation would be a farce. You can't tempt someone with something they already have, and you can't seduce a person with something they don't want or desire. The temptation was real, intense and legitimate. Jesus didn't possess the kingdoms of the world, and he wanted them. It's his mission. It's the Director's passion. It's why Jesus is so focused on the kingdom.

The devil centred the last great temptation on the nations of this world because he recognised how much Jesus wanted them. God the Father, Son and Holy Spirit will bring the kingdoms of this world under one authority but not from the hand of Satan in the wilderness. This final temptation is authentic. The nations of the world had to change hands, but it had to be under the banner of God, not the influence of Satan.

In the theatrical version, the wilderness scene is often isolated from the continuing story. Matthew tells us Jesus went into the wilderness to face the devil and his temptations. So, we immediately assume this episode refers to the sinless nature of Jesus and his ultimate sacrifice. We tick that box and move on as though the wilderness encounter has nothing to do with the rest of the script. Amen. Jesus resisted the devil and passed the test. He can now go to the cross as a perfect sacrifice because he 'has been tempted in every way, just as we are – yet he did not sin' (Heb. 4:15).

The Director's cut, on the other hand, doesn't surrender the story that easily. It won't allow this event to be quarantined or compartmentalised into some systematic theology.[13] There is another voice to be heard. In the Director's cut, the wilderness victory wasn't just an isolated incident to test the loyalty of God's son. Its reach touches everything Jesus did from that moment forward. For the sake of the kingdom of God, Jesus had to go into the wilderness and face the devil head-on. If Jesus hadn't gone into the desert at the start of his ministry, we wouldn't be reading half the stories we treasure today.

Luke presents the wilderness event as a power play. Jesus enters the desert *full* of the Holy Spirit, but he comes out in the *power* of the Holy Spirit.[14] 'Power' is just another word for 'authority'. Jesus gained authority in the wilderness. God didn't send Jesus into the desert to see how his boy behaves under pressure; he sent him out there to shut the devil up. God equipped Jesus at his ordination. He then takes him into the wilderness for promotion. It was more than a revelation of character.

Into the Light

Jesus can now display the extraordinary works of the kingdom of God in Israel. He can now walk the streets, taking back what the devil stole. He can reverse the evil and free the nation from spiritual oppression. His remit also includes freedom from human and political subjugation, but the leaders and the country need to repent if they want to experience that messianic hope and expectation. With each temptation, the foundation of Satan's kingdom crumbles. When Jesus leaves the wilderness and comes back to town, he may have lost weight, but he still returns a much bigger person. His shadow has grown beyond his human stature.

Let's trace the steps of Jesus from the wilderness through the nearby towns of Galilee. He won the battle; now, he collects the spoils. In the Gospel of Mark, the first announcement Jesus makes when he steps out of the wilderness is a declaration of victory. "'The time has come,' he said. "The kingdom of God has come near. Repent and believe the good news!'" (Mark 1:15).

The soundtrack of the theatrical version often plays the 'suffering servant song' when the text mentions repentance. We presumably think Jesus is alluding to his impending death and resurrection: 'You will enter the kingdom when you believe in me and my sacrifice on the cross.' But this is not what Jesus is saying. That's our interpretation, not his. This is not some cryptic suffering servant announcement based on a future event. It's a shout of victory from Jesus to the Jewish actors on the stage. It's the gospel of the kingdom. It's the royal refrain. Jesus is telling them to have faith.

> The kingdom is obtainable right now. Believe this. I am here to show you what it looks like and to make this happen. Come with me. I muzzled the devil; now let's take back the land. The kingdom of God is at your fingertips. It is near. Repent. Turn. Reach out and grab it.[15]

After this announcement, Jesus consistently demonstrates what life in the kingdom of God looks like. It's everything the people desired. They wanted health, prosperity, love, freedom, security, acceptance, along with the blessing of God and his mercy. Jesus walks through their streets, giving it to them. Everywhere Jesus goes, we find him casting out demons, healing the sick and, like the prophets of old, he calls out, 'Repent. Pick up the script. The kingdom is yours; don't you want it? The show must go on.'

We also see the extent of the wilderness victory each time a demon encounters the Son of God. They keep coming out of the woodwork confessing, 'What do you want with us, Jesus of Nazareth? Have you come to destroy us? I know who you are – the Holy One of God!' (Mark 1:24). It's a cry of fear and defeat. The demons know they're facing an untameable, superior foe who can't be bought.

In the wilderness, the devil twice goaded Jesus with self-doubt: 'If you are the Son of God' (Matt. 4:3,6). Ironically, when Jesus steps out of the wilderness, we find all the devils confessing it for him. 'Whenever the impure spirits saw him, they fell down before him and cried out, "You are the Son of God"' (Mark 3:11).

Did this knowledge come by revelation? Are the demons that smart and all-knowing? No! They knew Jesus because he just wrestled their master to the ground and tied him up. Jesus can now walk through the streets as champion over the demonic forces in Israel. There's obviously been a power shift, and Jesus is the victor. Sounds like the inauguration of a new era, doesn't it?

'As surely as I live,' says the Lord,
'Every knee will bow before me;
    every tongue will acknowledge God.' (Rom. 14:11)

Intermission

At this juncture of the story, the ministry of Jesus is moving from glory to glory. Jesus has won significant victories. The kingdom of God is being preached and demonstrated. It's an excellent start. 'I will send my son, whom I love; perhaps they will respect him' (Luke 20:13).

But we know the story doesn't end here, and the absence of the cross is not the issue. The issue is the kingdom of God on earth. It still isn't established within the borders of Israel. The Jewish people still linger between the fourth and fifth phases of the morality clause. The nation no longer worships idols, but the kingdom of God isn't just about what we deny, it's about what we affirm. It's not about what we stand against, as much as what and who we support and celebrate. Israel had the religion. They held tight to tradition and were quick to condemn those who rocked the boat but, like eleven of the disciples, they weren't inclined to step out and walk on water. Many of the leaders were corrupt and self-seeking. The fact that the central message of John the Baptist was 'repent' tells us something of the nation's spiritual condition.

Jesus reinforces John's message. He too submits to John's baptism of repentance (even though he is without sin). Whenever Jesus preached the gospel of the kingdom, his first instruction was, 'Repent!' This repentance would usher in the kingdom. It wasn't some stop-gap exercise preparing people for the cross. It's connected to the 'royal motif', not the 'suffering servant song'.

If they repented, the nation would see the reality of their messianic hope in their generation. Hezekiah and Isaiah repented before God when they stood between the fourth and fifth phase of the morality clause, and God miraculously freed them from Assyrian invasion. Hezekiah didn't even have to send in the army. These two leaders just humbled themselves before God and repented of the nation's sin.[16]

Another factor to consider is the proliferation of demonic activity among the Jewish people. Jesus continually silenced them and cast them out, but the question is, why did they have such a hold on the population? Demons don't just jump on whoever they want to control. People have to surrender.[17]

Demons have to be invited. The invitation isn't sent out by post or written on a card. Sin is the invitation. Sin is the open door. At first, you think you can control your sin, but then it gets away from you, and other powers ride on the back of it.

The glory of God is his presence. The presence of God is a manifestation of the kingdom on earth. Jesus is the presence. Reject the presence, and you reject the king. Reject the king, and you forfeit the kingdom. Each time Jesus is rejected in the gospels, things change. His ministry shifts gears. The message becomes more hidden and enigmatic. Parables become his main form of public teaching; they weren't meant to illumine but to obscure; only the disciples received a further explanation.

The 'suffering servant song' and the 'royal motif' are both pencilled into the script, but God didn't carve the order in stone. The actors' performance on the stage is the deciding factor. The actors are as free to choose as Adam and Eve were free to decide in the garden of Eden. If they want the 'royal motif' in their towns and cities, they have to welcome Jesus and repent. If they refuse, the kingdom will still arrive on stage, but not in their generation. God the Father, the Director of the production, is ready for either scenario.

Search and Destroy

It's been a long, rocky road up to this point in Jewish history. Caesar was not the answer to their messianic hope, and Rome is not their kingdom of choice. No one wants to be oppressed. These aren't the glory days envisioned by the prophets or the blessings promised in the covenant. Many generations have come and gone on this world stage, and the production still flounders. The kingdom of God is buried deep in Jewish soil, and the Director wants to dig it up.[1] 'In those days John the Baptist came, preaching in the wilderness of Judea and saying, "Repent, for the kingdom of heaven has come near"' (Matt. 3:1–2).

When John announces how near the kingdom is, he's talking about messianic hope. The king is here, and he's ready to establish the kingdom of God on Israel's stage right now, in this generation. We don't often hear it preached, but it was right that the first-century Jews should anchor their hope on a Davidic king who would rule when he first stepped on to the stage. Their desire was not unscriptural or misguided. It was accurate and sound. It was the divinely inspired revelation of God. It's what God revealed to them and wanted them to know. It was the hope God disclosed to them over the centuries. We need to hear their voice, not silence it. The Director wasn't playing games with the actors. 'Ha-ha, the joke's on you. You thought he was going to reign now, but no, you'll have to wait thousands of years for that to happen.'

This idea often skulks about in the theatrical version, but it's not in the Director's cut. The time is ripe. This is to be the harvest generation; a season of Jubilee. It's why God led the Magi to Bethlehem announcing, 'Where is the one who has been born king of the Jews?' (Matt. 2:2). They didn't travel all that way looking for someone to die for their sin.

The nation desperately desired a messianic king. They prayed it would happen in their time, and Jesus was the answer to that prayer.[2] The door to the kingdom is the king.[3] The key that opens that door is repentance. This is the gospel of John the Baptist, and it's the gospel of Jesus the Christ. It's not something God wanted to delay for some future generation. It was available right now for them and the world. John was preparing the way for a reigning Messiah, not a suffering servant.

When Jesus started his ministry, the script was wide open. It could go in one of two directions; either the 'royal motif' or the 'suffering servant song' would dominate. The outcome would be determined by the actors' response to God's one and only Son. If they hadn't rejected him, we would be living in a different world today.

The Fraud Squad

Whenever a messianic figure steps on the stage the Pharisees and other Jewish leaders send out envoys to explore the possibility: are the reports real or fabricated? Do they live up to the messianic expectations recorded in Scripture? Do they see themselves as the Messiah sent by God? Like military police, the Fraud Squad examines the credentials of John the Baptist.

Now this was John's testimony when the Jewish leaders in Jerusalem sent priests and Levites to ask him who he was. He did not fail to confess, but confessed freely, 'I am not the Messiah.'

They asked him, 'Then who are you? Are you Elijah?'

He said, 'I am not.'

'Are you the Prophet?'

He answered, 'No.'

Finally they said, 'Who are you? Give us an answer to take back to those who sent us. What do you say about yourself?'

John replied in the words of Isaiah the prophet, 'I am the voice of one calling in the wilderness, "Make straight the way for the Lord."' (John 1:19–23)

Later, the Fraud Squad comes to question Jesus. His answers often angered them or left them speechless. They couldn't figure him out, so we find the Jewish leaders continually lurking in the crowd, questioning, prodding and looking for some crack in his messianic armour. Early on, when Jesus didn't bend to their Sabbath regulations, they were swift to reject him. 'Then the Pharisees went out and began to plot with the Herodians how they might kill Jesus' (Mark 3:6).

At this point, the 'suffering servant song' quietly inches its way into the soundtrack. It is subtle, almost imperceptible because there is still some hope. God is poised at the drawing board to make the final edit, but love is patient.

We can see why John the Baptist and Jesus were calling the people to repent. The leaders of the temple were the spiritual heartbeat of the nation, but many of them were stuck. The arteries running from Jerusalem to the general population were contaminated. Israel wasn't just under the duress of Rome; they were shackled by the yoke of human religion, posing as kingdom. Jesus was trying to break this yoke off the Jewish back.

They tie up heavy, cumbersome loads and put them on other people's shoulders, but they themselves are not willing to lift a finger to move them. (Matt. 23:4)

Woe to you, teachers of the law and Pharisees, you hypocrites! You travel over land and sea to win a single convert, and when you have succeeded, you make them twice as much a child of hell as you are. (Matt. 23:15)

Come to me, all you who are weary and burdened, and I will give you rest. Take my yoke upon you and learn from me, for I am gentle and humble in heart, and you will find rest for your souls. For my yoke is easy and my burden is light. (Matt. 11:28–30)

The word 'yoke' was a common metaphor used at the time of Jesus. It's another word for 'doctrine'; a person's specific interpretation of Scripture. If we used the phrase today, we would say things like 'the yoke of Calvinism', or 'the yoke of Arminianism'. Each denominational slant would be called a 'yoke'. We often find Jesus comparing his yoke to the popular beliefs of the day. 'You have heard . . . but I say to you.'[4] Jesus wanted to free the nation from all the religious accoutrements and additions to God's law. His yoke honours the spirit of the law, but it refuses to make that law into an idol or the end goal.

The Turning-point

The game-changer for the Director is when the star of the show is publicly dishonoured, first by his family, then by the Fraud Squad.

When his family heard about this, they went to take charge of him, for they said, 'He is out of his mind.'

And the teachers of the law who came down from Jerusalem said, 'He is possessed by Beelzebul! By the prince of demons he is driving out demons.' (Mark 3:21–2)

It just doesn't auger well when the main cast believe the star of the show is a spawn of Satan and his own family think he's gone a bit loopy. God is patient, but he's also aware when the thing becomes unworkable.

The irony is that Jesus arrived to govern as their king and free them from the Romans. He came to take up the royal sceptre and rule. Jesus started at the grassroots, reawakening the general population to the kingdom of God. He brought the blessing and the hope of God with him. He was progressively rescuing and digging up the kingdom assignment: the one Israel had previously buried and forsaken. Jesus even battles the spiritual and religious forces that were warring against it and against the Jewish people. He would eventually deal with Rome, but first things first.

The process was the same as God laid out and exhibited in the Old Testament. Repent, get spiritually right with God, pick up the script, then watch as the Almighty pushes back your enemies. However, before Jesus could take it that far, the nation rejected him and his claim.

The power Jesus displayed over evil spirits is what prompted the Fraud Squad to dismiss him publicly. Everywhere Jesus goes, after the wilderness experience, demons dramatically expose themselves, confess who Jesus is, and leave at his command. The Jewish leaders had no precedent for this.

Jesus commands demons with such ease and authority the Fraud Squad assume he has made a pact with the devil.

To them, it appears to be a set-up, a spiritual scam. So, instead of repenting and embracing the king and the kingdom, they just point the finger and shout, 'Sorcerer!' They had no idea how insulting this was to Jesus, the Father and the Holy Spirit. They didn't have a clue what Jesus went through to gain this place of authority. It cost him. The wilderness temptation was real, but Jesus stayed the course. The flesh was tempted, but he kept himself steady in the Holy Spirit. The accusation of the Jewish leaders was so unfounded and deplorable that Jesus tells them where this kind of allegation will lead them.

> 'Truly I tell you, people can be forgiven all their sins and every slander they utter, but whoever blasphemes against the Holy Spirit will never be forgiven; they are guilty of an eternal sin.'
>
> He said this because they were saying, 'He has an impure spirit.' (Mark 3:28–30)

This was the *coup de grâce*. It was the turning-point of the whole production: 'He came to that which was his own, but his own did not receive him' (John 1:11). From this point forward, the 'royal motif' starts to fade into the background. The 'suffering servant song' will now dominate world history. The painful edit has begun, and no one can turn back the pages. It will severely affect the star of the show, the actors on the stage and the world audience.

The allegation centres on authority. So Jesus takes them back to the wilderness encounter. As John the apostle tells us, the Son of God came to destroy the works of the devil, not to enlist in his army.[5] Serving Satan was one of the temptations Jesus rejected.[6]

So Jesus called them over to him and began to speak to them in parables: 'How can Satan drive out Satan? If a kingdom is divided against itself, that kingdom cannot stand. If a house is divided against itself, that house cannot stand. And if Satan opposes himself and is divided, he cannot stand; the end has come. In fact, no one can enter a strong man's house without first tying him up. Then he can plunder the strong man's house.' (Mark 3:23–7)

The theatrical version doesn't always make the connection between these words and the wilderness victory, but this is what it's all about. Jesus didn't regard the wilderness temptation as a test of character; he saw it as an opportunity. God sent him out there at the beginning of his ministry to meet the enemy face-to-face and neutralise him. This is why the authority of Jesus over demons is so efficient and operative. To the Jewish mind, the wilderness was the dwelling place of Satan and his demons.[7] Jesus is telling the Jewish leaders, 'I went into Satan's house (the desert), and I tied him up (I was stronger than the temptations). Now I can and will plunder his house (heal the sick and cast out devils)!'

Intermission

Jesus was taking ground for the kingdom of God and its establishment on the world stage of Israel. When the Jewish leaders accuse Jesus of sorcery, and his own family thinks he's overtaxed himself and is out of his mind, the Director knew this generation wasn't ready for a reigning Messiah. God had encountered this kind of behaviour a few centuries earlier when the actors rejected him as king.[8] The heart of the nation was clogged and unwilling to change or turn. Their resistance, lack of faith, and behaviour negated the reality of their messianic hope.

God's plan from the very start was a God-breathed community displaying his love, goodness and unity to an orphaned planet. If the steering committee of the Actors Guild rejects the star of the show and ignores the script, just what is the Director to do?

The Painful Edit

Once again, God is reluctantly forced to shut the production down. Phase 5 of the morality clause will sweep the stage and purge it one more time. The messianic expectation of Israel isn't going to happen in that generation because they scorned the king. They will be held accountable for every prophet they and their ancestors have rejected and killed throughout their entire history. The axe is massive; it's going to fall, and the consequence will be catastrophic. The Babylonian exile lasted seventy years; this one will last two thousand years. It's one thing to deny a messenger; it's quite another to dismiss the king.

> This generation will be held responsible for the blood of all the prophets that has been shed since the beginning of the world, from the blood of Abel to the blood of Zechariah, who was killed between the altar and the sanctuary. Yes, I tell you, this generation will be held responsible for it all. (Luke 11:50–51)

The change in the script is painful. Jesus will be nailed to a Roman cross. Forty years later, Rome will devour the Jewish nation. Thousands of Jewish citizens will be crucified during the Roman siege of Jerusalem. Neither would have happened at that time if the people had repented. Rejecting the king of the kingdom not only changed the script and the ministry of Jesus, but it also altered the destiny of Israel. The suffering servant will now walk their streets. Jesus will soon die for the sin of the world, but the nation of Israel will also undergo a brutal death. The painful edit is now carved in stone. It didn't have to happen this way. Jesus was ready to rule, but they rejected his claim. You can hear the pathos and regret as Jesus steers toward centre stage.

> As he approached Jerusalem and saw the city, he wept over it and said, 'If you, even you, had only known on this day what would bring you peace – but now it is hidden from your eyes. The days will come upon you when your enemies will build an embankment against you and encircle you and hem you in on every side. They will dash you to the ground, you and the children within your walls. They will not leave one stone on another, because you did not recognise the time of God's coming to you.' (Luke 19:41–4)

> Jerusalem, Jerusalem, you who kill the prophets and stone those sent to you, how often I have longed to gather your children together, as a hen gathers her chicks under her wings, and you were not willing. Look, your house is left to you desolate. For I tell you, you will not see me again until you say, 'Blessed is he who comes in the name of the Lord.' (Matt. 23:37–9)

Destinies are being rewritten. The messianic hope of a Davidic king ruling from Jerusalem is put on hold until the Director witnesses a change of heart: a people who live the first commandment and value the presence of God in their camp. If you want the kingdom, you can't reject the king.[1]

Concealing the Message

The painful edit compels Jesus to alter his teaching style. Jesus has ears to hear, so he fine-tunes his strategy to echo the soundtrack. As the 'suffering servant song' increases in volume, Jesus modifies his approach to ministry. Before this moment, Jesus had spoken plainly. He used sermons and analogies to clarify the message; just read the Sermon on the Mount.[2] However, after the sorcery accusation, Jesus starts to conceal the message in parables. The theatrical version often assumes the parables were meant to clarify divine truth, but that's not how Jesus saw it. Listen carefully to what he tells the disciples.

> He told them, 'The secret of the kingdom of God has been given to you. But to those on the outside everything is said in parables so that,
>
> "they may be ever seeing but never perceiving,
>   and ever hearing but never understanding;
> otherwise they might turn and be forgiven!"' (Mark 4:11–12)

This statement is a quote from the prophet Isaiah.[3] In both cases, the nation was racing towards Phase 5 of the morality clause because of their unbelief and unrepentant hearts. Jesus now hides the secrets of the kingdom from those who aren't ready to receive them. He warned the disciples, 'Do not give dogs what is sacred; do not throw your pearls to pigs. If you do, they may trample them under their feet, and turn and tear you to pieces' (Matt. 7:6).

At the time of Jesus, Jewish teachers would often quote a list of random Scriptures to make a theological point or practical application. The teaching method was called 'stringing pearls'.[4] The pearls, of course, were the individual snippets of Scripture used in the list. What Jesus is telling the disciples is, 'Don't give away the secrets and truths of the kingdom to those who have not positioned themselves to receive and act upon them. Know your audience.'

Gethsemane

Now, we know the painful edit affected more than the way Jesus taught. The 'suffering servant song' was a hymn nobody wanted to sing: not the Director, not Jesus, nor the Jewish nation. God the Father wanted Israel to receive his Son and honour him.[5] Jesus desired the 'royal motif' as much as the Director and the Jewish nation. The 'suffering servant song' was not the way anybody wanted it to happen. Jesus never asked his Father to crank up the volume when this song started to play. Instead, he shouts up to heaven, 'Can you turn that music off?'

> Then he said to them, 'My soul is overwhelmed with sorrow to the point of death. Stay here and keep watch with me.'
>
> Going a little farther, he fell with his face to the ground and prayed, 'My Father, if it is possible, may this cup be taken from me. Yet not as I will, but as you will.' (Matt. 26:38–9)

> And being in anguish, he prayed more earnestly, and his sweat was like drops of blood falling to the ground. (Luke 22:44)

From the birth of Jesus to the accusation discrediting his divine authority, options were open. The cross at that time was a possibility but not a certainty. This is why Jesus prays, 'If there is another way of going about this Father, let's go for it. You spared Isaac;[6] can you do the same for me?'

If the original acting company rejects the star of the show, there is nothing more the Director can do to display the kingdom of God on earth. The Jews were the primary actors. If they disqualify themselves, who is left to reveal the kingdom? So God offered himself in Jesus Christ. He gave them his heart. What more could God give them to get the show back on the road?[7] He was ready to fulfil everything they desired and read about in their Scriptures. This was their moment. God's Son was the prize of heaven come to earth: Immanuel, God with us. God gave them their king.

God didn't spare his Son for two related reasons. One is that he had to recruit new actors. This hardly gets a mention in the theatrical version. The Director was making way for the Gentiles to step on to the stage. He was providing the means whereby they could be grafted into the vine and become sons and daughters of Abraham (citizens of the new covenant). If the Director couldn't work with the original cast, he could adjust the contract to bring in a new acting crew in the hope that they would fulfil his purpose and witness upon the earth.

The second reason God doesn't spare Jesus or release him from the painful edit is explained very well from our pulpits. It's the one highlighted in the theatrical version. Jesus died for the sin of the world, not just the Jewish nation. It's a whole new contract. Jesus went to the cross to recruit a new cast. At first, Jesus came for Israel; now he's going to die for the entire planet. The show must go on.

Intermission

The cross is the most magnificent, most dramatic scene of the entire production: past, present and future. The sacrifice is real. It is horrendously painful, but Jesus surrenders with such divine dignity.

The four gospel writers never let up on the kingdom issue. The subject keeps popping up in the most unusual places. At times the Gentiles are more enamoured with the authority and kingship of Jesus than many of the Jews.

When Pilate interrogates Jesus, the conversation centres on the kingdom of God; ironically, Pilate sentences Jesus to death because of this royal claim. He even hammers it to the cross in Hebrew, Latin and Greek: 'JESUS OF NAZARETH, THE KING OF THE JEWS'.[8] It was prophetic – a Gentile unwittingly honours Jesus as the king of the Jews in all languages. It's something the Jewish elite never did. A Gentile declares what the Jews keep tripping over.[9] The 'suffering servant song' and the 'royal motif' crescendo at the cross and they are in perfect harmony. A new cast is being formed; it's a new community. The believing Jews who kept to the script will hand out the invitations. The show will go on.

Reaching for Crumbs

Now, I don't know about you, but I find it a challenge trying to squeeze every biblical statement, event and law into one seamless, airtight package. There's always that one mischievous verse or statement that raises its head and kicks against the theological structure I've erected. So what can a person with limited intelligence do? Well, we tend to ignore it or try to un-explain it. One of those verses is the dogmatic proclamation Jesus declares to a Gentile woman, 'I was sent only to the lost sheep of Israel' (Matt. 15:24).

If this was a one-off statement, we could easily pass it by and still live a good Christian life. We tend to do this with many of the words and phrases we read in the Bible, especially those that rock the boat we're sitting in. None of us is going to let the ship sink because of one little hole. We always seem to find a patch somewhere. However, this statement is not a small cavity. For Jesus, this exclusivity appears to be company policy. It's not a slip of the tongue or an editorial glitch. Listen to what he tells the disciples before he releases them into the population.

Do not go among the Gentiles or enter any town of the Samaritans. Go rather to the lost sheep of Israel. As you go, proclaim this message: 'The kingdom of heaven has come near.' (Matt. 10:5–7)

It doesn't sit comfortably with the theatrical version, does it? How can Jesus come only for the Jews and then die for the sin of the world? Why does he tell the disciples not to go to the Samaritans after he's already interviewed a Samaritan woman who triggers a messianic revival in her town?[1]

Well, everything was in flux. The script was going through the painful edit, a new contract was being ratified, and Gentiles are randomly interviewed for the sequel. Significant changes in policy and planning are executed during the few years Jesus ministered in the towns of Israel. The greatest show on earth was going through a transition, but it was going to survive the revolt. The present actors may toss the script to the ground, but the Director has a rewrite in his hand, and no one will outlast or derail the production. His reputation depends on it.

The exclusivity highlighted in the story of the woman who gathers crumbs shows us another thing we often overlook, and that is the Lord's flexibility. He is relational. He is God. He does what he wants when he wants. If he wants to bend his own guidelines, he will, but he always veers towards love, not away from it. I suppose this is what we call 'mercy'.

Under the Table

The story of the woman born in Syrian Phoenicia often grates against our Western civilities.[2] It bothers us that Jesus could be so seemingly rude, especially towards someone who is desperately concerned about their daughter's welfare. It's just not Christian, is it? First, the woman comes begging for mercy, but Jesus ignores her. He doesn't talk to her or acknowledge she is there. Then the disciples get annoyed – not with Jesus but with the woman. She wouldn't shut up. So they ask Jesus to send her packing. The Son of God finally looks at her and says, 'I was sent only to the lost sheep of Israel' (Matt. 15:24). Then he walks off. Of course, Jesus never lies, but he is cryptic at times. In his concise way, Jesus is telling her, 'My mission is to the Jewish nation. You fall outside that remit. I need to get them back on script. My authority is limited to the children of Abraham.'

If you ever wondered about bureaucracy in the Bible, this story is a good example. Bureaucracy is the closest we ever get to a black hole. If you have encountered it, you know how frustrating it is. You wait in an office for thirty minutes and finally get to the counter. Then the person says, 'I can't help you. You're in the wrong department.' They give you a number to call. You dial it, press option three on the keypad and wait as the music lulls you to sleep. Twenty minutes later, a recorded voice comes on the phone. 'Sorry, there is no one available to take your call; try again later.' You obey because you have no other option. The next day you try again. After two hours, you finally break through only to hear: 'Just send in your A254 form, and we will process it.'

What? Of course, you have never heard of an A254 form, and now you have to go online to print one off. Your angst shifts to rage when you discover the website is down. Then your wife comes in the room asking how all that hair got on your desk. She hadn't noticed the bald patches on your scalp. You fight down the explosion of expletives bouncing around in your head. You don't vocalise them because you're a Christian, but you quickly discover how effective bureaucracy is in stimulating that part of your brain.

An American proverb says that the squeaky wheel gets the grease. This woman is persistent. She wasn't going to let some administrative detail stand between her and her child. She was a squeaky wheel. The response of Jesus to her request seems to add insult to injury: 'It is not right to take the children's bread and toss it to the dogs' (Matt. 15:26). However, in this passage the word 'dog' is used as a metaphor, not a label. In Jewish culture, dogs were unclean animals and weren't usually part of the family. They often lived outside the home. This is the point. It wasn't an insult to speak of this woman as a dog. Jesus was just explaining his mission at that time was focused on the Jewish family.

Now, this is a kingdom statement. It has to do with authority. The bread is everything the kingdom represents and provides. Health is part of that meal.[3] The Israelites are the children. They are the first to eat. It's their calling and destiny. However, this woman is streetwise enough to cut through all this bureaucratic red tape. '"Yes it is, Lord," she said. "Even the dogs eat the crumbs that fall from their master's table"' (Matt. 15:27).

This answer was a great response. 'Yes, Lord, I'm not ethnically a Jew, but I dwell at the table. I'm in the land. Maybe I can't sit at the table because I'm not part of the immediate family, but I am a resident. Can't you give me a small taste of the kingdom and heal my daughter?'

The reply of Jesus is affirming, 'Woman, you have great faith! Your request is granted' (Matt. 15:28). The whole episode is about authority and jurisdiction. It is a kingdom issue, but it is also prophetic. The script is in transition, and the Gentiles are slipping more and more into the story.

Ordering a Takeaway

The narrative of the centurion's ill servant is another example. This Gentile lives in the land of Israel, and he understands authority, unlike many of the Jews. Surprisingly, he never actually meets Jesus face to face. He sends Jewish elders to see if

Jesus would come and heal his servant; 'Give me some of the crumbs under the table. I want som-adat.'

Jesus goes to meet him, but before he arrives, the centurion sends a message asking him just to speak a word of command. He understands what authority is all about. Of course, Jesus is impressed.[4]

The irony is that a Gentile recognises and affirms the authority of Jesus with the same intensity as the Jewish leaders reject it. So the centurion eats the crumbs that fall under the table while the children go away hungry. The children weren't neglected; they just couldn't accept or recognise the one serving the meal. The feast is the kingdom of God manifested on Israel's stage. It is their messianic expectation realised in their generation. Unfortunately, the Jewish leaders couldn't put their feet under his table. This attitude is what alters the script. Jesus announces it in the most unpleasant terms.

> When Jesus heard this, he was amazed and said to those following him, 'Truly I tell you, I have not found anyone in Israel with such great faith. I say to you that many will come from the east and the west, and will take their places at the feast with Abraham, Isaac and Jacob in the kingdom of heaven. But the subjects of the kingdom will be thrown outside, into the darkness, where there will be weeping and gnashing of teeth.' (Matt. 8:10–12)

Ouch! This had to hurt. If we want to live in the kingdom, we have to recognise the authority of the king. There is no way around it.[5] Jesus is the star of the show. When Jesus talks about the Gentiles eating 'at the feast in the kingdom of heaven', he isn't talking about the sweet by and by, he's talking about life on this earth. The 'outer darkness' spoken of is the world outside the kingdom: the world that refuses to honour God or welcome him into the centre of their camp. This is what the word 'outer' is referring to: outside the kingdom at any age. The kingdom is the light on a hill; the darkness is where the light doesn't shine.

The theatrical version often assumes Jesus is talking about heaven and hell when he says things like 'outer darkness' or 'gnashing of teeth'. Usually, these phrases are applied to the after-life, but not all the time. These terms aren't the exclusive property of eschatology or final destinations. The focus is the kingdom of God; are you in or out?[6] It doesn't matter what side of eternity you are on. Are you living in the light or outside of it, in the dark? Jesus is talking about the kingdom of God being established in their generation, and what it will be like if they miss it.

Jesus and Crumb Collectors

The exclusiveness of Jesus wasn't about Jewish ethnicity or divine selection. The question is, how much authority did Jesus have when he walked the roads of Israel? How far did the influence of Jesus reach? Well, we've already encountered some of the limits. Before the cross, Jesus had authority over the Jewish nation. He didn't have jurisdiction over other lands.

Previous to the cross/resurrection event, the devil could tempt him with the kingdoms of the world because the authority of Jesus was limited to the actors on the stage. Jesus had authority in Israel because of the covenant the Hebrews signed at Mount Sinai. Israel agreed to let God into their camp. It was a binding contract, as binding as God's view of marriage. God is married to Israel, and he will not let her go. He is jealous for her.[7] They are his, and he's not going to write them off.[8]

Jesus also has authority on the stage. The land of Israel is a substantial part of the contract. The stage is crucial for the kingdom of God on earth. It's a divine promise to Abraham and his descendants, and that will never change.[9] We sometimes spiritualise it because a physical, specific location doesn't easily fit into our ultra-spiritual theology, but it sure fits into the theology of the inspired writings we call the Bible.[10]

Jesus also had the authority of a prophet, and the power bestowed on him by the Holy Spirit at his ordination. So on one level, when Jesus says he was sent only to the Jews, it wasn't because he doesn't care about the world or doesn't have the entire planet as the goal of the mission. He is just working within the sphere of his authority at that particular time. Jesus does heal a few Gentiles, but these people are on the stage. By faith, they forced their way into the kingdom. These are the first Gentiles Jesus met (including the Samaritan woman at the well[11]) who caught a glimpse of the kingdom of God and said, 'I want som-adat.' Little did anyone know how prophetic these encounters were regarding the kingdom.

The Holy Spirit sent Jesus into the wilderness to bind Satan and knock out a few teeth. God leads him to Golgotha to put Satan down. Jesus walks out of the tomb with authority over death and hell.[12] Then he makes a statement that changes everything for the Jews, the actors, the audience and the world.

All authority in heaven and on earth has been given to me. Therefore go and make disciples of all nations, baptising them in the name of the Father and of the Son and of the Holy Spirit, and teaching them to obey everything I have commanded you. And surely I am with you always, to the very end of the age. (Matt. 28:18–20)

The word 'given' speaks of something not previously possessed. You can't be given what you already hold in your hand. Jesus was promoted when he surrendered to the painful edit. Satan was bound in the wilderness, but the cross finished him off. Satan still 'prowls around *like* a roaring lion', but Jesus kicked out all his teeth (italics mine).[13] Satan can deceive, but he can no longer bite us if we chose to resist him.

Jesus wouldn't receive the nations of the world from the hand of Satan, but he would accept them from his Father. The devil said he would give Jesus the kingdoms of this world if Jesus worshipped him. The devil's way is easy if you don't love God. God's way was brutal but universally effective. The mystery of the cross is an explosion of love and hope.[14]

Jesus no longer instructs the disciples to stay within the boundaries of Israel.[15] His authority is now universal. So he tells all of them to go and invade the planet with love. I am with you. I am God. I am love. The world is your parish. Don't just win converts, make them active disciples in the kingdom.

Intermission

Today, we step out into the audience and invade it with the love of God. Jesus has the authority, and we have the divine right to speak for him in every nation of the world because he has obtained it and has given us the right to do it.

I'm Outta Here

I used to live in a tent. It was called a tepee. It's the kind of thing hippies did back in the 1960s and 1970s. We just couldn't help it. As a matter of fact, I lived in two different tepees. The first one was in Kansas during my drug days before I became a Christian. The second one was in Colorado after I was saved and delivered. In a funky sort of way, they were prophetic reflections of my life at the time.

Each tent needed 17 straight poles, 18 feet long. They weren't easy to find in Kansas. What I finally acquired was all crooked and gnarly. I slapped a dirty carpet on the ground for flooring and, like the tepee dwellers of previous centuries, I dug a small pit in the middle for a fire. Unfortunately, I was clueless about open flames and tepees. Half the time, you wouldn't know if I was living in a tent or a chimney. The peace pipe seemed to be the only fire I could control. I'll say no more about that. Fortunately, those peace-pipe days are over.

The second tepee I lived in was different. The Almighty blessed it. His presence was there, and I was rejoicing. I pitched it in a field offered by a local farmer. There was wild asparagus, a river, horses and trout. It was a dream come true; I had the *joie de vivre*.[1]

Poles were much easier to find in Colorado than in Kansas. I went to the local lumberyard, hoping I could order some. The man behind the counter said, 'Funny you should ask that. Last year someone came in and ordered that many tepee poles but never picked them up. You can have them all for ten dollars.' Well, this was a gift from heaven. I could see God's fingerprints every step of the way.

At that time, I was working in a Salvation Army thrift store. For some reason, we had a glut of fur coats. People donated them, but no one was buying. I got them all for five dollars each – another gift.

I also learned how to manage the fire. Visitors could leave their gas masks at home. Tepee ventilation was no longer a problem. I could now burn an open fire in the middle of the tent without asphyxiating myself and everyone around me. At night the tepee glowed like a lantern. It was magical. Step inside, and it was wall-to-wall mink, fox, seal and rabbit; not that I would advocate for that now, but I still smile, just thinking about it. Winter, however, was cold and brutal, so I eventually sold the tepee and moved back into one of those square boxes we call a house; sadly, I was on the road to domestication.

Once in a while, I still get the urge to be wild and free. Whenever my wife and I watch the movie, *Dances with Wolves*, I dream about that tent in the field. I tell my wife she could be my little prairie-princess: just put a few feathers in her hair, and I could teach her how to skin a buffalo. Funny, she never took me up on that idea.

Now you may consider this is zany, but what's really crazy, when you think about it, is when the almighty, living God, Creator of the universe – the one who knows all the stars by name and holds them in his hand – does exactly the same thing. He comes to Moses and says, 'Get me some poles. Get me some animal furs. Get me some linen curtains. Make me a tent, and when you finish it, I'm going to step down from heaven and move in.'[2] Now, this is mind-boggling. He even brings his own fire.[3]

We sometimes talk about putting God in a box; however, this time, God puts himself in a box. The box is called the holy of holies. It was a cube, approximately 15 by 15 by 15 feet. God's only reason for dwelling there was to be in the middle of the camp with his people. Later in Jewish history, God moves from the tent into the temple. Did he want to live in the temple? No! God couldn't wait to get out of that prison. The moment Jesus died, God was out of there.

> And when Jesus had cried out again in a loud voice, he gave up his spirit.
> At that moment the curtain of the temple was torn in two from top to bottom. The earth shook, the rocks split and the tombs broke open. The bodies of many holy people who had died were raised to life. They came out of the tombs after Jesus' resurrection and went into the holy city and appeared to many people. (Matt. 27:50–53)

The theatrical version often says God tore the curtain so we could enter into the holy of holies or, in other words, come into the direct presence of God without harm. There is nothing wrong with this picture. The cross certainly made this possible. However, the Director's cut takes a different slant. God wasn't trying to get us into his box; he was busting out of it.

As soon as Jesus breathed his last breath, God said, 'I'm outta here!' He ripped that curtain open and shot out of that box so fast the ground shook. Any rocks in the way split just like the curtain. He even took some of the righteous dead with him.

It was a celebration of freedom. Nothing was going to impede the getaway. 'Free at last. Free at last. Thank God Almighty (myself), I'm free at last!'

Before the cross/resurrection event, humanity wasn't holy or righteous enough to be in the direct presence of God. Of course, there were a few exceptions, but God the Father was very selective about who and how individuals could approach him. The law, the tabernacle and the sacrifices were the buffers God chose to protect people when he was in the camp. They were divine gifts of grace and love.

After the cross/resurrection event, God no longer requires these protective cordons. Our righteousness no longer depends upon ourselves but on him. Jesus is our righteousness. We are complete in him.[4] We no longer need a physical barrier to keep us safe. God no longer requires a temple, law or the various sacrifices to shield us because we now stand in the righteousness of God; the righteousness of Jesus Christ.[5]

Before the cross, any interaction with the Holy Spirit was limited and provisional. Now, the Holy Spirit can live inside of us forever because Jesus made us righteous, pure and holy. We have become the temple of the living God.[6] We are the holy of holies. This is what the painful edit did for every human on the planet who will align themselves with Jesus Christ.

Jesus took our sin away. It doesn't matter what we think about it. It never did. What matters is what God thinks about it, and he says the sacrifice of Jesus is enough for every believer to live in his presence without being damaged. Grace, upon grace, upon grace. We are the righteousness of Christ. The painful edit transformed everything.

Intermission

Up to this point in the biblical story, a manifestation of God's kingdom has had a difficult time breaking into the world. The mustard seed was planted, but where is the tree? A few times it was chopped down before it could blossom.[7] When the Director sent his Son, he was looking to restore a community. When that community rejected him, the Director established another community. It isn't mentioned in the Old Testament by Moses or the prophets. It was a closely guarded secret. That secret is the church.

PART FOUR

THE CHURCH AND
THE KINGDOM

The Next Generation

Now let's take a journey back to 28 September 1987. It was a Monday. I will never forget it. Statistics tell us twenty-seven million people were waiting with bated breath anticipating its arrival. I remember it so well. The long eighteen years of silence was over. Since 1969 we hoped for a revival, and it was finally upon us.

I remember sitting in front of the television screen with a dinner tray on my lap wishing the *BBC News* would hurry up and quit chattering about the world's failures. Then at precisely six-thirty that evening, it happened. After all those lingering years, it flashed upon our screens in big, blue letters: *Star Trek: The Next Generation*. Once more, we were allowed to climb on board the starship *Enterprise*. If that doesn't put a smile on your face, I don't know what will.

The biggest thrill, however, was the opening scene when Captain Picard looked straight into the camera with a head as hairless as a Klingon's elbow. From that moment onward, I was a changed man. I now live in the revelation, 'Bald is beautiful!' The contribution he made to the follically challenged on this planet is historic. Move over Captain Kirk; a new captain is on the bridge. I'm sure Picard's appearance ended thousands of comb-overs that year. Hat sales must have plummeted as many brazenly exhibit their shiny domes with renewed dignity and pride. Strange how those with hair now shave it off just to emulate the look. Yee-haw!

The Franchise

As you can see, some people are passionate about their entertainment. Movie and television franchises draw an incredible fan base. When one is cancelled, the audience response can be quite vociferous. The *Star Trek* franchise has been going now for over fifty years. Our cinemas and television screens still display its many incarnations. The original series only lasted three years. The studio axed it in 1969, but the reruns garnered such a large cult-following that the studio revived it. It's now one of the longest-running franchises of the industry. For over five decades, it has inspired and entertained us.

Similarly, we know that the first time God's production, the greatest show on earth, was cancelled, Jeremiah walked the streets of Jerusalem weeping. Tradition tells us he even wrote a book about it; it's called 'Lamentations'. Many of the actors, like Daniel,[1] pleaded with the Director to bring the show back again. Seventy years later, it finally happened. God graciously reinstated many of the previous actors along with their children's children, but unfortunately, the ratings never recovered.

Not until Jesus elevates the role of the Holy Spirit do we see the production revive and flourish. We watch as the Holy Spirit invades the stage. The Pentecost scene is one of the few times we hear the audience cheer and applaud with anticipation.[2] The franchise is reborn. It's a whole new programme, but the objective never changed. The greatest show on earth will be unveiled and performed one way or another. The earth will witness and honour God when they finally get a clear vision of what he is like and who he is. The Son reveals his glory. The Holy Spirit reveals the glory of the Son, but the primary goal of the production is to display God's glory in and through a human community: the chosen inhabitants of the earth.

To make this performance a success, God has invested everything. Extraordinary adjustments breathe new life into the show. Through the millennia we have viewed the production's various screenings, but this time there's a significant rewrite. We could call it *The Greatest Show on Earth: The Next Generation.*

A Game of Cards

Now, let's imagine that in the middle of the production the Director invites the twelve disciples to a friendly game of cards.[3] We find each of them sitting comfortably around the table. It's Peter's turn to deal. As they scrutinise their hands, they decide what card to keep and what to throw away. Matthew glances over at Thomas. Thomas looks a bit indecisive, so it could go either way for him. Peter wears his heart on his sleeve, so we know when he has a winning hand. The glint in his eye and the smile on his face are sure giveaways. We won't mention the time he got up and started dancing, whooping and hollering around his chair. Some things are best left unsaid. Suffice it to say, most of the disciples decided to drop out of that game.

Nathaniel is not very good at cards. He has no guile and wants the others to win (not much fun in that). Judas is rather cagey. He keeps looking around, scratching at his sleeve. Of course, James and John are quite intense when it comes to competition. They are the only ones who torch the deck when they lose. Their mother isn't much help either; she has a habit of interrupting the game. Sometimes you can hear her whisper,

'Jesus, can you let my boys win now and then?' The other disciples find this behaviour annoying.

Conversely, the Director gives nothing away. He can sit there with a royal flush and not even blink. His countenance and posture never change, no matter how long he has to sit there. God is patient. He knows what he holds in his hand, but no one could read it from his expression. God keeps the cards close to his chest until it's time to lay them on the table. Timing, for him, is everything. He watches everyone and plays his hand accordingly.

This picture illustrates how God works in history. It's the way he played the game when he opened the curtain on the church. No one at the table expected him to lay down that hand. There was a wild card in the deck, and it stunned all the players. For the first time, the Director breaks the mould. The actors are no longer typecast as Jews. Jewish exclusivity is now a relic of the past. Anyone can audition for an acting part. It's a game-changer for the production and the world. The new acting company is called the body of Christ: Jew and Gentile, slave and free, male and female.[4] All ethnic, gender and cultural barriers are withdrawn. The stage is now open to welcome a new troupe. Paul said this secret was so well hidden, not even the prophets of the Old Testament saw it coming.

> In reading this, then, you will be able to understand my insight into the mystery [secret] of Christ, which was not made known to people in other generations as it has now been revealed by the Spirit to God's holy apostles and prophets. This mystery [secret] is that through the gospel the Gentiles are heirs together with Israel, members together of one body, and sharers together in the promise in Christ Jesus. (Eph. 3:4–6)

Although I am less than the least of all the Lord's people, this grace was given me: to preach to the Gentiles the boundless riches of Christ and to make plain to everyone the administration of this mystery [secret], which for ages past was kept hidden in God, who created all things. (Eph. 3:8–9)

Jews and Gentiles are now holding the same script, reading from the same page. All the promises of the past are now a part of the new heritage. *Faith* is the operative word, not the origin of birth. Gentiles are no longer the spectators chewing on popcorn, judging the show. These new believers in Christ are the show.

The church has received the baton of the kingdom. It's passed to us. It is now in our hands. Jesus predicted it.

I tell you that the kingdom of God will be taken away from you [Jews who rejected Jesus] and given to a people who will produce its fruit. (Matt. 21:43)

I will give you the keys of the kingdom of heaven; whatever you bind on earth will be bound in heaven, and whatever you loose on earth will be loosed in heaven. (Matt. 16:19)[5]

Peter expands on this in one of his letters. He begins with the original declaration God gave to the Hebrews on Mount Sinai and applies it to the church.

You are a chosen people, a royal priesthood, a holy nation, God's special possession, that you may declare the praises of him who called you out of darkness into his wonderful light. (1 Pet. 2:9)[6]

Intermission

The original acting company was a chosen people; we are now chosen people. They were to be priests to the world; we are now priests to the world. They were a holy community; we are now a holy community. They were to manifest the kingdom of God on earth; that task has now fallen to us. The show was once on a fixed stage, but now it's circling the planet. The church is the street theatre of the kingdom. Communities around the globe watch the performance. *The Greatest Show on Earth: The Next Generation* is now playing, or will be playing, on a screen near you. Will this divine reboot improve the ratings of the franchise? Are we, as the church, manifesting the kingdom of God any better than the previous actors, I wonder?

Sign on the Dotted Line

The Bible talks about covenants; today, we talk about contracts. We know God makes agreements with the human race, ethnic groups and individuals. This I find incredible. It's a humbling thought. Both Testaments exclaim, 'What is mankind that you are mindful of them?'[1]

Has God made a contract with you? If so, it's probably to your benefit to review it now and then. It's undoubtedly the most crucial contract any of us will ever sign. I hear a lot of Christians say we should claim the promises made in the Bible. I agree, but we need to know what promises are in the contract God made with us. Not every deal is the same. Scholars tell us God has two types of agreements in his files. One file he labels 'promissory'. The other file is marked 'obligatory'. These categories help us understand our place and authority in the kingdom.

When God makes a promissory covenant, he takes all the pressure off us and puts it upon himself. We don't have to do anything to make it happen. We're under no obligation. God will do it all despite us. I like this kind of contract; so does he. It's neat and tidy. It won't fail because God takes full responsibility. It's the kind of contract God made with Noah and the human race. 'I will remember my covenant between me and you and all living creatures of every kind. Never again will the waters become a flood to destroy all life' (Gen. 9:15). We don't have to do anything. God's written it in the contract, and it will always stand; it's signed, sealed and delivered.

God also made a promissory covenant with King David: 'Your house and your kingdom shall endure for ever before me; your throne shall be established for ever' (2 Sam. 7:16). The contract didn't require anything on David's part. It was a covenant sealed with a promise from God. These covenants and others like them are straightforward and dependable.[2]

The first thing we notice when we open the promissory file is how tidy, efficient and ordered it is, but when we open the file labelled 'obligatory', we find a quagmire of legal wrangling. There are clauses marked out, others pencilled in by grace. Some pages are tear-stained and wrinkled. We filter through all the adjustments for breach of contract and stagger at the number of red-letter comments highlighting unfulfilled expectations. This file is a legal nightmare. The problem has nothing to do with God. It has everything to do with us.

In the obligatory file, we find the contracts that hold both parties responsible. On God's side, the promise is conditional: 'I will do this if you will do that. If you don't do that, then I won't do this.' These are the scary ones. It's an unsettling business when the almighty, living God invites you to sign on the dotted line. Your pen-hand shakes; not because God is malicious, or won't fulfil his side of the bargain. We tremble because we know ourselves. We know our track record. We aren't as faithful and steady as he is. So, with trepidation, we scribble our name knowing deep down, outside of God's grace, this will not bode well.

The most renowned obligatory contract is the one God made with Moses and the Hebrew people at Mount Sinai.[3] This contract required the actors to stay on script. We know Israel often failed to live up to their side of the bargain. We don't need to rehearse the story again, but there are some details worth exploring.

From the very start, it's obvious things could be better. The morality clause was often invoked for breach of contract, but it was never meant to be the ongoing pattern of the production. Who wants to give all their energy and resources to corrective discipline and disappointment? The Director wasn't going to spend his earthly career trying to corral a company of actors who were undisciplined and spiritually feral. It was unworkable. Ticket sales were down, and no one was rushing into the cinema saying, 'I want som-adat.'

A Short Reverie

Have you ever thought about living in a different place and time? My wife would have loved to live in a period drama, especially during the years of Jane Austin (1775–1817). *Pride and Prejudice* is her all-time favourite story, book and film. She loves Mr Darcy. She couldn't care less about Captain Picard and the future displayed in *Star Trek*. We are different that way.

However, in sacrificial love, I have sat through her movie at least ten times in the last fifteen years (I'm talking about the six-hour BBC television series). She even read me a few chapters of the novel. I hung in there for a while, but eventually I just had to say, 'Enough! No lace. No lace, Mrs Porter, I beg you.' Of course, those who have read the book or have seen the film (ten times) know this is a paraphrased quote from Mr Bennet

256   *The Church and the Kingdom*

to Mrs Bennet. It seems even the characters of the book knew when enough was enough.

I tell this story to illustrate that I have never heard anyone mention they wanted to go back and live in ancient Israel. A few, perhaps, during the three or so years of Jesus, but nobody is attracted to ancient Israel. It seems not even we Christians want som-adat.

He Makes it Easier

Now when a movie flops, directors probably find a bit of solace rehearsing past successes. Opening a file full of positive reviews is comforting. When heaven opens the promissory file, it's a celebration of triumph for all the parties involved. God can promise no more global floods, and it's a done deal. There are no red marks or negative assessments on that contract. There is no need to modify any of the terms or review the fine print looking for some loophole. Even God's signature lends to the show's success. Don't you wish you could sign all your con-tracts with a rainbow?[4] That is so cool. This kind of agreement just sits there neatly in the promissory file with all the other attractive covenants. You open that file, and you're met with the aroma of success; the Shekinah glory shines from the pages; God's anointing is all over it. But, what is God to do with the contracts in that other file?

The Director can hire a different cast, but would a new community fare any better under the old terms? Humanity is humanity; ethnic origins can't erase that fact. If the Jews failed under the previous contract, then why presume a Jew/Gentile cast would perform any better bound by the same conditions? Well, as always, the Director was way ahead of the game.

Back in the Old Testament just before the Babylonians swept the last actor off the stage, God was already hammering out a better arrangement for a future cast. It was a momentous, radical declaration.

'The days are coming,' declares the LORD,
  'when I will make a new covenant
with the people of Israel
  and with the people of Judah.
It will not be like the covenant
  I made with their ancestors
when I took them by the hand
  to lead them out of Egypt,
because they broke my covenant,
  though I was a husband to them,'

                                    declares the LORD.

'This is the covenant that I will make with the people of Israel
  after that time,' declares the LORD.
'I will put my law in their minds
  and write it on their hearts.
I will be their God,
  and they will be my people.' (Jer. 31:31–3)

A new deal was on the way. The old contract wasn't producing the goods. God was faithful, but he couldn't depend on the other party. The obligatory contract served a purpose, but it was never intended to be the ultimate game plan of the kingdom.[5] Notice there is no mention of Gentiles in this Old Testament prophecy. So far, it's still exclusively Jewish; it's a new contract for an old acting company. At the time of Jeremiah, God wasn't ready to reveal his hand regarding the church. He was waiting to see how the future actors would respond to his Son. When the nation rejects Jesus, that's when the Gentiles and the Jewish believers steer into the new deal.

Here's a potted version of our legislative history. First, God gives us one law, and we break it. So he gives us ten laws to curb our behaviour and steer us towards love. We violate them. Then he gives us 613 commands to keep him in the centre of the camp. We break those. God knows we can't follow a written constitution. It's not in our nature. The knowledge of good and evil drives us towards independence, not community. So this new deal will free both Jew and Gentile from the written code.

This time the Director isn't giving us more regulations to keep him in the camp. He's not out to make it harder for us to connect with him. God is going to make it easier. He wants his kingdom on earth, and his kingdom is not about laws and codes; it's about relationships, community and love. Love does not need a judge or a lawyer to stimulate it. Jesus moved with compassion in the Holy Spirit. It's one of the ways the Father spoke to him and gave him direction. He didn't need a written code to prompt him. God is love.

The best part of this new contract, however, isn't going to be found in the details or the fine print but the file God stores it in. The Director is shifting it from the obligatory file to the one marked 'promissory'. This is tremendous. The new contract does not require a morality clause because the onus is now on God and not us. The Director has moved the kingdom contract into the file of his more fruitful endeavours. It's the heart of the new covenant. God is taking control. Instead of the actors having to obey an external code, he's writing it on the actors' hearts. The law was all about love and our relationship with God and each other.[6] The Christian is reborn to follow love through and by the Holy Spirit in them, not a list of rules to keep God in the camp.

> In the same way, after the supper he took the cup, saying, 'This cup is the new covenant in my blood, which is poured out for you.' (Luke 22:20)

> For what the law was powerless to do because it was weakened by the flesh, God did by sending his own Son in the likeness of sinful flesh to be a sin offering. And so he condemned sin in the flesh, in order that the righteous requirement of the law might be fully met in us, who do not live according to the flesh but according to the Spirit. (Rom. 8:3–4)

> Such confidence we have through Christ before God. Not that we are competent in ourselves to claim anything for ourselves, but our competence comes from God. He has made us competent as ministers of a new covenant – not of the letter but of the Spirit; for the letter kills, but the Spirit gives life. (2 Cor. 3:4–6)

> So the law was our guardian until Christ came that we might be justified by faith. Now that this faith has come, we are no longer under a guardian. (Gal. 3:24–5)

Intermission

By faith and commitment, we agree to the new terms. All we have to do is surrender. By faith, we climb on to the life raft of the kingdom, just like the patriarchs of old. Jesus paved the way for us on the cross. God signs the contract with his own blood, not a rainbow. What a sacrifice. What a deal. What a plan. What grace.

Embracing Change

I once stood in a shopping mall when a busker started to play the violin. It was beautiful. She knew her instrument. About three minutes into the performance, another violinist joined her. Then I heard the sound of a flute coming up behind me as the musician walked towards the violinists. A man with a cello appeared out of a shop and started bowing the bass line. By this time, the shoppers were gathering around enjoying the music and the spectacle.

Before we knew it, there was a small orchestra performing in front of us. All the musicians emerged unexpectedly from the audience. We were mesmerised. It wasn't just the sounds we heard; it was also the message. It was the coming together from the crowd and making something more significant than the sum of its parts. It triggered the wholesome side of our imagination. It was inspirational. The mall, however, erupted when the dancing troupe sprung from their various stations around the shops. The applause was deafening. This is how the Director sees the church.

Believers committed to Jesus Christ come out from among the worldwide audience and take their place in the kingdom of God. We each have our talent and specific gifting. We live and play together amid an audience. The soundtrack of this new production is grace, grace, grace and more grace. The script is put to music. The Holy Spirit writes it on our heart. Every Christian is part of this orchestra. It's born of heaven. It's playing on earth. Japan, China, India, Russia, Europe and the most obscure audiences of this planet listen to it. It's a new day, a new contract, a different stage with a diverse acting company but the goal is still the same. The Jews were to manifest the kingdom of God on the stage of Israel. The church has been handed the same remit, except the boundaries of the stage are now localised worldwide.

Last Days Era

People often say these are the last days; most of the time they are thinking about the apocalypse, the mark of the beast and the end of the world. The Bible, however, has a much broader definition. Biblically, the 'last days' is an era, not a few years marking time till the four horsemen saddle up.

The era started with the incarnation and is still progressing more than two thousand years later. No doubt the apocalypse is a compelling subject, but the term 'last days' relates more to the franchise of the kingdom than it does to the end of the world. For the New Testament writers, the last days were the present moment in which they lived.

In the past God spoke to our ancestors through the prophets at many times and in various ways, but in these last days he has spoken to us by his Son. (Heb. 1:1–2)

He was chosen before the creation of the world, but was revealed in these last times for your sake. (1 Pet. 1:20)

So why did these first Jewish Christians call their present situation the 'last days'? These were the last days for something, but for what? Well, one thing's for sure, it was the last days as they knew it. It was the last days of the written law. It was the last days of the animal sacrifices. It was the last days of the temple. It was the last days of the obligatory contract. It was the last days of Jewish exclusivity. It was the last days of a national stage, and it was the last days of the nation.[1]

Intermission

All that Israel had known from their conception was in transition. It was a cultural change that rocked the foundations of everything they had been taught. Throughout the book of Acts, the changeover from Israel to the church wasn't easy for anyone. Even Peter, Paul and the other apostles struggled with it.[2]

The Director has laid his cards on the table. It's the dawn of a new era. It's a different day, a new contract, new actors, a new stage. The Holy Spirit indwells us. No more curtains or holy of holies in a temple. We are the holy of holies. We are a holy nation, the new priesthood of the kingdom.

Messianic Prophecies

Before we continue, let's stop here and ask some hard questions.

- What if the Jews had received Jesus as their king at the beginning of his ministry?
- Would we witness something equivalent to the millennium without the cross?
- Would God still have allowed his Son to die if the Jewish leaders and nation had embraced him?
- How would the law be written on our hearts?
- How would God make us righteous enough to receive the indwelling of the Holy Spirit, as we witnessed at Pentecost?
- How would the new covenant be ratified?
- Would Jesus have died of old age like every other human being?
- Would a natural death be enough to deal with our sin and free us from the law of sin and death?[1]

I don't know.

Sometimes I think we barely understand these issues in light of the cross, let alone outside of it. As I said earlier in this book, we are speculating about something that never happened.

God has secrets, and he holds those secrets close to his chest. He only plays his cards when the time is right and when he needs to do so. All I know is that if the Jews had received Jesus as their Messiah, we would be living in a different world today; which brings us to other questions you've probably been asking yourself. What about all those messianic prophecies recorded in the Old Testament or the ones applied to Jesus in the New Testament? Would they be negated if the Jews had received their Messiah?

First, I'd like to point out that not all the messianic prophecies have come to pass. Some we have projected into the far distant future. These are the ones Jewish people trip over when we speak of Jesus as their Messiah. They ask,

- Where is the kingdom?
- Where is world peace and justice?
- Why is the Jewish nation under duress?
- Where is the universal harmony promised in the book of Isaiah?[2]

The point is, if the Jews had received Jesus as their Messiah, we would have witnessed the fulfilment of the 'royal motif'. The prophecies concerning the 'suffering servant song' would've been the ones projected into the distant future if we chose to acknowledge them at all.[3] I say this because many of these ancient prophecies weren't recognised or interpreted the way the Christian church has adopted them. We applied many of them to Jesus after the cross/resurrection event, not before it happened. The disciples couldn't imagine the Messiah nailed to a cross. Listen to Peter's response when Jesus brings up the idea. 'Peter took him aside and began to rebuke him. "Never, Lord!" he said. "This shall never happen to you!"' (Matt. 16:22).

They all struggled to grasp the idea of a suffering Messiah, even when it came from the mouth of Jesus. The disciples travelling on the road to Emmaus were no different. They were bereft of solace because they were never taught or suspected the 'suffering servant song' was in the script. Jesus is the only one who instructed them of this idea. Their hearts burned within them as they looked into the new hand that was dealt upon the table. Even Saul the Pharisee and master theologian thought the idea was heretical until he encountered the risen Christ.[4]

The 'suffering servant song' was one of God's secret treasures buried in the text. It's in the Scriptures, but the revelation was on hold. Most of the Jews before the cross/resurrection event believed the suffering servant was Israel, not their messianic expectation. Why was it concealed from Jewish eyes who studied the Scripture night and day through all those previous generations? It's because God wasn't ready to reveal it. It didn't have to take place in the age of Jesus. It was pencilled in the script, but the timing wasn't set in stone.

You may be asking, 'But what about the statement of John the Baptist?' 'Look, the Lamb of God, who takes away the sin of the world!' (John 1:29). Isn't this about the suffering servant? Wasn't this proclaimed before Jesus embarked on his ministry? No doubt the theatrical version interprets it this way, but not the Director's cut. Consider what John also said of Jesus in the Gospel of Matthew.

> His winnowing fork is in his hand, and he will clear his threshing-floor, gathering his wheat into the barn and burning up the chaff with unquenchable fire. (Matt. 3:12)

John the Baptist isn't talking about the after-life or the suffering servant who will make atonement for the world's sin on a cross;

he's talking about a saviour who will execute judgement against sinners now. Even the context of Matthew's Gospel affirms this. The winnowing fork statement is the concluding declaration of a speech John made to the Jewish leaders.

> You brood of vipers! Who warned you to flee from the coming wrath? Produce fruit in keeping with repentance. And do not think you can say to yourselves, 'We have Abraham as our father.' I tell you that out of these stones God can raise up children for Abraham. The axe has been laid to the root of the trees, and every tree that does not produce good fruit will be cut down and thrown into the fire. (Matt. 3:7–10)

Christian scholars agree that John's announcement about the Lamb of God would not be understood or interpreted as a reference to a suffering Messiah.[5] Some suggest the statement was perhaps influenced by Jewish, non-biblical sources that describe the Messiah as a warrior ram who saves the flock from enemies.[6] We don't know what was going through John's head but what we do know is that the link between the suffering servant and the Messiah wasn't in the psyche of the Jewish nation before the cross/resurrection event. Even the message to Mary from the angel Gabriel had nothing to do with a suffering servant; it was just the opposite.

> He will be great and will be called the Son of the Most High. The Lord God will give him the throne of his father David, and he will reign over Jacob's descendants for ever; his kingdom will never end. (Luke 1:32–3)

In the gospels, Jesus is the one who introduced the suffering Messiah concept to his followers.[7] As the 'suffering servant song' increased in volume, Jesus started to inform the disciples what the painful edit was going to look like.

> He then began to teach them that the Son of Man must suffer many things and be rejected by the elders, the chief priests and the teachers of the law, and that he must be killed and after three days rise again. (Mark 8:31)

We also tend to crank up the volume of the 'suffering servant song' when Simeon prophesies about Jesus in the temple. It's another mind-loop. We immediately think of the future cross/resurrection event, but his prophecy is ambiguous enough to embrace either the 'royal motif' or the 'suffering servant song'. His prophetic words are valid for either event.

> For my eyes have seen your salvation,
>   which you have prepared in the sight of all nations:
> a light for revelation to the Gentiles,
>   and the glory of your people Israel. (Luke 2:30–32)

> This child is destined to cause the falling and rising of many in Israel, and to be a sign that will be spoken against, so that the thoughts of many hearts will be revealed. And a sword will pierce your own soul too. (Luke 2:34–5)

The statement that Mary would also be pierced by a sword (metaphorically speaking) isn't pointing to the cross. In context, Simeon is telling her that the thoughts of her heart will also be revealed like those of the other citizens of Israel. The sword could refer to a number of things that aren't directly related to the future cross/resurrection event. In the Gospel of Luke, Jesus often said things about Mary and his family that seem rather detached.[8] His family, at times, thought Jesus had lost the plot.[9] Hearts were being tested and exposed, including those of Mary and the family of Jesus.

Simeon's speech veers closer to the winnowing fork prophecy of John the Baptist, not a suffering Messiah. But one thing is sure: Simeon wasn't waiting on or hoping for a suffering servant. His hope was a messianic king who would rule in their generation; a king like the one the Magi proclaimed.

The widow Anna is also linked to Simeon's prophecy. She interprets and summarises his words, but there is no mention or hint of a suffering Messiah in her statement.

> Coming up to them at that very moment, she gave thanks to God and spoke about the child to all who were looking forward to the redemption of Jerusalem. (Luke 2:38)

> She talked about the child to everyone who had been waiting expectantly for God to rescue Jerusalem. (Luke 2:38, NLT)

Intermission

The stage was wide open for the 'royal motif' or the 'suffering servant song'. We know how it played out, but we don't know what would've happened if the Jews had received Jesus as their Messiah. Only God knows that, but the point is it could have gone either way.

The Full Gospel

The title of the old Irving Berlin song tells us, 'There's No Business Like Show Business'. Perhaps he's right. If we had the opportunity to be a film star I think most of us would say, 'Yeah, bring it on. Go for it!'

We Gentiles eagerly jumped on to that new stage more than two thousand years ago and haven't looked back. Recruitment is now in our DNA. Jesus told us to go and make disciples of all the nations, so we went. We are still going as we send out our top recruiters and missionaries. We unashamedly declare the goodness of God, and the redemption afforded us through the cross. This is both scriptural, and Holy-Spirit-led. One by one, we invite the people of the world on to the stage, but what gospel do we actually preach? What gospel do we live by, or follow?

Anyone who reads the New Testament will eventually notice the alleged rift between what Jesus proclaimed as gospel and the statements of Paul. For Jesus, the gospel is the kingdom of God (how to live and manifest the kingdom). To Paul, the gospel is faith in the death and resurrection of Jesus Christ (how to enter the kingdom saved).[1] Jesus stresses the community; Paul focuses primarily on the individual. These two gospel declarations aren't mutually exclusive, but they do generate their own specific mindset, especially when we elevate one and devalue the other.

> Now, brothers and sisters, I want to remind you of the gospel I preached to you, which you received and on which you have taken your stand. By this gospel you are saved, if you hold firmly to the word I preached to you. Otherwise, you have believed in vain.
>
> For what I received I passed on to you as of first importance: that Christ died for our sins according to the Scriptures, that he was buried, that he was raised on the third day according to the Scriptures. (1 Cor. 15:1–4)

What is the gospel? If we asked anyone in our church this question, I'm sure most people would say something like Paul did in the above Scripture. Why? Because this is what we are taught and what we are used to – it's the theatrical version. It's our mind-loop.

The Director's cut, on the other hand, widens the screen. It embraces Paul's primary emphasis without projecting the gospel of Jesus to some future event or demoting it to some Jewish theological anomaly. The gospel is about the community and the individual. It's about the kingdom and becoming citizens of the kingdom. It's not just getting people saved.

Jesus came and preached the gospel of the kingdom to an audience that lost sight of it. He proclaimed the kingdom of God and repentance because he was calling Israel to get behind the plan.

> Pick up the script and walk the path you volunteered to follow back at Sinai. The kingdom is within you.[2] It's in your genes. It's in your ancestry. It's in your midst. You are the chosen ones.

The Jews weren't strangers to the gospel of the kingdom; they just weren't co-operating. Paul and the apostles, on the other hand, were preaching to a different audience. They preached to both Jews and Gentiles in light of the new contract. It was the 'last days' message.

> Then Paul and Barnabas answered them boldly: 'We had to speak the word of God to you [the Jews] first. Since you reject it and do not consider yourselves worthy of eternal life, we now turn to the Gentiles. For this is what the Lord has commanded us:
>
> "'I have made you a light for the Gentiles,
>   that you may bring salvation to the ends of the earth.'"
>
> When the Gentiles heard this, they were glad and honoured the word of the Lord; and all who were appointed for eternal life believed. (Acts 13:46–8)

The difference between the Jews and the Gentiles is that the Gentiles didn't have a history of the kingdom to fall back on. It wasn't something they or their ancestors carried or understood. It wasn't in their past or their spiritual DNA. The old covenant didn't apply to the Gentiles. They never read the script; they were in the audience munching popcorn. Why call them to repent of something they had never participated in. All the Gentiles had to repent of was their sin, not a breach of contract.[3] They never saw the old covenant or participated in the law. As a matter of fact, the early church fought hard to keep the law away from them.[4] Remember, it was only Jesus who rose from the dead – not the old system. The king is the doorway to the kingdom, not the law. Who would've thought?

However, the believing Jews also had to sign the new contract to receive the kingdom because their custodial rights had been withdrawn. The kingdom was no longer an active birthright or immediate inheritance without Jesus. They understood the kingdom, but they didn't fully understand Jesus, the king. The revised contract changes you from the inside out – you will be born again.[5] It's stamped and written on the heart. Participants are led by the Holy Spirit, not the written law of Sinai. A new community will arise from the ashes. Jew and Gentile are living together in the same kingdom, under the same promises as equal brothers and sisters.

So the apostles preach the gospel of the cross/resurrection event to both the Jews and the Gentiles because that is what both groups needed to hear in these last days, but it is not the end game. The gospel of the kingdom didn't die a death on the cross. Jesus went to the cross to establish the kingdom. He didn't come to abolish the kingdom remit.[6] The kingdom of God will be manifested on this planet so that everyone can see what God is like and understand who he is. His primary desire and witness to the world was always centred on a community, not specific individuals.

Jesus never projected the kingdom to some far distant future event or the second coming. The church, both Jew and Gentile, is the new torchbearer: the light on the hill, the salt of the earth, the carrier of the kingdom at the present moment.

> your kingdom come,
> your will be done,
>   on earth as it is in heaven. (Matt. 6:10)

This is the first request Jesus told the disciples to ask when they pray. Each time they bowed the knee or looked up to heaven, it was always there between them and their heavenly Father. Surprisingly enough, even after the cross event, Jesus continues to focus on the kingdom, not individual salvation.

> He presented himself to them and gave many convincing proofs that he was alive. He appeared to them over a period of forty days and spoke about the kingdom of God. (Acts 1:3)

Like the disciples on the road to Emmaus, their hearts must have burned within them, listening to Jesus preach the kingdom in his glorified body. No wonder they were motivated to wait for the Holy Spirit at Pentecost. It stirred them enough to prompt the question, 'Lord, are you at this time going to restore the kingdom to Israel?' (Acts 1:6). I think we all would have asked this question after a forty-day course on the kingdom from the mouth of God, the risen Christ.

The theatrical version reacts to the disciples' question as though they were on a different planet. 'When are these people going to get it into their head that God isn't interested in Jewish politics and the land of Israel? I mean, come on, guys, when are you going to wake up and smell the coffee?'

This reaction is very short-sighted and uninformed. God is very concerned about the Jewish people and the land of Israel. Remember the apostles, at this time, were in a state of transition. The baton of the kingdom was being handed from Israel to the church. Greater clarity regarding the new contract, the additional actors, the stage and the manifestation of the kingdom of God was yet to come. Notice also that they didn't ask when the kingdom would be manifested on earth; they wondered when it would be displayed on the stage of Israel. They had yet to comprehend the new card God had laid out on the table. Jesus answers their question.

It is not for you to know the times or dates the Father has set by his own authority. But you will receive power when the Holy Spirit comes on you; and you will be my witnesses in Jerusalem, and in all Judea and Samaria, and to the ends of the earth. (Acts 1:7–8)

Jesus didn't say the manifestation of the kingdom was relegated to some extended far-off date, unattainable until God says, 'Go for it.' He also didn't say they shouldn't expect it on the stage God promised to Israel. With regard to all that has been discussed so far, here is what Jesus is telling his disciples.

The kingdom will come back to the stage[7] with the Jewish people, but not at this particular time because the baton of the kingdom is being passed on to the church (Jew and Gentile). Israel is not written off forever; just for an unspecified time. So, go and manifest my kingdom through the church, holding on to the new contract, respecting the alternate stage; receive the Gentile actors. The manifestation of the kingdom of God isn't consigned to some future event; it is now. Get on board and live it and preach it to the ends of the earth.

So, throughout the book of Acts and the rest of the New Testament, we find the apostles preaching both the kingdom and the death and resurrection of Jesus Christ. They never drop the kingdom remit because God gave it to them in the Old Testament, and Jesus rebranded it and kept hammering it into them in the New Testament. The gospel of the cross event was the inauguration into the new deal; the gospel of the kingdom was the goal for the life and praxis of the church. Notice how the apostles combine both concepts as one gospel (the full gospel).

But when they believed Philip as he proclaimed the good news of the kingdom of God and the name of Jesus Christ, they were baptised, both men and women. (Acts 8:12)

Paul entered the synagogue and spoke boldly there for three months, arguing persuasively about the kingdom of God. (Acts 19:8)

Now I know that none of you among whom I have gone about preaching the kingdom will ever see me again. (Acts 20:25)

For two whole years Paul stayed there in his own rented house and welcomed all who came to see him. He proclaimed the kingdom of God and taught about the Lord Jesus Christ – with all boldness and without hindrance! (Acts 28:30–31)

Intermission

I often hear people talk about the 'full gospel', but I never hear them relate it to the gospel of the kingdom. They usually attach the term to spiritual gifts. However, the full gospel is actually the gospel of the kingdom and the gospel of the cross/resurrection event. This is the full gospel. We tend to divide it, and we often ignore or undervalue the importance of the kingdom assignment for our towns, cities, mission and our present community. The goal is to live and participate in the kingdom; not just to flash our 'salvation badge' around the sanctuary on a Sunday morning.

In the book of Exodus, the wedding between God and Israel took place at Mount Sinai. The rest of the Old Testament is about the marriage. In the New Testament, the wedding takes place at Calvary, then comes the discipleship (the marriage). The wedding day is not the goal; the goal is the marriage.

Last Will and Testament

The church pays a lot of attention to the words of Jesus, especially the last words of Jesus to his followers: 'go and make disciples of all nations' (Matt. 28:19). We frame it. We hang it on our wall. We highlight it in our mission statements, and we go. It is our mandate, our purpose, our goal. We rejoice when there's a soul saved. We measure success by the numbers sitting in the congregation – especially the new converts. Not everyone can go to the overseas mission field, but we sure love to honour and support those who do. This is the theatrical version: our mind-loop. Of course, there's nothing wrong with the theatrical version, but it does tend to drown out some of the other voices in the Bible – even the voice of Jesus.

The Great Commission recorded in Matthew is our prime directive. These are the last words Jesus spoke to the disciples, but what about the last words Jesus spoke to his Father? Do they hold the same weight when it comes to the mission of the church? Just because his final prayer, on the night of his capture, doesn't directly address the disciples or us – it undeniably concerns us. The question is, do the *last prayer* and the *Great Commission* hold the same weight when it comes to the mission of the church?

Now I Lay Me Down to Sleep

To begin with, if I knew I was going to die a brutal death in the next few hours, I'd follow the example Jesus set at Gethsemane: 'Father, if you are willing, take this cup from me; yet not my will, but yours be done' (Luke 22:42).

This is a good, honest prayer. It's simple, reasonable and endearing. To follow it with an 'amen', though, is somewhat anticlimactic, don't you think? I believe I'd also be asking God about the things closest to my heart. I'd be praying for those I was leaving behind. I'd pray for my family. I'd pray for the work God called me to do. I'd pray my last will and testament: the legacy I was going to bequeath into other hands. 'Father, get me out of this' seems a bit of a let-down when we consider the life Jesus lived. Would you want this to be the last message posted on your Facebook page? This is the sort of question I wrestle with when I think of who's praying. But then, one day, I noticed this verse in the book of John that turned everything around.

> When he had finished praying [the prayer of John 17], Jesus left his disciples and crossed the Kidron Valley. On the other side there was a garden [the garden of Gethsemane], and he and his disciples went into it. (John 18:1)

So this tells us that just an hour or so before Jesus stepped into Gethsemane, he had already laid out his last will and testament before God his Father, and it was a good one. That night, prior to the garden arrest, Jesus had already put all his affairs in order. The Gethsemane prayer was the tail end of a lengthier dialogue Jesus had had with his Father.

John 17 is the longest, most intimate prayer Jesus ever offered in the New Testament. It's often referred to as the high-priestly prayer. So just before Jesus goes to the cross he speaks to God about the things closest to his heart. He prayed the one thing he hoped to see for all his sacrifice and effort. It was a community thing. It was kingdom, in thought, practice and deed.

> I will remain in the world no longer, but they are still in the world, and I am coming to you. Holy Father, protect them by the power of your name, the name you gave me, so that they may be one as we are one. (John 17:11)

> My prayer is not for them alone. I pray also for those who will believe in me through their message, that all of them may be one, Father, just as you are in me and I am in you. May they also be in us so that the world may believe that you have sent me. I have given them the glory that you gave me, that they may be one as we are one – I in them and you in me – so that they may be brought to complete unity. Then the world will know that you sent me and have loved them even as you have loved me. (John 17:20–23)

This is what burned in the heart of Jesus before he surrendered to the cross. This is the legacy he wanted to leave behind. It's what he hoped to accomplish and witness for all the work and sacrifice. It is his last will, his passion, his desire. It's the heart of the new covenant. It's the aspiration of the Director. It is the mission of the new actors.

To Jesus, the community living in love and harmony with God at the centre is still the target. It is God's most significant witness to the world. We preach Jesus, but people need to see the kingdom manifested in the church to confirm the message we so readily proclaim. The gospel *of* Jesus and the gospel *about*

Jesus are one gospel. We can't emphasise one aspect above the other, or the revelation loses credibility. When we ignore the gospel of the kingdom, we tend to focus on conversion, not discipleship. Discipleship and transformation are the goal of the full gospel. The last words of Jesus to his Father in John 17 and the last words of Jesus to his disciples in Matthew 28 reveal the heart of Jesus regarding the church and her mission. In practice, we tend to elevate one above the other. The theatrical version is comfortable with this hierarchical positioning. The Director's cut, however, holds them both in tension and gives them both equal weight.

Intermission

This orphaned world is dying to see the kingdom of God on this planet; a community united in unconditional love with the tangible presence of God in the centre of the camp bestowing his blessing. Whenever I read the prayer of Jesus in John 17, I can't help but ask myself, 'Lord, has your prayer ever been answered? If not, then why not? What's holding it back? There must be more than this.'

Pentecost

Pentecost is a pilgrimage feast. Out of the seven yearly cele-brations required of the Jews, three of them were centralised in Jerusalem.[1] Full participation expected you to pack your wagon, hitch the donkey and make the journey. In the Jewish mind, the temple was the highest place on earth. So no matter where you came from, you were always going up to Jerusalem, never down. Today when a Jewish person immigrates to Israel, it's called making *Aliyah* (the act of going up). It doesn't mat-ter if your home is in the Alps or on the moon, if you go to Jerusalem you are going up. This perception sets the tone of the pilgrimage. No matter where you come from, you are ascend-ing the mountain to encounter the living God.

Now, there are specific songs we sing every year during our holy days, especially at Christmas and Easter. The Jews are the same. They had fifteen songs they would sing on the road. In most Bible translations they are aptly called the songs of ascent (Pss 120 – 134): the pilgrimage songs. They progressively focus and prepare a person's heart before they step through the gates of the outer court. These psalms guide you spiritually as you travel a physical road.[2] They transform the corporal journey into something mystical.

As your feet kick up dust, your heart is moving closer to heaven. The divine echo provokes you to release the hurtful and harmful things you carry with you along the way, whether it be distress, sin, distraction, anxiety, enemies or fear. Through the words of these songs, the pilgrims are encouraged to dump all their negative baggage as they travel up the road to encounter God. What's done on the journey is just as significant as what you participate in when you reach your destination. You prepare your soul on the way. Your heart races on before you.

> How I suffer in far-off Meshech.
> > It pains me to live in distant Kedar. (Ps. 120:5, NLT)[3]
> I look up to the mountains –
> > does my help come from there?
> My help comes from the LORD,
> > who made heaven and earth! (Ps. 121:1–2, NLT)
> I was glad when they said to me,
> > 'Let us go to the house of the LORD.' (Ps. 122:1, NLT)
> When the LORD brought back his exiles to Jerusalem,
> > it was like a dream!
> We were filled with laughter,
> > and we sang for joy. (Ps. 126:1–2, NLT)
> But the LORD is good;
> > he has cut me free from the ropes of the ungodly.
> May all who hate Jerusalem
> > be turned back in shameful defeat. (Ps. 129:4–5, NLT)
> How wonderful and pleasant it is
> > when brothers live together in harmony! (Ps. 133:1, NLT)

These fifteen short psalms are progressive. They speak about God's provision, Jerusalem, and the blessedness of discovery in the temple. As the pilgrims see the gates of the city, they are ready to enter. Their demons have been dealt with on the journey, so they serenely sing:

> I have calmed and quietened myself,
>> I am like a weaned child with its mother;
>> like a weaned child I am content. (Ps. 131:2)

The pilgrims are now spiritually free and fully present when they climb the steps of the temple. They are ready to participate in the festivities and receive something more from the hand of God the Almighty.

> Praise the LORD, all you servants of the LORD
>> who minister by night in the house of the LORD. (Ps. 134:1)

No wonder God chose the pilgrimage feast of Pentecost to introduce the Holy Spirit in such awe-inspiring power. God wanted that first audience to be open and ready to receive the message of Christ. He was preparing their hearts on the road before he overwhelmed them in the temple. The Director was setting up the props long before he made this curtain call. It's why Jesus told the disciples to stay in Jerusalem.[4] The timing was everything. Pilgrimage is what set the scene for this climactic event on Israel's stage.

Jesus had already planted the disciples in Jerusalem. They were on the road for the Passover feast. Their pilgrimage was in the waiting. They prayed and sought the face of God in expectation of the Holy Spirit. They prepared themselves to receive from God like all the other travellers who were pushing their way into the city precincts. This Pentecost will be the commemoration; the official ceremony when the mission of the kingdom will pass from the hands of Israel to the church. The new era is upon them.

We know the story well.[5] Fifty days earlier, God left the temple in a rush; ripping the curtain, splitting the stones and raising the dead.[6] He likes to make a scene now and then. God was out of there, big time, but now he's back. He returns the same way he left. Like a rushing, mighty wind God breaks into the upper room. The Shekinah glory (the cloud by day and the fire by night) rests on the head of each disciple. God is no longer on some distant mountain or shining forth from the holy of holies. He is now very much present with the new cast. He is upon them, and he is in them.

James tells us the tongue is the trickiest body part to control.[7] This time the Director is leaving nothing to chance. Nobody is going to mess up the sequel of *The Greatest Show on Earth: The Next Generation*, at least not on the day of its world premiere. Jewish pilgrims from the surrounding countries were present, and God had their attention.

Jerusalem that day was like visiting the United Nations in New York City. Everywhere you turned you would hear voices speaking words you couldn't understand. Each delegate spoke in their home language. The only difference between this Pentecost festival and the United Nations is that the United Nations has interpreters. However, the Director has a great special effects artist. The Holy Spirit didn't need an interpreter; the Spirit just put the different languages into the mouths of the disciples. It was a reversal of what God did at the Tower of Babel.[8] At the tower, he was separating people into nations; here, in Jerusalem, he is bringing them together. This is the kingdom of God.

As we know, thousands signed on the dotted line that day, Jerusalem was buzzing like a beehive. A new community was born again, but what next? The new actors had signed up for the show, but they couldn't go home without a script. They needed a bit of tutoring so they could play their part in the kingdom. Fortunately, no one was in a hurry to leave. They were excited and alive. The glory of God was upon them and working in them. Logistics, however, was a problem. The idea of pilgrimage is that you go up to Jerusalem, but then you actually leave. Pilgrims, in those days, didn't carry credit cards or bank details. They had enough cash and provisions to sustain them only for the few days they were away from home. It was meant to be a temporary sojourn. They are visitors, not immigrants, but it was starting to look like a refugee camp. What do you do with thousands of pilgrims who decide to stay? It's like hosting Woodstock,[9] but no one goes home when it's all over: a big problem.

So they met daily in homes and ate dinner. People sold houses and lands to provide the needed finance to support them. They were all of one mind and heart. They were making disciples, not just converts. The Holy Spirit was alive in their midst, and they loved God. They liked what they heard from the apostles. They gave with joy. They caught a vision of the kingdom of God on earth, and they abandoned themselves to it, and him. God showed them what it was like living in the kingdom. Jesus, the great physician, was healing them spiritually and physically. You can imagine the smile on Luke's face as he tells the story.

> They devoted themselves to the apostles' teaching and to fellowship, to the breaking of bread and to prayer. Everyone was filled with awe at the many wonders and signs performed by the apostles. All the believers were together and had everything in common. They sold property and possessions to give to anyone who

had need. Every day they continued to meet together in the temple courts. They broke bread in their homes and ate together with glad and sincere hearts, praising God and enjoying the favour of all the people. And the Lord added to their number daily those who were being saved. (Acts 2:42–7)

Intermission

When the audience catches a glimpse of what the kingdom of God on earth looks like they come running. It is the alternative culture, and they are attracted to it. This is what it's like when God is in the centre of the camp. People are ignited by his love. They care for each other and rejoice in the process. They share their resources. God heals them and blesses them. He is a good Father. This God is what people have been looking for all their life. When they see an authentic expression of the kingdom, they want som-adat.

Pilgrimage

Acts 2 is often held up as a model for the perfect church. I don't entirely agree with this evaluation, but it is the model of an ideal moment in church history. We see people and God moving together in the power and the sacrificial love of the Holy Spirit. This is the kind of show the director is trying to produce. It's what God intended for Israel from the very start. We can see why a display of the kingdom of God, exhibited in a counter-cultural community, is good news for our towns and cities.

It speaks louder than the voice of any one evangelist behind a pulpit or on a street corner. Of course, we need evangelists. We should all have some fire in our heart to tell others of the goodness of God and his great salvation, but if our Christian community isn't reflecting the reality of what Jesus prayed for in his last will and testament, then something will be lost in the telling. We can't undervalue the gospel of the kingdom. It is a significant element of the full gospel, and everyone suffers when it's neglected. We may never see the perfect church congregation this side of eternity, but we should at least aim for more, ideal church moments. I don't need to tell you why the church is not perfect because we all know that answer. We may not like it, but it's relatively evident. If my life is not set on pilgrimage, then I am and will be a problem.

> All these people were still living by faith when they died. They did not receive the things promised; they only saw them and welcomed them from a distance, admitting that they were foreigners and strangers on earth. People who say such things show that they are looking for a country of their own. If they had been thinking of the country they had left, they would have had opportunity to return. (Heb. 11:13–15)

> Dear friends, I urge you, as foreigners and exiles, to abstain from sinful desires, which wage war against your soul. (1 Pet. 2:11)

If ever I lose sight of who I am, who I represent, and the culture and family I've been adopted into, then I will be a problem. We know no one has ever lived a perfect life in this fallen world except Jesus, but there is no reason why I can't progressively live a better life and become more like him. There is no reason why I shouldn't seek the manifestation of the kingdom of God here on earth right now. There is no cause why I should not be advancing from glory to glory, renewing my mind, boldly stepping out in faith and love, and living a life in tune with the Holy Spirit and the voice of the living God.

As a pilgrim on a lifelong pilgrimage, I hold on to the fact that the journey is just as important as the destination. The legacy I leave behind will be foundational for the next generation. All the people commended in Hebrews 11 never lost sight of the pilgrimage they were on. So they faced and overcame their demons with the help and guidance of God. They were dropping all their fear, unbelief, and sinful ways along the road behind them, and when they reached their destination, they were ready to fall into the arms of God. 'Well done, good and faithful servant!' (Matt. 25:21).

I hope you know by now that I'm not talking about salvation through works. I'm talking about living a life worthy of the salvation we have been so freely given and valuing what Jesus values. I'm talking about obedience to the king, who has welcomed us into his kingdom. Paul calls it worship, not brownie points.

> I urge you, brothers and sisters, in view of God's mercy, to offer your bodies as a living sacrifice, holy and pleasing to God – this is your true and proper worship. (Rom. 12:1)

When I make the comforts of this world the focus of my attention, I can't help but gather worldly baggage. It clings to me like bugs on flypaper. Spiritually, I start to look like Pilgrim in *Pilgrim's Progress*, weighed down with a backpack full of the world's values, culture and attitudes.[1] If I forget I'm a pilgrim and live like a settler, I will bring all that rubbish into the local church, and that is a problem.

Let me put it like this, if you want a perfect congregation, don't invite me, because I'm still a work in progress. I believe I'm growing and becoming more like Jesus, and I think I'm a better person now than I was last year and hopefully will reflect more of God in the next, but I still have a way to go. This is what pilgrimage is all about. It's a forward, upward movement, not a downward spiral. The only thing that will keep me from fulfilling what God wants of me in this life is if I look back, turn around, settle down and feed on the world. It is difficult to walk in love and unity in the kingdom of God while holding hands with a system that calls us to pick up the manual of the knowledge of good and evil and put numero uno first.

A life of pilgrimage doesn't surrender to what we see with our eyes. The pilgrim is always looking forward to the destination. Then we pray it, live it, contend for it to become a tangible reality right here, right now, on the road we are walking on. The pilgrim grabs on to what lies ahead and drags it to their current time and location. The pilgrim gets a vision of the future hope and plants that reality in the present moment. This is the heart of a pilgrim. What else would prompt Jesus to focus his life on the kingdom if it wasn't, or couldn't be, a present reality?

Is the church perfect? No! Will it be? Yes! However, pilgrimage is a movement. What is done on the road right now matters to God, the world and the next generation. Pilgrims think: 'There is no perfect church congregation, but there are ideal moments the church can experience.' So perhaps we should set our hearts on the ideal moments and not despair when the church disappoints us. Let's pray and work towards an increase of ideal moments like at Pentecost or past revivals. Who knows, if we get enough of them we might surprise ourselves – we may even see a fuller answer to the prayer of Jesus.

Intermission

I can't remember if I was ever handed a Christian tract before I committed myself to Jesus Christ, but I have given out hundreds. What bothers me is that sometimes we can be so spiritually right and yet miss the big picture. I don't remember any tract mentioning the gospel of the kingdom. Most of us claim to be in it or influenced by it, but a definition is hard to find. Some say its reach goes much further than the church, some say it is the church, but in practice, no matter what we believe, how has it affected our lifestyle? Our evangelism? Our attitude towards each other and other communities of the Christian faith? Are we, as Christian people, revealing who God is and what he is like in our towns and cities any better than the forerunners of the previous covenant?

Somewhere along the line, it seems something was lost in the transition. Between the Bible story and the world today, it appears we have left something behind that shouldn't have been pushed aside; something we shouldn't forget. It is, and was, the last days for many things, but it is not the last days for the gospel of the kingdom. It's what Jesus and the apostles preached. It is still the good news this world needs to see in practice today. They need to witness it, not just hear our doctrines and explanations about it. Theoretical discussions may charm the academy, but they won't attract the world.

So where has the gospel of the kingdom gone? It appears to have been swallowed up in the message of personal salvation: the cross, resurrection and faith in the king. We hold on to what Jesus did for us but hold loosely to what he wants to do through us as citizens of his kingdom. I am fascinated by the fact that Jesus never relegated the gospel of the kingdom to the back burner even after he rose from the dead. His message never wavered. He still believed the manifestation of the kingdom was the good news the world needs to see and encounter. It was the responsibility of the Jews on the stage of Israel. It is now the duty of the church on stages throughout the world. Do we believe it? Do we see it? How do we recognise it?

The Great Divide

I have a secret. Some people are aware of it, but out of humility, I don't advertise it; the only exception is when I release it through books, magazines, interviews, Facebook and the occasional sermon. Otherwise, it's just that little clandestine fact I keep close to my chest. I'm looking at it now as it hangs above my desk, all notarised and so, so official.

> Registration Deed of Noble Title
> The Principality of Sealand officially declares that
> Lord Richard Porter
> has been awarded this individual Noble Title from the
> Royal Family

Yee-haw! I am a Lord of Sealand. I feel a rush of blue blood each time the document catches the corner of my eye. It helps me stand a little taller than all the rest. It affirms how vital, thriving and wise I am among my peers: Lord Richard of Sealand. I asked my wife if she would start introducing me as Lord Richard when I enter a room. For some reason, she just won't do it. Can you imagine? Who, in their right mind shuns a person of royal entitlement? I ask you?

When I first heard of Sealand, a micronation off the English coast, I was fascinated. The story and vision is the stuff of novels and fantasy. But when I discovered I could buy a royal title and become a lord I thought, 'Alright! Sign me up.' So I paid for the designation, and I am now Lord Richard Porter of Sealand. I am entitled, invested, and I belong!

A Kingdom Divided?

We all like to belong to something unique and special. We love to be valued as individuals in a community no matter how small or big it is. Just ask the Lord of Sealand; he'll tell you all about it. We find satisfaction cheering on our favourite sports team and celebrating when they win. I was raised in Illinois, so I bought a Chicago Cubs baseball cap. I like the Cubs because many of their games seemed to be a comedy of errors. However, miracles happen. In 2016 they won the World Series. Shocker!

This was the first time they had won the pennant since 1908. Even though I live in Northern Ireland, that weekend I wore my Cubs baseball cap into the church. I told everyone this was the first win in one hundred and eight years; I could wear the hat with pride. Surprisingly, they understood. All the other times, I just wore the cap to keep the rain off my head.

This kind of competition is healthy and fun. There's satisfaction waving a banner even when your team loses. It gives us a sense of belonging. But what happens when factions, competition and rivalries enter the doors of the church? Halfway through the first century, we find kingdom children drawing lines in the sand, forming new tribes, choosing chieftains and declaring their allegiance.

I appeal to you, brothers and sisters, in the name of our Lord Jesus Christ, that all of you agree with one another in what you say and that there be no divisions among you, but that you be perfectly united in mind and thought. My brothers and sisters, some from Chloe's household have informed me that there are quarrels among you. What I mean is this: one of you says, 'I follow Paul'; another, 'I follow Apollos'; another, 'I follow Cephas'; still another, 'I follow Christ.' (1 Cor. 1:10–12)

Brothers and sisters, I could not address you as people who live by the Spirit but as people who are still worldly – mere infants in Christ. I gave you milk, not solid food, for you were not yet ready for it. Indeed, you are still not ready. You are still worldly. For since there is jealousy and quarrelling among you, are you not worldly? Are you not acting like mere humans? For when one says, 'I follow Paul,' and another, 'I follow Apollos,' are you not mere human beings? (1 Cor. 3:1–4)

No one aspires to be a face in the crowd. We want to stand for something. No one cheers insignificance. So we pitch our tents under flags, causes, ideologies and specific leaders, but so often we choose and navigate the waters poorly. Our desire to be unique and noteworthy can cloud who we actually are. It's easy to lose sight of where we fit into the big picture.

There's no need to trace a detailed history of the church's track record over the last two thousand years. Suffice it to say, this last days era has been intriguing. It wasn't long before the Gentiles separated from the Jews and the Jews from the Gentiles. Then the Eastern Church slipped away from the West and the Western Church from the East. As we jump to the sixteenth century, we witness the Protestant Reformation. From there we've been exponentially dividing like amoebas in a petri dish. These divisions have left ragged tears on the pages of history. Few happened amicably in love, joy or peace.[1] The world audience looks on and wonders what this church thing is all about. It appears the kingdom has as many relational, infighting problems as the world.

Is this what the Director had in mind under the new contract? Is this part of the script? Is this the answer Jesus hoped for when he prayed? Are we doing any better manifesting the kingdom of God than our predecessors? I'm not qualified to point the finger or to state who is right or who is wrong throughout our history. Of course, I have my own beliefs and specific banners to wave. Many times I parade them unconsciously. No one lives in an ideological vacuum. We all pilot our spiritual plane toward some runway. Today there are thousands of Christian landing sites: independent churches, traditional and current denominations, various flavours within each persuasion as we divide and multiply. Hopefully, each rift is seeking to follow Jesus with renewed passion. However, no matter how noble or righteous our intentions, the audience will usually shake their heads and walk away.

If we were all on the same page, and at the same level of maturity, we would be more concerned about God's reputation in the audience than our own in-house disputes. If God himself holds back justice and judgement because of what the audience might think of him, shouldn't we consider how the viewers will interpret our actions?[2] You'd think over the centuries we'd at least learn how to divide in love. I hardly want to mention the times we split over personalities or minutiae preferences. The audience may be temporarily amused, but they sure don't want som-adat.

> If a kingdom is divided against itself, that kingdom cannot stand. If a house is divided against itself, that house cannot stand. (Mark 3:24–5)

These are the words of Jesus. Each of us can draw our own conclusion whether we're a divided kingdom or not. We know the kingdom of God is unshakeable and will never collapse but are we demonstrating the full potential of the gospel Jesus and the apostles preached? What we witness from the stage is not seen from the vantage point of the viewers. Jesus addresses this issue in the Sermon on the Mount.

> You are the light of the world. A town built on a hill *cannot be hidden*. Neither do people light a lamp and put it under a bowl. Instead they put it on its stand, and it gives light to all in the house. (Matt. 5:14–15, italics mine)

The kingdom is supposed to be attractive and appealing in both covenants. The Shekinah glory is intended to be all over it because God is in the middle of the camp. It is illuminated by the goodness and the love of God. It's a community united and fuelled by the Holy Spirit, uncompromisingly revealing who God is and what he is like by our love for each other.

The kingdom of God should be a beacon, a lighthouse drawing the people of the world. The audience should be running to our door, saying, 'I want som-adat. I want to live under your banner.' But the town on a hill has been camouflaged. The light is on a dimmer switch, and the audience has difficulty finding it.

Have you noticed that after the painful edit, Jesus no longer speaks of the kingdom as a light shining from a hill? It's now half-hidden and buried in the ground.

> The kingdom of heaven is like treasure *hidden in a field*. When a man found it, he hid it again, and then in his joy went and sold all he had and bought that field. (Matt. 13:44, italics mine)[3]

It's quite a plunge from the mountain top to a hole in the ground. Notice how Jesus applies the word 'hidden' in each of the above statements. The first time, Jesus tells us God doesn't want the kingdom hidden under a bowl, later he tells us it's now hidden and buried in a field somewhere. No wonder missions flounder when we neglect and veil half of the gospel.

God wants the kingdom to shine like a supernova, not be swallowed up in a black hole. People may accidentally stumble upon the buried treasure and desire it, but it's no longer that easy to find. In both of these illustrations, Jesus is speaking of what the kingdom should be and what has happened to it. In what field is the kingdom hidden? In the old covenant, it's hidden in Israel. In the new covenant, it's buried in the church. Every congregation, denomination, house group or para-church organisation is part of this field.

The treasure is buried so deep in some sections you need a pickaxe to dig it up. In others, you trip over it as soon as you walk through the doors. When congregations split and display the attitudes of the world, the light of the treasure falls a bit deeper into the sinkhole, and every church assembly suffers for it. When we neglect unity and love towards each other, we tarnish God's reputation in the world. The audience just looks on and says, 'I don't want to join that club.' A person can go out the next day and preach Jesus all they want, but if the kingdom is partitioned and segregated, the reality of what Jesus stood for is that much harder to communicate.

In another kingdom parable, Jesus speaks of a wealthy CEO who gave sums of money to his employees and told them to invest it while he was away.[4] Sometime later, the CEO returns to check on their progress. During the first two interviews, he's pleased to hear they both made a profit. However, the third employee is lazy and wicked. Out of *fear*, this employee *buried* the money he was to invest. The CEO was not happy and fired him on the spot.

God isn't pleased when we *bury* his kingdom, or his gifts, or his investments. It's sobering to think Jesus didn't save us to sit around and enjoy the ride. He's looking for profit. He's lovingly guiding us to produce fruit, to show the world our salvation is authentic. Perhaps I can say it like this: 'There will be minimal gain if we bury the kingdom but, even worse, there's no reward.'

Intermission

We have inherited a kingdom. God gave us the keys to the estate. When we value our traditions, church government and specific doctrinal stances above unity and love in the body of Christ, we have lost sight of the Director's script. We stumble and trip on the baton that God entrusted into our hands.

When we examine our own field, we tend to focus on the gold. It's what we cherish and try to preserve each time a congregation bitterly separates and divides, but the people on the street don't value what we value. All they see are the broken bottles, stones and weeds; a field they don't even want to walk through. What people think of God and his reputation in the world matters. It matters to him, and it should matter to us. We need to embrace the full gospel.

We have inherited a kingdom. God gave us the keys to the estate. This orphaned planet has enough dysfunctional families. Jesus never intended his church to be one of them!

A Paradigm Shift

Belfast was my longest tenure as a pastor. I served there for twenty years. The congregation did everything you would expect from a Christian church, but we did it from within our sphere of influence under a denominational banner. I also worked with Teen Challenge.[1] It's a worldwide para-church organisation helping people with addictions. I know the hell it is to be hooked on drugs, and I know how Jesus delivered me from that hell. If anyone needs to see the kingdom of God, it's these individuals.

Each Tuesday evening a group of us would park the Teen Challenge bus in our neighbourhood. From there we served hot drinks, provided food and talked to the various people we met on the street. We also handed out information and the occasional tract. Some of those we spoke to were on drugs. Many of the people had friends and family members suffering from addiction, depression and mental illness. Paramilitaries also had their brand of influence in the community.

One night as I stood in front of the bus, I was overwhelmed by the need, and troubled by the spiritual darkness hanging over the area. It seemed as if no one could lift their head above the cloud. They were stuck and demoralised. Many were living in broken homes, dependent on government welfare. Suicide was prevalent. A manifestation of the kingdom of God is good news for our towns and cities, but if it's buried, then what?

> When he saw the crowds, he had compassion for them, because they were harassed and helpless, like sheep without a shepherd. (Matt. 9:36)

That night I felt it. This verse about the sheep kept running through my head. His love engulfed me. It seemed Jesus was standing right there next to me whispering in my ear.

> Richard, see the Elim Pentecostal Church on the corner. My kingdom is there, but where do you see it in this community? Do you see the Church of Ireland across the street? My kingdom is there, but where do you see it on these streets? Look over at the building where you worship and serve. My kingdom is there, but where do you see it in the homes surrounding your congregation? Look over at the Methodist Church. My kingdom is there, but where is it in the community I have planted you in?

When I went home that night, I had a mind-loop. Three ideas kept repeating themselves over and over in my head. For me, it was a paradigm shift.

1. I'm no longer to measure the impact of the church by what goes on inside it. I'm to measure achievement by what happens outside in the surrounding neighbourhood. The size of the congregation, the preaching, the programmes and worship is no longer to be the medal I wear on my chest. If I don't see the kingdom on the streets, then the treasure is still buried and hidden in a field. What matters is how the

kingdom of God is engaging and engulfing the community around us. Where is the evidence of the kingdom of God outside the church doors?

2. I felt God tell me that I was no longer to spend all my energy building up a denomination, or a congregation. Yes, I will love and be faithful to the people God called me to serve, but I am also to step out of that boat and live kingdom. I am to honour, pray for and share resources with all the denominations and congregations in my area – even if I don't embrace their particular slants of doctrine or practice. They are not the enemy. If the Holy Spirit lives in us, then we are in the kingdom. The only way we get the Holy Spirit is through Jesus Christ. This is the bottom line. This I will honour. I will love and embrace any brother or sister in the kingdom no matter what flag or banner they wave.

3. I believe God said, 'Richard, you can't do any of this by yourself, not even with your congregation. A kingdom divided cannot change the culture surrounding you. The monster is far too big. The culture of the church has to change before it can change the culture of a city.'

Well, these thoughts went off like dynamite in my head. It took me from getting someone saved to changing a culture. It focused my heart on the full gospel, not just one part of it. The vision is big. The goal looks impossible. I lack the resources. I stand before God and the world naked, weak and vulnerable. I feebly hold on to a script born in heaven, but I lack the wisdom and at times the strength and courage to act it out. This must be of God!

So I run with it. I'm out of the boat. I lay down my personal, ministerial ambitions and leave the flags and banners behind me. I don't dishonour them; I just don't wave them with the same fervency. I now eat and breathe under one flag: the kingdom of God manifested on earth as it is in heaven. I'm content to be a face in the crowd. I no longer try to coerce my wife to announce Lord Richard when I enter a room. I don't accommodate the pang of failure or rejection when someone leaves my congregation to go to another church. God bless them – they're still in the kingdom. I'm not in competition. The gospel of the kingdom has eclipsed my parochial ambitions. I have picked up the script and have been living the kingdom remit ever since. It's what has motivated me to write this book. That's what motivates me still.

The next morning I confessed, 'I don't even know the other ministers in my community.' Obviously, this unintentional exclusivity isn't part of the kingdom script. If you want to change the culture of your city, you have to change the culture of the city's churches. Sounds grand, doesn't it?

How can a person turn a fleet of ships that have been travelling full speed ahead for hundreds of years? The mind boggles. God had to do some substantial brain and heart surgery in me to turn my own boat around. It's humbling. It's taking the lowest position. It's stooping down and washing feet. It prefers others above myself. It's picking up the cross and dying. It's a sacrifice, and it hurts. At times I question if I'm compromising too much or going too far. No Christian leaps off a cliff if they doubt God's hand will be there to catch them. To live kingdom, at times, feels like jumping off the edge, but I'm learning; If we aren't holding tight to the script, we won't even take the first step.

Intermission

There have been so many failed attempts and disappointments regarding unity in the church that many shudder and shut down at the mention of it. Others give it lip service, but the idea doesn't inspire or drive them towards it. I once talked to a pastor about church unity in East Belfast. He said, 'Don't waste your energy. I tried it, and it didn't work.' Then he prayed that I would give up the idea because it was a waste of valuable time. However, love is not so easily thwarted or disenchanted. Jesus never gave up. I will follow him. Love never fails!

Kingdom Pastors

No one trains or conditions us to value the gospel of the kingdom over our tribal instincts – except Jesus. So, the week after my God encounter, I started to make appointments with the individual pastors of the area. In my feeble attempt, I thought I would try to melt a few of the significant icebergs that tend to sink the ship. We often focus on them when we hear the word 'unity'.

The First Iceberg

The question often asked was, 'How can I do this without compromising myself and the people I represent and serve?' I told them we don't have to compromise our beliefs to walk together. We honour what God honours and humbly admit none of us has a full understanding or a monopoly on the truth. In God's eyes, we are brothers and sisters of one family trying to make sense of the mystery and change our city together. If we confess and follow Jesus and have the Holy Spirit in us, we are part of the same family.

Consider the seven churches in the book of Revelation.[1] Each one had issues, doctrinal stances and praxis. Jesus was the one who commended their strengths and admonished their failings. Their neighbours had no part in this. Can you imagine the hurdles they would've jumped to walk together? I'm sure the church of Ephesus, who were known for their intolerance of evil and false people,[2] would have had an issue with the church of Pergamum[3] or Thyatira[4] who welcomed false teachers into their congregations and gave them places of influence. The Sardis church, who were numbly comfortable in their dead orthodoxy,[5] would probably disdain the zeal and love displayed in the church of Thyatira.[6] Thyatira may have felt sorry for the lukewarm Laodiceans.[7] The church at Smyrna had few resources but were rich in God.[8] The church of Laodicea were just the opposite.[9]

What surprises me, though, is that Jesus told John to send this letter to all seven of these churches unedited.[10] Smyrna read how the congregation in Philadelphia did church. The church of Sardis was informed of Ephesus. They saw each other's dirty laundry, trials, strengths and weaknesses, even their financial reports. They were in this thing together. Jesus stood in the midst of them all. They were one family under his care.[11] They each had a personality, but they all served and existed under one banner. One king ruled them.

Jesus never told them to correct each other or to wag the finger on Facebook, Instagram, Twitter or YouTube. Philadelphia wasn't called to change Laodicea. Ephesus wasn't instructed to restore Thyatira. Each church (or denomination) was to deal with its own internal issues. They were answerable to Jesus, not the church down the road. The church down the street served as an example but not as a saviour or a judge. If Jesus hadn't given up on any of them at that particular moment in history, then why should we separate and give up on each other at a time such as this? It's arrogant and foolish to say, 'I don't need you. I will go it alone because you don't come under my particular brand of Christianity.'

As I spoke to the individual pastors, I kept reiterating that this is not about changing each other or compromising who we are; it's about love and unity. It's about a kingdom united in our city, sharing resources, wisdom, honouring each other, supporting one another, helping each other, walking together in love, working and praying together to bring a witness of the full gospel into our neighbourhoods and towns.

The Second Iceberg

'How can I do this tied to a denomination? I don't answer to myself. I'm a servant on a huge ship.' Again I answer, 'Let Elim be Elim. Let Methodist be Methodist. Let Baptist baptise, and the charismatics prophesy in tongues. People are different. The kingdom of God has many facets to accommodate each of them.'

The Apostle Paul said we are all part of one body. We each have a different function and role to play in this body. The body needs every part. When one part hurts or severs itself, it affects everyone. It's crippling.[12]

I would say to the pastors, take care of your own house but don't value it above the broader kingdom. We need each other if we are going to win and change the culture of our city. We need to see each other's strengths and weaknesses to grow, not to condemn, judge, or cut ourselves off from each other. Denominations can be healthy. They're the runways we land the plane on. It works, but we have to be careful not to bury the treasure. The witness of the church suffers when a denomination or church congregation becomes exclusive and judgemental and starts to carry on as though the other parts of the body aren't relevant. We can't change the culture of our community alone. We are not called to be independent entities in competition with or in isolation from each other. A house divided cannot stand.

The Third Iceberg

'What will this cost me? I'm juggling so many balls at the present moment. I can't imagine adding something new to my list.' Here is where it starts to get sticky. Up to this point, the conversation has been academic and theological; now it's practical and demanding. The question is, am I willing to pay the price? I told everyone if we don't believe what Jesus believed, and carry that belief with the same passion, then we won't pay the price.

God the Father believed that a community united in love, with him in the centre bestowing his blessing, is what the world needs to witness. It's the alternative culture – the culture born in heaven, the life raft for a fallen world. Jesus was obsessed with the kingdom mission. He lived, died and rose from the dead to make it happen. He ratified it in his last will and testament. His blood endorsed it. The apostles preached it, decrying schism, promoting love and unity in the body of Christ. They grasped the full gospel. They lived, served, prayed, and sacrificed their lives for the kingdom.

We as the church need a revelation of the treasure, and the field that holds it. We need to see the treasure through God's eyes. It's time for us to dig it up. Examine it. Pray about it. Allow God to spell the revelation into the palm of our hand. Pick up the revised script. Value it. Honour it. Run with the baton. Take the basket off the light. Let the treasure shine with the glory of God like a city on a hill. Turn the key. In obedience, go through the door and become as passionate about the kingdom as the Saviour we claim to follow. It's radical. It seems impossible, but it is God-breathed. It's the one thing Jesus told us to put at the top of our list. 'But seek first his kingdom [the gospel of Jesus] and his righteousness [gospel about Jesus], and all these things will be given to you as well' (Matt. 6:33). The blessing of God will be upon you.

When the Holy Spirit opens our eyes, we will buy the field. We will pay the price. Not because we want the field, but we desire the treasure that's hidden in it. The treasure is the kingdom of God manifested on our shores. In these last days, the field is the church. For this season, we can't possess one without the other. To get the treasure, we have to pay the price and buy the field. The field is more extensive than any single congregation or denomination.

The church is to manifest the kingdom of God on earth. No independent group can do it alone. The light shines from a hill when we walk together in love. Our brokenness will always come back to bite us. Love, unity and the presence of God is what will distinguish us from all the other communities on the planet and in our cities.[13]

After the Thaw

A few months later, after many words and prayers, the Kingdom Pastors was birthed. There were fifteen of us: thirteen church leaders and two para-church directors. We met one morning a month to get to know each other, pray and discuss the way forward. These were small but significant steps; at least we were starting to journey together. It wasn't always smooth sailing, but the ship never sank. Over time we began to climb out of our boats and walk on water towards each other. What started as an exercise of faith soon developed into a bond of friendship. Do you think God was smiling?

We arranged a gathering with a group of other pastors, and nine hundred people from all denominations joined together to pray God's blessing on our city. At one of our meetings, I heard the Congregational minister confess to the Church of Ireland minister: 'I never had much success in maintaining a pensioners group. Could I bring my few members to your church because you're good at it?'

I grinned at that one. I thought, 'Now we're starting to think kingdom.'

One of the other leaders said, 'I used to drive by all your buildings and didn't know any of you. Now when I drive by I think, "God bless you. I'm glad you're in the community."'

This was a kingdom statement if ever I heard one. God was working in us. Acceptance, love and understanding were silencing competitiveness and fear.

One night I skipped my own church meeting to go to the Elim Church down the road. During the service, the pastor got up and said, 'Tonight I want to welcome Reverend Richard Porter who's visiting from the Church of the Nazarene, and I just want you to know he is a friend of our congregation.' This was a kingdom statement. A pastor whose name I had barely even known twelve months earlier honoured me as a friend and a brother.

We as Kingdom Pastors held services together. We walked through the city streets together, praying for peace, salvation and healing. At various times we invited other congregations to come and pray for Belfast. Hundreds of people attended. God blessed it. He was there. This was the beginning of kingdom thinking and action, but these were still baby steps. The kingdom remit was now on our list, but it still wasn't a top priority. However, I'm grateful for the wonderful kingdom moments it generated, and I thank God for my brothers and sisters who shared them with me.

The Illusion of Lack

Do you ever think God is holding out on you? We probably wouldn't say it out loud, but at times we might wonder. Our dreams usually exceed our resources. The tension between what we hold in our hand, and what we want it to accomplish, is often untenable. We pray for more leaders, more workers, more money, more space, more time, more young people, families, fathers, mothers, grandparents. We think community outreach and service would be much better and more effective if only we had the resources. We wonder why we are crawling when we should be running from glory to glory.

Fortunately, not everyone has this problem, but many congregations struggle to stay alive. Some inner-city churches among the poor find it hard to keep their doors open. We had two different congregations in East Belfast close down recently because they didn't have the people, energy or finance to go on. The sad part is, so few of us knew they were struggling until the doors closed. Is the Director holding back the props? Where's the answer to their prayers? Their unique footprint in the city has now been washed away. Does anyone mourn the death as we watch a once-thriving church replaced by another restaurant or speciality shop?

A kingdom divided cannot stand. I'm learning that division is not always antagonistic. It has many faces. The uncontentious, respectable ones go by the names of 'apathy', 'passivity' and 'unresponsiveness'. In the Sermon on the Mount, Jesus made some extraordinary declarations. Listen to what he told the crowd that day regarding scarcity.

> Ask and it will be given to you; seek and you will find; knock and the door will be opened to you. For everyone who asks receives; the one who seeks finds; and to the one who knocks, the door will be opened. (Matt. 7:7–8)

Don't we all ask, seek and knock? Weren't the churches who've closed their doors fervently clasping their hands and calling out to God, hoping to receive from heaven? Did God withhold the PIN number when he handed them his credit card?

I can understand how lack and need draw us deeper into trust, faith and dependence, but I find it difficult when the need leads to decay. Did God want to replace with a tombstone a church struggling to serve and love him? We can't change the culture of a city until we change the culture of the city's churches. The gospel of the kingdom is still the greatest show on earth, but what happens if it remains hidden in the field? God have mercy on our towns.

On the surface, the statement 'ask, seek and knock' is uncomfortably *carte blanche*. I use the word 'uncomfortable' because 'ask and you will receive' doesn't always line up with our experience. I can't judge the level of faith required to hit the jackpot, but we wouldn't even bother to ask if we didn't have some confidence and faith in God, so there must be more going on here – something we haven't fully grasped. Fortunately, Jesus sheds a bit more light on the subject.

Which of you, if your son asks for bread, will give him a stone? Or if he asks for a fish, will give him a snake? If you, then, though you are evil, know how to give good gifts to your children, how much more will your Father in heaven give good gifts to those who ask him! So in everything, do to others what you would have them do to you, for this sums up the Law and the Prophets. (Matt. 7:9–12)

God is a good Father, and he gives us good gifts, but what does that have to do with the golden rule? 'Do to others what you would have them do to you.'

The reason we have a hard time making the connection between 'ask, seek, knock' and the 'do unto others' is that many of us are stuck. We are taught to build our own kingdom under our own chosen banner. Deep down, many of us want to be Lord of Sealand (or whatever we wish to call our domain). We all humbly frame our documents and accolades and hang them above our desks. We sign our books, distribute our sermons and write our blogs. We inwardly react when someone litters on our shore. We become the protectors and the guards as we recruit others to support us in our particular mission.

There is no lack in the kingdom of God. There may be a lack in isolated congregations, but God never intended his church, born of the Holy Spirit, to work and live independently of each other, especially those located in the same town, village or city. 'I am of Paul', and 'I am of Apollos' is not kingdom. Nor will it ever be. God withholds nothing from us.

He who did not spare his own Son, but gave him up for us all – how will he not also, along with him, graciously give us all things? (Rom. 8:32)

Lack in the kingdom of God is an illusion. God has provided everything we need to fulfil his purpose, but he doesn't give it all to one independent congregation. He disperses it in the kingdom; among all the assemblies.

> Knock, and it will be opened unto you! Do to others what you would have them do to you.

Our apparent lack is a divine nudge to think and live kingdom. It's not easy to knock on the door of a stranger and ask for help. On the other hand, there's no shame knocking on the door of a friend, especially a friend we love and who loves us. By our love for each other, the world will know we belong to God.

In the kingdom of God, independence is not a virtue. Yes, we knock on the door of heaven, but the answer may lie behind the church door down the street. If we want to change the culture of a city, we first have to change the culture of the city's churches.

> Seek, and you will find. Knock, and the door will be opened. Do to others what you would have them do to you.

We desperately need a revelation of the kingdom of God: the full gospel. We, at times, step up to the starting line and pray together, but that's just the beginning; it's not the race. If unity is anchored somewhere near the bottom of our priority list, then the ship will never turn or change a culture. For Jesus, a kingdom united in practical love took precedence over everything because it is number one on the Director's list. Why is it not a chief concern for many of us, his followers?

We've been handed an extraordinary script. It's the greatest show on earth, and the world needs to see it now. The kingdom is what will attract the world. It's a significant part of the gospel. We will always be outnumbered and overwhelmed in our towns and cities if we don't passionately pick up the baton and run with the full gospel: the gospel about Jesus (the cross/resurrection event) and the gospel of Jesus (a unified kingdom in all its diversity).

Intermission

We have yet to witness the kind of anointing, revival, blessing and awakening there would be in a town or city of a unified church; one working together and displaying the goodness, harmony and love of God, an alternative culture, an alternative community. Many on our streets don't have the tools to excavate the treasure that lies in our field. In some places, it's buried too deep. We need to dig it up for them. Show them what the kingdom of God on earth looks like in our towns, streets and cities. How can we speak of love and the restoration of the family unit, when we fail to display those qualities among ourselves as the family of God?

> Whoever claims to love God yet hates a brother or sister is a liar. For whoever does not love their brother and sister, whom they have seen, cannot love God, whom they have not seen. And he has given us this command: anyone who loves God must also love their brother and sister. (1 John 4:20–21)

Through the Looking Glass

'How old are you?'

'I'm seven and a half exactly.'

'You needn't say "exactually,"' the Queen remarked: 'I can believe it without that. Now I'll give *you* something to believe. I'm just one hundred and one, five months and a day.'

'I can't believe *that*!' said Alice.

'Can't you?' the Queen said in a pitying tone. 'Try again: draw a long breath, and shut your eyes.'

Alice laughed. 'There's no use trying,' she said: 'one *can't* believe impossible things.'

'I daresay you haven't had much practice,' said the Queen. 'When I was your age, I always did it for half-an-hour a day. Why, sometimes I've believed as many as six impossible things before breakfast.'[1]

I love this quote from Lewis Carroll. Do you think Jesus believed six impossible things before he started his day? If we want to live a lifestyle comparable to Jesus and what he experienced, we have to expect and believe the impossible. As I read the book of Acts and the four gospels, the more I realise what a kingdom lifestyle looks like. It is full of wonder, childlike faith, and random, miraculous surprise.

The Dock Cafe

I'm one of a number of chaplains in the Dock Cafe. It sounds slightly pretentious, doesn't it? You don't find chaplains in other cafes so, what's the deal? Well, the Dock Cafe is an original kingdom project situated in the centre of Belfast.[2] We host volunteer chaplains from all denominations, both Catholic and Protestant. If you know anything about Northern Irish society you can appreciate how radical, free-thinking and revolutionary it is to take this step.

We serve food, teas and coffees all without price. Customers take what they want and pay what they want in the 'honesty box'. First-time customers are usually shocked and inspired when they hear this. It's an alternative culture; a culture they hadn't seen before. We've been operating in the Titanic Quarter area of Belfast for over ten years now. Tripadvisor lists us as the number one coffee shop in the city.[3]

We average about two to three hundred customers a day: tourists, students, residents, workers and people travelling from various parts of the island. We support a few paid staff and host over sixty volunteers a week. Many of the volunteers haven't embraced the Christian faith yet, but they often tell me they like what's going on here and want to be a part of it somehow. They have seen the treasure, and they want som-adat. Our wonderful volunteers are part of the mission field.

One day a Muslim man came in and asked me to pray for him. I said, 'It would be an honour, but you know I am a Christian, and I will pray in the name of Jesus as the Son of God?'[4] His reply surprised me, 'I've asked you to pray because I believe there is something special about you and this place.' Well, as you can imagine, I almost fell over. When a Muslim man comes up to you and says, 'I want som-adat', you know the full gospel must be leaking out somewhere. He saw the treasure in the field, and he wanted it. He wanted the crumbs that fell under the table.

I led him into the prayer garden (a corner cordoned off in the cafe) and asked him what he wanted Jesus to do for him. He said he had just applied for a job and would love to have it. I knew God had set this one up, so I prayed a short, simple prayer: 'Father, in the name of Jesus, please show my new friend here how much you love him and give him this job. Amen.' As soon as I said, 'Amen' the phone in his pocket rang. Seriously! As he listened, I watched his smile transform from joy to glee. After he rang off, he told me that was the boss calling him in for the final interview. That's when his friend, who was standing next to him, jumped in and said, 'Could you also pray for me?' Hmmm, it seems he also wanted som-adat.

It wasn't my preaching on some street corner that drew these Muslim men; it was a manifestation of the kingdom of God in the middle of the city. It was a community united in the love of God, in the presence of the Holy Spirit that awakened them.

I do a short devotional talk and prayer with our team each week before the doors of the Dock Cafe open. Some time ago, during our prayer time, I sensed the tangible presence of God upon me, which is always a wonderful experience. It started me thinking about the Apostle Peter and his shadow. People brought out the sick and those possessed of evil spirits, hoping his shadow would fall across them and heal them.[5] However, there was nothing supernatural about Peter's shadow. It was the tangible presence of the Holy Spirit in him, and upon him, that made all the difference. When people are near someone who values and carries the presence of the Holy Spirit upon them, things happen. Peter and the Holy Spirit were walking the path together, changing lives, and Peter didn't even have to say anything.

So that day, as customers arrived in the cafe, I meandered between the tables and silently prayed, 'Lord, do these people sense your presence as I do right now? Do you still work this way? Please let them encounter you and know how much you love them.' I did this for about twenty minutes and then passed by the volunteer washing dishes in the back room. He had no idea I was there. Again, I prayed, 'Lord, does my friend here sense your presence as I do right now? Do you work this way? Could you show him how much you love him?'

God remarkably answered that prayer, but I didn't know it then. As my wife and I were driving home that evening, she said, 'Richard, the dishwasher said something strange to me today. He said he was standing at the dishwasher when, all of a sudden, it felt like someone poured a bucket of warm water on his head, and it covered his whole body. He said he had never sensed anything like it before in his life. It was so peaceful. He even looked around to see who was doing this, but no one was there. Odd, isn't it?'

Well, I was rejoicing as I told my wife about the prayer that morning. When someone encounters the Holy Spirit, things transpire inside of them. Until that moment, our dishwasher friend had never joined in the morning prayer meeting with us, but now he comes all the time. Our friend got a glimpse of the treasure, and he wanted som-adat. There is an anointing that comes when God's people work together. It's so easy to tell people the gospel about Jesus after they encounter the gospel of Jesus – the gospel of the kingdom. Sometimes you don't even have to use words.

How good and pleasant it is
    when God's people live together in unity!

It is like precious oil poured on the head,
    running down on the beard,
running down on Aaron's beard,
    down on the collar of his robe.
It is as if the dew of Hermon
    were falling on Mount Zion.
For there the LORD bestows his blessing,
    even life for evermore. (Ps. 133)

Open Skies

I try to support and take part in ventures that host the kingdom and welcome everyone. Open Skies is one of those events. For three days in August, people from various churches and backgrounds from around the world come to worship and pray together. I've had the privilege to speak at one of the seminars and pray with some of those attending.

The week after the festival ended, I received a phone call at home. It was from one of the men I had prayed with at Open Skies. Somehow he'd got my phone number and wanted to tell me how he was helped and encouraged by the prayer and seminar. I thanked him for his thoughtfulness and encouragement. Then he broke down and cried. I silently waited, not sure what was coming next. He quickly composed himself and confessed, 'I just never thought I would see the day when a Catholic like myself living in Southern Ireland would be praying for God's blessing with a Protestant in the north.'

Well, for me, that one phone call was the highlight of the entire festival. It was another milestone on the road God has set before me. The Holy Spirit in God's people longs for a united family. There's a deep and growing hunger these days (at least in Northern and Southern Ireland) to connect with each other and break down the walls that separate us. If we want to change the culture of our towns and cities, we have to tip the scales and embrace the kingdom. It's a lifestyle that wars against the status quo. Orphans aren't attracted to dysfunctional families. The world does not applaud marital breakdowns, or celebrate a community that claims to love its enemies but can't love each other.

Intermission

We continue to pray for the manifestation of God's kingdom on this planet. Jesus didn't tell us to pray for a partial glimpse of the kingdom but for the whole shebang: 'on earth as it is in heaven'. We have been waiting and praying this prayer for over twenty centuries. Jesus initiated this prayer. It's a prayer born from heaven. It's the will of the Father. Why don't we see it? Could it possibly be that God is waiting for us to answer his prayer instead of us waiting for him to answer ours? The greatest show on earth requires a director, but it is also dependent on actors who will follow the script.

Tipping the Scales

'Why are you doing this?' Anjezë, a little Albanian woman, was often asked this question.[1] Her answers varied, but the motivation never altered.

- I do this because God loves you.
- I love you.
- My God taught me.
- I care for you.
- I want to be like Jesus.
- I see Jesus in these people.

Now, being a follower of the Messiah myself, I can understand the love of God working in a person's heart. Christians are often travelling the globe doing good deeds. Even those who don't confess him perform loving acts of service to benefit the human race. This we welcome and cannot fault. The image of God in each of us dribbles out somewhere at various times, whether we chose to acknowledge the source of outflow or not. Anjezë, of course, is Mother Teresa. We've all heard of her, and we are familiar with her work among the homeless people of Calcutta. When the world's media took notice of Mother

Teresa, one of the reporters also asked her that well-worn question, 'Why are you doing this?' Her answer to him was like an arrow of light shot into a dark room. 'I do this because no one else is doing it.'

Today there are many following Mother Teresa's example in Calcutta, but why haven't we heard of others doing this before Mother Teresa hit the streets? Why would anyone even ask her that question, 'Why are you doing this?'

Well, in my naivety, I narrow it down to one thing: Mother Teresa tipped the scales. I find, in this world, there is often a cut-off point to love and kindness. It's not publicised, it's just acceptable. How far will I go when it comes to forgiveness, hospitality, or the welfare of another person? Where do I draw the line on my giving? How selective am I with regard to the people I choose to serve and love? We usually stop giving when it is socially acceptable to do so. That's the world's limit. Many hang out in this arena because it's comfortable and relatively safe. It costs us something, but there's always enough left on our plate to smile about and have a good meal afterwards.

If we live in this camp, it's guaranteed no reporter is going to come up and ask us, 'Why are you doing this?' We may be momentarily applauded for our sacrifice and our prudence, but no one will take that much notice. Why? Because we are living within the world's acceptable limits. It's what people expect to see in a person who has their spiritual and moral compass turned on. We're just balancing the scales.

Respectability has its cost, and that cost is mediocrity. If we want to leave a mark for Jesus in this world, then we have to tip the scales. We have to jump over the world's conventional boundaries and run where the world refuses to go. As a church, we need to run like this together.

Jesus said and did a lot of radical, disturbing things that jar against our common sense. He just wasn't that interested in balancing someone else's scales. Consider this statement, 'If anyone wants to sue you and take your shirt, hand over your coat as well' (Matt. 5:40). Now that's a scale-tipper. I'm sure if anyone actually followed through and offered more than the court required, someone would ask, 'Why are you doing this?'

Here's another scale-tipper: 'If anyone forces you to go one mile, go with them two miles' (Matt. 5:41). It was a Roman law that a soldier could demand this of you. The Romans were the occupying force. It didn't make sense to help him beyond what the law required. If anyone went two miles, I'm sure someone would have asked, 'Why are you doing this?'

Many other statements rock the boat of acceptable, moral behaviour: love your enemies,[2] put no limitation on the number of times you forgive someone,[3] consider others and their needs more important than your own.[4] Wow! For many, this is absurd. However, the world takes notice of those who actually do it, Christian, or otherwise. Perhaps this is one of the reasons we read of people like George Müller, Corrie Ten Boom, Martin Luther King, or Jackie Pullinger. They tipped the scales.

Every day we choose the kind of life we live. If we want more of God, we have to make more room for him in our life. We either tip the scales or comfortably live within the boundaries of mediocrity. Listen to how Jesus illustrates the choice.

If you love those who love you, what credit is that to you? Even sinners love those who love them. And if you do good to those who are good to you, what credit is that to you? Even sinners do that. And if you lend to those from whom you expect repayment, what credit is that to you? Even sinners lend to sinners, expecting to be repaid in full. But love your enemies, do good to them, and

> lend to them without expecting to get anything back. Then your reward will be great, and you will be children of the Most High, because he is kind to the ungrateful and wicked. (Luke 6:32–5)

What do you notice in all these words? Reading between the lines, I hear Jesus saying, 'Be radical. Seek first the kingdom of God and don't be conformed to this world. Tip the scales and leave God's mark of love on this orphaned planet. Stand united as one family. Share the resources God has given. Think kingdom. Love each other.'

If the church can't love each other, then we will have a difficult time tipping the scales.[5] We can camp under our religious banners and promote Jesus as we know him, but the world needs to see the culture of heaven on their streets. It's radical because the planet is dysfunctional. Heaven is not dysfunctional, and the church shouldn't be either. When we live kingdom, Christianity will no longer be a world religion; it will be a world phenomenon. It will be a culture the world can't fault, deny or emulate because it's born from above. It's not of this world.

> No one has ever seen God; but if we love one another, God lives in us and his love is made complete in us. (1 John 4:12)

> A new command I give you: love one another. As I have loved you, so you must love one another. By this everyone will know that you are my disciples, if you love one another. (John 13:34–5)

The Director has been pointing the camera in one direction throughout the entire production. From Genesis to Revelation, he keeps calling us back to the script. All the resources we need are in the kingdom. The kingdom of God is the alternative culture that tips all the world's scales, but we can't do it alone. The good news for the world is not our independent churches or denominations. The world needs the full gospel: the gospel about Jesus, and the gospel of Jesus, the gospel of the kingdom.

Intermission

As the church continues its march through the last days, how far will we go to see the kingdom of God manifested on this planet? Which town or city will take the script and run with it as one body? Can we tip the scales further than the previous generations? What would our towns and cities look like if every Christian woke up in the morning and asked God how we could tip the scales together? What impossible thing can I participate in and pray about before I sit down to my morning cereal?

What radical, out of the box thing could we do, or our local church participate in, that reaches beyond the world's limits of love, forgiveness, unity and service? How can we give like the widow in the temple, and not like the Pharisees?[6] How long will it take us to elevate unity in the body of Christ, to lift it from the bottom of our priority list and make it our chief concern? Many in this world need to see the gospel of the kingdom so they can accept the gospel about Christ. The treasure was never meant to be hidden in a field. Who will dig it up and let it shine as a city on a hill?

Getting out of the boat we've invested in isn't easy. Sometimes I too am afraid of the cost. Love often demands more of me. I will have to sacrifice my desires. I will have to pick up my cross and lift it a bit higher. I will have to be a real disciple and not just a passenger floating comfortably by, dipping my hand in the water now and then. God planted us in this world to learn how to love. Failure is when I close down and refuse to turn the other cheek.[7] We can't say we love God and not love people, especially those in the body of Christ. We can't worship in Spirit and truth without sacrifice.[8] The only sacrifice God honours in his kingdom is the one fuelled by love.

Walking on water is a miracle. Walking on water together is how we tip the scales and change the culture of our towns and cities. This is how we steal the show away from the kingdom of Satan and the world. Remember, we aren't wrestling against flesh and blood but against wicked spirits (Eph. 6:2).

Lord, don't let us sit comfortably watching the waves and drift off into some mind-numbing religion the world winks at but never asks the question, 'Why are you doing this?' Inspire us to seek first the kingdom of God and not leave it buried in the field. Let us unite and show the world what you are like and who you are in the community you have planted us in. Let this be the generation that dazzles the onlookers with the glory of your treasure. Let the audience come running to the lifeboat, crying out, 'I want som-adat.' May the beauty of your kingdom overshadow the attractions of this world. Help us tip the scales for your glory and honour in our community.

Heaven's Silence

Somehow it has filtered into popular culture that all we will do in heaven is strum a harp and placidly float around on the little cloud assigned to us. Heaven has become some airy-fairy sort of place, utterly different from what we're used to in this life. There we will participate in a 24/7 worship service for eternity. No guitars. No drums. No pets. Don't walk on the grass and no fishing. This, of course, is an unsophisticated, comical picture of the after-life.

I love to worship Jesus. I love everything about him, who he is and what he does, but if all I have to look forward to is an eternal sing-along, or sitting on a cloud somewhere in the ozone, I'd probably be looking for the diving-board.[1] I'd be better jumping than just sitting there. I can't get excited about a church service that doesn't have a closing benediction and a door nearby. Can you imagine Michael the archangel saying, 'Let's now turn to hymn number eight billion, five hundred and twenty-three million, four hundred and fifty-six thousand, seven hundred and twenty-one. OK, all together now.'?

I know this is facetious, but a lot of ideas regarding our final destination are laughable, some of them even frightening and I'm not just referring to the bad place.[2] Many wish the Bible told us more about the after-life. Any book that tries to fill in the details is usually a bestseller. The authors who have been there and back after their death and resuscitation experience are frequently applauded and sought after.

The Apostle Paul tells us no one has ever seen, heard, or could possibly imagine what God has planned for us who love him.[3] That's an incredible statement; however, Paul also tells us these mysteries are being revealed to us by the Holy Spirit.[4] The subject is rather cloudy, but one thing is indisputable, we won't find anybody sitting around wishing they knew how to play the harp or beating themselves up because they forget to bring their cell phone. There will be no disappointments. But what fascinates me the most is that the biblical details focus more on the kingdom of God than they do on heaven or hell.[5] God never drops the kingdom remit even when we step through the doors of eternity.

The Unravelling

From the time of Jesus till now we've all been living in the last days. It is a time of grace like the world has never known.[6] Jesus died for our sins and rose from the dead. The Holy Spirit is poured out on all people,[7] revealing the secrets and the workings of God.[8] Confessed sins are instantly forgiven.[9] The new covenant and all that it entails is changing us from the inside out. This is our day. This is our Jubilee.[10] It is a season of abundant, amazing grace.

The fact that the last days have gone on for so long is another revelation of God's grace: love is patient. All we have to do is believe and respond, seek and find. Salvation, redemption, sanctification, holiness and the eternal life of God are freely available. Through Jesus Christ, anyone can reach out and be born again; Christ in us the hope of glory, righteous before God, a child of the kingdom, a new creation.

This is the season we live in at the present moment, but it is still just a season. Right now, the door is wide open, but there is coming a day when that door will close. We don't know the exact time this will happen. There are many prophetic statements regarding it and a plethora of interpretations describing it. The closed door is often called the 'final judgement', the 'second coming' or the 'great white throne'.[11] It's the moment Jesus says, 'Well done, good and faithful servant' or, 'I never knew you. Away from me.'[12]

There is also another term the Bible frequently uses to describe the last moments of this world as we know it. The phrase is in both Testaments. It's called the 'day of the Lord'.[13] Right now is our day, but God's day is approaching. There is coming a time when God will say, 'Enough! I am now going to set everything right in the universe.' This will be humanity's point of no return. It will be glorious or terrible; it depends on which side of the door we are on when the hinges start to creak.[14]

Revelation

The book of Revelation is all about the creaking door. It's a letter describing how this world is to end. It's the fountain we drink from when we try to grasp the outcome of humanity. Our fascination with it is understandable. The subject is apocalyptic in scale, and the way it is written invites a world of speculation. No wonder it's the final message of the Christian Bible. What an ending. Your kingdom shall come, your will shall be done on earth as it is in heaven.

The first thing most people notice when they read Revelation is that the entire book is structured on the number seven. There are seven churches, seven spirits, seven lampstands, seven stars, seven seals, seven horns and seven eyes. There are seven angels, seven trumpets, seven thunders, seven heads, seven crowns, seven plagues, seven bowls and seven hills. You can't escape it. It's an avalanche of sevens. It's the current driving the book forward. It's the Jewish way of telling us the ship is heading onward to perfection. The boat is ready to dock. We will soon disembark on Eden's shore. Not only will there be a new heaven and a new earth,[15] but God will be in the centre of the camp forever.[16]

The books of Genesis and Revelation are the literary bookends of the Bible; not just in their placement but also in their theology. Revelation is the mirror-image of the first creation story. They are both built on the number seven. In Genesis, all things come into being; in Revelation, everything that was created unravels and disappears. In Genesis, the stars are placed in the sky; in Revelation, they fall from the heavens.[17] In Genesis, God creates the seas; in Revelation, the seas disappear.[18] In Genesis, God creates day and night; in Revelation, day and night are rolled up and tossed away, no longer needed.[19] God is making space for a brand-new creation.[20] Eventually, the lifeboat is going to drop us off on this shore. It's our final destination.

So we watch as the door swings shut on the first creation. It starts when the Lion of Judah, the Lamb that was slain, lifts the scroll from the Father's hand.[21] As Jesus snaps open each of the seven seals, you can hear the door of this fallen world groan on its hinges. The goal is to remove the seven seals and open the scroll. Why is this so important? It's crucial because the scroll is the universal reset button. It triggers an unimaginable, cosmic reboot.

> Then I saw in the right hand of him who sat on the throne a scroll with writing on both sides and sealed with seven seals. And I saw a mighty angel proclaiming in a loud voice, 'Who is worthy to break the seals and open the scroll?' But no one in heaven or on earth or under the earth could open the scroll or even look inside it. I wept and wept because no one was found who was worthy to open the scroll or look inside. (Rev. 5:1–4)

You can feel the tension as the drama heightens. If the story ended here, we would all be weeping. The day of the Lord commences with the breaking of the seals. It represents the time God steps in and eliminates evil worldwide. The kingdom of God is consummated on earth. It will be precise, just as the Director envisioned it. No more Satan and his hordes. No more crime. No more violence, chaos, victims, addictions or sin. Everything will be in harmony with the love of God.

If no one opens the scroll, there will be no room for the new heaven and the new earth. What we see on the news around the world each and every day would never end. We'd be stuck in an eternal mind-loop. Death would be laughing as our hope is put off day by day for the rest of eternity. Creation would continuously groan under the weight of unrealised expectation.

The scroll is the final page of the script; the climactic scene of the entire production this side of eternity. If no one is worthy to open it, then we are all left hanging. The greatest show on earth will be like one of those frustrating movies that leave you suspended without resolution. So, John wept. Of course he wept!

However, the Director isn't going to let the production end on such a low note. He has unlimited resources to invest, so he's surely not going to pull the plug at this crucial moment. This scene was written for only one person: the star of the show. The misdirection and irony serve only to heighten the drama and the role Jesus plays in both the old and the new creation. So we watch as the camera zooms in on the Son of God.

> Then one of the elders said to me, 'Do not weep! See, the Lion of the tribe of Judah, the Root of David, has triumphed. He is able to open the scroll and its seven seals.'
> Then I saw a Lamb, looking as if it had been slain. (Rev. 5:5–6)

Jesus Christ is worthy. The elder tells John to look at the Lion, but when John turns, all he sees is the Lamb. On the cross, the Lamb reboots the kingdom in this creation. With the scroll, the Lion is going to establish it in the new creation. We watch as the catastrophic events unfold. The contents seep between the cracks as the seals are peeled off one by one. Heaven's inhabitants hardly know what to do with themselves as the last seal falls to the ground.

> When he opened the seventh seal, there was silence in heaven for about half an hour. (Rev. 8:1)

This is momentous. It's unimaginable. Silence in heaven? The angels stop their vocal worship. The 'holy, holy, holy' of the Seraphim[22] and the living creatures[23] ceases. Prayers are hushed. The twenty-four elders close their mouths and keep to their seats. The stillness is a gasp of awe and wonderment. Heaven is catching its breath. Finally! Finally! God is going to make room for the new creation. They've all been anticipating this day since our ancestor Adam took the first bite of the forbidden fruit. Justice is going to 'roll on like a river, righteousness like a never-failing stream' (Amos 5:24). At last, it begins.

A Chip off the Old Block

Revelation is another one of those biblical books that require an 'R' rating. Just like the book of Judges, it is full of violence, but this time God is the instigator. It's the epic disaster movie: meteors striking the earth, pandemics, populations wiped out, earthquakes, fire, smoke, drought, terror, war and disaster. It's the end of life as we know it. No one is having fun in this book, not even God. However, all of heaven is cheering it on. It has to be done.[1]

Yet, in the middle of all this, the one thing we can't overlook regarding earth's closing days is the original cast. In the book of Revelation, the Jews are back on the page. John tells us 144,000 of them will play a significant role in these final scenes. They are called God's servants and his prophets.[2] Two of Israel's best actors also make a comeback if we accept the traditional understanding that Moses and Elijah are the two witnesses in Jerusalem.[3]

Nevertheless, Revelation isn't the only New Testament book that speaks encouragingly about the Jews and their relationship to the Messiah. The Apostle Paul also has a lot to say.

And even they [the Jews], if they do not continue in their un-belief, will be grafted in, for God has the power to graft them in again. For if you were cut from what is by nature a wild olive tree, and grafted, contrary to nature, into a cultivated olive tree, how much more will these, the natural branches, be grafted back into their own olive tree.

I do not want you to be ignorant of this mystery [secret], brothers and sisters, so that you may not be conceited: Israel has experienced a hardening in part until the full number of the Gentiles has come in, and in this way all Israel will be saved. (Rom. 11:23–6)

Only God knows when the 'full number of the Gentiles' will come to Christ. The statement that 'all Israel will be saved' is wide open for interpretation. Suffice it to say, the Jews are not forgotten or left on the sideline. Paul makes this very clear. They still have a leading role to play in the drama, but when? Does the scroll have to be opened before it takes place?

We can't deny that 1948 was a remarkable year. The original cast is back on the stage after a two-thousand-year diaspora. It's unprecedented. We also can't dismiss the existence of messianic Jews and the Jewish individuals who are turning to Christ. I lived, prayed and served in Israel for two years. I have met many Christians who regularly pray for the peace of Jerusalem and the Jewish nation. They hope that one day the Jews will recognise Jesus as their Messiah. However, this is a bumpy road for both parties. Regrettably, we Christians have inherited a long history of anti-Semitism in the name of Jesus Christ.[4] Many of us wish it wasn't written on our page, but it's there. At times, the sins of the parents do filter down through succeeding generations.

Our history with the Jews is like an unflushed toilet. We wish we could wipe the slate clean, but they have a good sense of smell. To them, Jesus is not a neutral figure. The cross has become a symbol of hate and oppression. Centuries of accusations and wounds take more than time to heal. Christian love is the catalyst; sincere repentance is the balm, but there are broader issues to consider when it comes to the Messiah and the Jewish people. Countless Christians are quick to send messages, leave tracts and proclaim the name of Christ, but we sometimes forget the unclean slate that follows us into that arena.

Making Them Jealous

Paul was also deeply concerned about the widening gap between Jew and Gentile.[5] His appeal in the book of Romans is both personal and passionate.

> I have great sorrow and unceasing anguish in my heart. For I could wish that I myself were cursed and cut off from Christ for the sake of my people, those of my own race. (Rom. 9:2–3)

Of course, Paul knew his sacrifice wouldn't save anybody, but still, he didn't enter the Jewish arena empty-handed. How many of us would willingly forfeit our salvation for someone else? We would probably give our life, but our eternal salvation?

Paul was tipping the scales. Love is the only thing that will open a wounded heart. When it comes to our relationship with the Jews, our love must be more renowned than the history we try to assuage. We too, have to tip the scales when it comes to the Jewish people, but how do we do it? Fortunately, Paul gives us a clue.

> Again I ask: did they stumble so as to fall beyond recovery? Not at all! Rather, because of their transgression [rejecting Jesus], salvation has come to the Gentiles *to make Israel envious.* But if their transgression means riches for the world, and their loss means

riches for the Gentiles, how much greater riches will their full inclusion bring! (Rom. 11:11–12, italics mine)

Ironic isn't it? Paul is willing to sacrifice his salvation for the Jewish nation, while the Jews (unknowingly) forfeit their salvation for the Gentiles. What's even more ironic is that the salvation we now possess is to spark envy in the Jewish heart. This is the clue. When the Jews get a clear vision of what they rejected and what we now possess, they will want it back. They will long for som-adat. It will all come around full circle. When the Jews embrace Jesus as their Messiah, it will have global repercussions.

I don't know how this sounded to the Christians in Rome when Paul wrote this, but it was a radical notion to the twelve disciples when they first heard about it. The news that Jew and Gentile were going to stand as equals on the same stage astounded them.[6] After two millennia, it still seems a preposterous, seemingly impossible notion. Can you imagine Israel being jealous of the church, all of Israel saved, Jew and Gentile standing on the same platform holding the same script, a communal witness that will challenge and bless the world audience? I mean, who has faith to believe this? Can any of us believe this impossible thing before breakfast?

But perhaps we need to ask a more practical question. Why aren't the Jews knocking on our door saying, 'I want som-adat? I want what you have?' Why haven't we seen this great Jewish awakening in the last two thousand years? Could it have anything to do with the kingdom of God? I'm not overlooking the fact that many Jews today are turning to Christ. I'm just saying they all need to see the kingdom, especially those who have embraced Judaism as God's answer for their life, and not Jesus as their Messiah.

The Jews expect many things of their Messiah. Sadly, they just haven't recognised them in Jesus.[7] It was true when Jesus walked the streets of Jerusalem, and it's true among Judaism's children today.

- Where is the promised global peace?
- Why isn't the knowledge of God filling the earth?
- Why aren't the prophecies of Isaiah and Ezekiel fulfilled?

These are the kinds of questions they ask. The queries are biblical. They are kingdom questions. It seems that throughout church history we have either rejected the Jews in the name of Jesus or tried to convert them in the name of Jesus – but how many times have they witnessed the gospel of Jesus, the gospel of the kingdom? This is what they want to see. But we often relegate their kingdom expectation to the sweet by and by or shelve it as a misguided interpretation of Scripture.

Where is the Kingdom?

Does anyone find it strange that the vast majority of Jews aren't jealous of anything we now possess? It seems what we offer isn't that attractive or inviting to them. We speak of Jesus, but what they want to see is the kingdom of God in our field, the culture of heaven on our streets.

If Jesus is the Messiah, then where is the manifestation of the kingdom of God? Show it to us. Produce it. Where's the proper fruit? Then we'll consider his claim.

The Jews need to see the kingdom of God planted in the church's soil and in our communities. The Jewish nation once held the responsibility of the kingdom. They possessed it, but now it's in the hands of the church. The Son of God has given us the keys. Jesus commissioned us to exhibit it like a light on a hill. It's the one thing we possess that will attract the Jews and make them jealous.

> I [Jesus] confer on you [the disciples] a kingdom, just as my Father conferred one on me. (Luke 22:29)

Our Jewish cousins need to see what this kingdom looks like and to touch it. They need to view a united family, born in love, exhibiting the unconditional love of their heavenly Father and the blessing of God in them and upon them. It's necessary for the Jewish people and the world. People need to see the fruit of God's presence amid the church and spreading out on to the streets.

Paul is telling us the Jews need the full gospel; not just the gospel about Jesus but also the gospel of Jesus, the gospel of the kingdom. It appears we are quick to tell them the one but quite slow to show them the other. As the old saying goes, 'You can lead a horse to water, but you can't make it drink.' There's truth in that saying, but what if we put some salt in its oats?

Jesus said, 'You are the salt of the earth. But if the salt loses its saltiness, how can it be made salty again?' (Matt. 5:13). The manifested kingdom of God in the church and on our streets is the salt. Our unity and love will change the culture of our towns and cities. It's what will make the Jewish people jealous, and shout, 'I want som-adat. Tell me again about the Messiah.'

The church was never meant to be Gentile only. It was called to be Jew and Gentile together. The church was born in Jewish soil. Jews were the first evangelists. They were the first converts. The Jews are the root. They wrote the Old and New Testaments.[8]

We Gentiles are grafted into that root. God's picture of the church is a family made from the believing members of the original cast and the redeemed population of the Gentile audience. The Gentiles were never meant to stand on the stage alone.

Intermission

The rift between Jew and Gentile has crippled us more than we imagine, and yet we hardly notice it. We have grown so accustomed to the status quo that the Jewish absence is of no great concern. For many it's just a side issue. We haven't considered what the Jewish inclusion will mean for the world and God's mission in and through the church. As Paul said, 'How much greater riches will their [the Jews] full inclusion bring!' (Rom. 11:12).

Does this ever enter the discussion when we talk of the church's mission to the world or to the Jew? I find it odd that we so easily ignore what Jesus considered to be the prime directive of his gospel. The manifestation of the kingdom of God is the most significant witness we have regarding the resurrection. It's what will convince our Jewish cousins that the claims of Jesus are valid.

Now I'm not saying the manifestation of the kingdom of God displayed in and by the church takes the place of the Holy Spirit. The church is ignited and made alive by the Holy Spirit. The Holy Spirit mysteriously confirms and reveals the reality of Jesus to the human heart.[9] However, when the church is not living in unity and love, it makes it much harder for the audience (both Jew and Gentile) to say, 'I want som-adat.'

The gospel of the kingdom confirms the reality of what we preach. Christ saves us, but the kingdom shows the world what it looks like to be saved. It's counter-cultural and attractive.

It's desirable. It's supernatural. It's what will open the door of the Jewish heart. If we desire to see a great awakening among the Jewish people, we first need to see a renewal in the church. Our unity and contagious love for each other in the presence of God is what will tip the scales.[10]

Dig up the treasure and put it on a hill for all to see. Don't leave it buried. Display the culture of heaven on our streets.[11] A field, or a battlefield, full of broken bottles and barbed wire won't do it. To change the culture of a city, we first have to change the culture of our city's churches. To win the heart of the Jew, we have to show them what the kingdom looks like in practice. When it comes to the mission, the kingdom of God actively displayed in our towns and cities is our most reliable witness to everyone on the planet of who God is and what he is like. It's worth more than a thousand sermons and tracts handed out on the street. We won't have to convince people of the reality and love of God; they will see it with their own eyes. It will awaken faith just like it did in the first chapters of the book of Acts.

The Last Hurrah

If you want to open a can of worms, mention the millennium. If you're still hungry, reach for the rapture.[1] Both cans reside on the same shelf. I hesitate to open either of them, but I'm reaching for the one labelled 'Millennium' because it's all about the kingdom. In these six verses, John introduces us to an unprecedented global event. It's governmental. It's theocratic. It's a power play no one can resist.

> And I saw an angel coming down out of heaven, having the key to the Abyss and holding in his hand a great chain. He seized the dragon, that ancient snake, who is the devil, or Satan, and bound him for a thousand years. He threw him into the Abyss and locked and sealed it over him, to keep him from deceiving the nations any more until the thousand years were ended. After that, he must be set free for a short time.
>
> I saw thrones on which were seated those who had been given authority to judge. And I saw the souls of those who had been beheaded because of their testimony about Jesus and because of the word of God. They had not worshipped the beast or its image and had not received its mark on their foreheads or their hands. They came to life and reigned with Christ for a thousand years.

(The rest of the dead did not come to life until the thousand years were ended.) This is the first resurrection. Blessed and holy are those who share in the first resurrection. The second death has no power over them, but they will be priests of God and of Christ and will reign with him for a thousand years. (Rev. 20:1–7)

Great minds discuss the doctrinal stances of pre-, post-, and amillennialism. Will the rapture of the church occur before or after the thousand-year reign of Christ? Will there even be a rapture? Is Jesus going to rule on earth for that specific period, or is the millennium a symbolic heavenly state with no historical reality? Why put Satan in prison, then let him out again? Who will be there? Will citizens have children? Will they be sinless? Why is the millennium even mentioned in the Bible?

There's no doubt these few verses provoke questions about citizenship, purpose, state of being, timing, reality, literal or non-literal, present and future. I know I have stepped into a murky pool at the mention of the millennium. However, the fact John records it just before earth's final battle and ultimate judgement is curious. What's even more intriguing is that the millennium is not about religion; it's about government. If anything, the millennium is the 'last hurrah' of the greatest show on earth this side of eternity.

God, the Director, has a script. The Jewish nation is the original cast. When the curtain came down on the first production, the audience wasn't that impressed, neither was the Director. The ratings were low. The intake at the box office was inadequate. So the initial run was cancelled. The script is now in the hands of the church (the next generation) under the direction of Jesus Christ.[2] God retains the members of the first cast who have faith in the star of the show and in the production, but he also recruits Gentiles to join them on the stage. As individuals, they all have to sign the new contract.

The church has come a long way over the last two thousand years, but we still have a long way to go. 'I follow Paul, I follow Apollos', has shadowed us through the centuries.[3] Our various flags and banners are still flapping about in the field, but there is a growing, Holy-Spirit-led awareness that we have to do this kingdom thing together. How far we will go is yet to be seen. The first production of the kingdom didn't reach its full potential. The second production is still a work in progress. The third production is the thousand-year reign of Christ – the millennium. The history of these three performances is progressive. With each production, God makes it easier for us – not harder. He wants us to succeed.

The Original Show

The first production focused on one race. Grace was breaking into the world but wasn't fully realised. The Jewish nation had to fight many of the battles that we, as the church, no longer have to wrestle with. Jesus won them for us. We are in no place to judge what the Jews have or haven't accomplished. God is their judge. God is their Father, and the show isn't over yet. They were ploughing the field, and the ground was hard. We follow on from their labour. We build upon their effort. The groundwork is done. If it wasn't for the Jews and the God who steered them, we wouldn't even be here. We should be thanking them profusely.

The Sequel

In the second production, God makes things easier for us. Jesus ushers in the age of grace. He frees us from a law-driven religion. The new contract is far more inclusive than the previous one. The Jews no longer have to shoulder the kingdom alone; God recruits Gentiles. They are now part of the cast. God moulds us from the inside out. He releases the Holy Spirit to us, upon us and in us. We have been given every spiritual blessing,[4] along with the gifts and the fruit of the Holy Spirit.[5] We have Christ himself.

This new production is bound to move things on from the earlier show. What's sad is that the original cast has become such a small minority. They have little influence, and their voice is rarely heard above the Gentile megaphone. The Director wasn't looking for a new root or a Gentile church. He was looking for the Jewish root to nourish and lead the Gentiles who were invited on to the stage. We're still on the road as we stumble towards maturity. The church is crippled and hardly notices a vital body part has been amputated.

The Third Instalment

When the millennium gets underway, God removes many of the obstacles that have plagued the two earlier productions. He chains Satan and his influence. Jesus arrives in person for his second star appearance. He now possesses all authority. For one thousand years, he displays what the kingdom of God should look like on this planet. Members of the cast are now ruling at his side. He has the final word in everything. All the nations of the world experience first-hand the love of God and what it's like to live under his reign in the kingdom. The hope of nations has come.

> For to us a child is born,
> > to us a son is given,
> > and the government will be on his shoulders.

And he will be called
    Wonderful Counsellor, Mighty God,
    Everlasting Father, Prince of Peace.
Of the greatness of his government and peace
    there will be no end.
He will reign on David's throne
    and over his kingdom,
establishing and upholding it
    with justice and righteousness
    from that time on and for ever.
The zeal of the LORD Almighty
    will accomplish this. (Isa. 9:6–7)

At last, the Director gives us an absolute picture of what it's like to live in the kingdom of God. No obstacle hinders it. God's people are unified. Jesus is in the middle of the camp. God's blessing and glory fill the earth. The citizens no longer live in fear. They don't have to pray for peace and justice because it's the foundation of earth's administration. No more dodgy politics, corruption, hidden agendas or selfish manoeuvrings. Jesus rules. The saints rule with him, and they are not impotent.

Blessed are the meek,
    for they will inherit the earth. (Matt. 5:5)
If we endure,
    we will also reign with him. (2 Tim. 2:12)

We can only imagine what the millennium looks like, but why is God giving us a thousand-year witness just before the arrival of the new heaven and earth? Why didn't he immediately jump to the final judgement and the new earth scenario? Well, for one reason, the Director isn't going to flip the switch between time and eternity before he knows who is going to stay on board the ship.

I don't want to enter into a lot of speculation, but it seems not every believer throughout space and time is present during the millennium – a debatable subject for many. The only ones identified are the resurrected martyrs and those who possibly survived the apocalypse. It seems natural that children will be born and go about their business under the rule of Christ. However, not everyone is spiritually redeemed because, when given the opportunity, many of them don't behave as redeemed people.

The moment Satan is released, he recruits thousands to stand with him. Fortunately, this coup doesn't last very long. In four short verses, Satan and his revolutionary army are put down never to rise again.[6] What this production stirs up or looks like from heaven or to those outside of space and time we don't know. Jesus has a way of separating the wheat from the chaff.[7] He will do it one last time when the curtain closes at the end of the thousand year reign.[8]

The millennium is one of the last pieces of the kingdom puzzle. The Director is tying up all the loose ends of the show. During the millennium, Jesus will fulfil all the prophetic statements both Jews and Gentiles have been anticipating since the days of the prophets. The production has had a long run, and God isn't going to stop until he sees the kingdom established on this side of eternity, even if it's just for a thousand years. A thousand years is enough time to make his point without misunderstanding. All we can say is that from the very beginning, the kingdom is a revelation of the heart of God, and it will be founded on this planet, one way or another. For a thousand years, Jesus reveals to this world what God is like and who he is through his community. He is a good Father.

The New Heavens and the New Earth

As eternity dawns on the new heaven and the new earth, the curtain closes. The audience is escorted out of the theatre for the very last time. The original stage is torn down. The dust settles. We have now witnessed the final curtain call of the greatest show on earth. The last hurrah has had its day. We have laid down our scripts and said goodbye to the mission, our banners, our denominations, our labour, our pains and this old body. What do we carry with us?

These three remain: faith, hope and love. But the greatest of these is love. (1 Cor. 13:13)

The lifeboat has finally docked on the shore of eternity. Interestingly enough, we haven't been whisked away to some other dimension where angels live. People have visited that place, but it's not our home or our final destination.[9] We won't be jumping from cloud to cloud with harps in our hands. God made a new heaven and new earth to be populated, not admired from some celestial vantage point. So, let's take a quick census to see who is going to be living there.

May he, as a result, make your hearts strong, blameless, and holy as you stand before God our Father when our Lord Jesus comes again with *all his holy people*. (1 Thess. 3:13, NLT, italics mine)

When the Son of Man comes in his glory, and *all the angels* with him, he will sit on his glorious throne. (Matt. 25:31, italics mine)

The Son of God is finally bringing everything together in heaven and on earth, but where is this new show going to take place? Well, he isn't moving all of us up there; he's bringing all of heaven down here. 'Hey, everyone, listen up. We're heading out. So, pack your bags. We're moving to earth.'

Jesus then comes with all his holy people and all the angels. Jesus leads them; he brings them all here to settle with us forever. Who is left in heaven if Jesus and all the people and the angels are down here? Does the Father stay behind? No! God, the Father doesn't try to bring us up there either; instead, he comes down to earth, forever.[10]

> I saw the Holy City, the new Jerusalem, coming down out of heaven from God, prepared as a bride beautifully dressed for her husband. And I heard a loud voice from the throne saying, 'Look! God's dwelling-place is now among the people, and he will dwell with them. They will be his people, and God himself will be with them and be their God.' (Rev. 21:2–3)

> [God] made known to us the mystery [secret] of his will according to his good pleasure, which he purposed in Christ, to be put into effect when the times reach their fulfilment – to bring unity to all things in heaven and on earth under Christ. (Eph. 1:9–10)

Even God the Father, the Director of the show, is going to dwell amid his people on this new/renewed planet.[11] This is how heaven and earth are brought together under the authority of Christ. The plan is finally consummated. Where it goes from here, God only knows. Praise his holy name. We have an eternity of discovery waiting for us just beyond the horizon.

> It is done. I am the Alpha and the Omega, the Beginning and the End. To the thirsty I will give water without cost from the spring of the water of life. Those who are victorious will inherit all this, and I will be their God and they will be my children. (Rev. 21:6–7)

Final Remarks

Well, this is the story, and it's a great one. It's more significant than any of us could imagine because God, the Director, is greater than any of our thoughts and words about him. What I've attempted to do in this book is put together a puzzle and reveal the picture on the box. In the centre of this picture is the star of the show. His face is human, yet he is God's only Son.

I've tried to give some direction and answers to the questions I've heard people ask over many years. These are the same questions I have asked at numerous times. Not everyone will agree with me; I don't expect them to, but I hope everyone who reads this book catches a glimpse of the bigger picture. I hope you have received a template to work from as you adjust, fill in and modify the details regarding the kingdom of God – I'm still doing this.

As with any revelation, you plant the seed and watch it grow. Perhaps we all have to do a little pruning along the way. I too am a work in progress. I know I have wandered a bit beyond the fringe in this book. I have put myself out on a limb and perhaps have strayed too far in my theology. Please forgive me; sometimes I can't help it. I'm still learning, and hopefully, I'm still teachable as I passionately pray,

Our Father in heaven,
hallowed be your name,
your kingdom come,
your will be done,
    on earth as it is in heaven. (Matt. 6:9–10)

I also pray that one day, on this side of eternity, we will see God's children boldly step out of the boat and seek more of those ideal kingdom moments in our towns and cities. May the revelation of the kingdom continue and grow in my own soul because it is the heart of God. The show must go on. It is the greatest show on earth, and I am compelled to seek it first. Hopefully, this seed is planted in all of our hearts. Love is invading this orphaned planet, and I, for one, want to be in the raiding party.

> For he has rescued us from the dominion of darkness and brought us into the kingdom of the Son he loves, in whom we have redemption, the forgiveness of sins. (Col. 1:13–14)

Yee-haw! Bless his holy name.

Notes

Part One: Setting the Stage

1 First Contact

1   Paramahansa Yogananda, *Autobiography of a Yogi* (New York: Philosophical Library, 1946).

2   Carlos Castaneda, *The Teachings of Don Juan: A Yaqui Way of Knowledge* (Berkeley: University of California Press, 1968); Carlos Castaneda, *A Separate Reality* (New York: Pocket Books, 1971); Carlos Castaneda, *Journey to Ixtlan* (New York: Pocket Books, 1972).

3   Jack S. Margolis and Richard Clorfene, *A Child's Garden of Grass* (North Hollywood, California: Contact Books, 1969).

4   Tom Wolfe, *The Electric Kool-Aid Acid Test* (New York: Bantam Press, 1971). This is a non-fiction book documenting Ken Kesey's road trip across America with the Merry Pranksters. LSD was legal at this time and they took every advantage to promote it.

5   Robert Crumb is a pioneer, underground comic artist (e.g. Zapp Comix, Mr Natural, and Fritz the Cat).

6   Norman Grubb, *Rees Howells: Intercessor* (London: Lutterworth Press, 1954).

7   Hal Lindsey, *The Late Great Planet Earth* (Grand Rapids: Zondervan Publishing House, 1964).

8   David Wilkerson, *The Cross and the Switchblade* (New York: Pyramid Books, 1962).

⁹   These were popular Christian singers and songwriters in the
    1970s.
¹⁰ Rom. 10:2.
¹¹ This is one of the essential texts of Hinduism.
¹² Eph. 6:17; Heb. 4:12.
¹³ Prov. 18:18; Acts 1:26.
¹⁴ Matt. 6:33.

2 Sinking the Ship

¹   Titanic Belfast was named the world's leading tourist attraction at
    the World Travel Awards, 2016.
²   E.g. secularised science, the theory of evolution, and the long geo-
    logical periods equated to Earth's past.
³   I'm not denying God created the world in seven, literal days. If
    God is God he could create it in one day if he wanted. All I'm
    saying is that the timetable of the creation event is not the main
    point of the narrative.
⁴   E.g. the word 'God' appears 35 times (5x7), 'earth' 21 times
    (3x7), 'heavens' 21 times (3x7), 'and it was so' 7 times. 'Light'
    and 'day' appear 7 times in the first paragraph. 'Light' is listed 7
    times in the fourth paragraph. 'Water' appears 7 times through
    paragraphs two and three. *Hayya*, the Hebrew word translated
    'beast' or 'living' appears 7 times in paragraphs five and six. For a
    more in-depth analysis see Umberto Cassuto, *A Commentary on
    the Book of Genesis: From Adam to Noah* (Jerusalem: Magnes Press,
    1961), pp. 12–16.
⁵   Gen. 2:20.
⁶   Gen. 2:17.
⁷   This is illustrated in Gen. 3 – 11.
⁸   In itself the knowledge of good and evil is not bad or malicious
    because God also has the knowledge of good and evil (Gen. 3:22).
    We don't know exactly what the phrase means. It is probably a
    Jewish idiom pointing to some form of self-government. Whatever
    it is, God told Adam it would kill him. We can't handle it; God
    can. It's kind of like handing a 5-year-old the keys to the car.

⁹ 1 Cor. 1:20; 3:19; Jas 3:15; Matt. 11:25; Rom. 1:21–3; Col. 2:23.

¹⁰ 2 Cor. 4:4.

¹¹ Eph. 1:10.

¹² Gen. 3:14,17; 4:11; 5:29; 9:25.

¹³ Gordon Wenham, *Genesis 1 – 15* (Waco: Word Books, 1987), p. li.

3 Shaking the Box

¹ Gen. 11:30.

² Gen. 12:5.

³ Abraham told Lot to choose which part of the promised land he wanted to live in. He specifically said go to the left or the right (Gen. 13:5–9). In the ancient Near East this was a clear designation. The choice Abraham offered Lot was not random. In the culture he lived, all directions were east-orientated. So when Abraham said go right or left it was from the perspective of someone facing east; so 'left' meant north and 'right' meant south. Abraham was offering Lot either the north or the south of Canaan. Lot went east (Gen. 13:11). See also Larry R. Helyer, 'The Separation of Abram and Lot: Its Significance in the Patriarchal Narratives', *Journal for the Study of the Old Testament* 26 (1983): pp. 77–88.

⁴ This is my amplified paraphrase of Gen. 15:2–3.

⁵ See Gen. 16.

⁶ Gen. 17:15–21.

⁷ E.g. Matt. 16:23.

⁸ Consider many of the Old Testament stories such as 1 Sam. 16:7 or 2 Kgs 6:17–18.

⁹ Gen. 3:12–13.

¹⁰ This is a Latin phrase theologians use to describe our fallen condition. *Incurvatus in se* simply means 'turned' or 'curved' inward on yourself. In other words, I am my number one concern. It's all about me.

¹¹ Rom. 1:17; Gal. 3:11; Heb. 10:38.

¹² Matt. 14:29.

¹³ See Gen. 15:6; Rom. 4:3; Gal. 3:6.

[14] Sarah surrendered Hagar to her husband to fulfil the promise. It was a step of faith and was in keeping with the culture of her day. We often interpret Sarah's action as a big mistake. It wasn't. She stepped out in the light she had; as of yet God hadn't told her the child would come from her body, but the child was to come through Abraham's body. Abraham sacrificed Isaac to the promise, but Sarah also made a sacrifice; she surrendered her husband to the promise. She is to be commended.

[15] 1 John 2:15.

[16] Ishmael would also father 'a great nation' (Gen. 17:20). The only difference between Isaac and Ishmael is that Isaac was the Director's choice for the greatest show on Earth.

[17] French phrase: 'the final blow'.

[18] See Rom. 4:17.

[19] If I were asked to illustrate the previous two thousand years of Bible interpretation, I think I would draw the church holding a Bible in one hand and a trowel in the other, trying to fill in the cracks. But this is the soil cults grow in. Denominational stances often stem from this practice. Like Abraham, I'm beginning to see that the deeper things of God are found in the gaps, not in smoothing out what lies on either side of them. Enigma and paradox are not enemies of faith. The gaps are often where divine seeds of revelation are planted.

[20] Rom. 12:2.

4 Passport Denied

[1] Gen. 25:21.

[2] Gen. 24:4.

[3] Gen. 24:6.

[4] Jewish scholars and rabbis often refer to Midrash (Bereishit Rabba 64:3) to explain why Isaac had to stay in the land: Isaac was a holy sacrifice (Gen. 22). They go on to explain that holy offerings to God must stay in the temple courtyard or else they will be defiled – thus Isaac had to stay in the Promised land.

[5] Gen. 12:10–11.

6 Abraham went down to Egypt because of famine (Gen. 12:10). Jacob fled to Haran to escape Esau's anger (Gen. 27:43–5). Joseph was forced into Egypt against his will (Gen. 37:28), which is later attributed to the will of God (Gen. 50:20). See also Gen. 15:13.

7 Gen. 46 – 47.

8 Gen. 26:16.

9 Gen. 26:16–33.

10 Gen. 26:22.

11 Gen. 26:25.

12 Gen. 26:25,32.

13 Gen. 26:26–31.

14 At times Isaac did follow his father's example. Abraham tells Pharaoh and King Abimelech that his wife was his sister (Gen. 12:10–20; 20:1–16). Isaac does the same (Gen. 26:1–33).

5 What's in a Name?

1 Gen. 25:26.

2 This action illustrates Jacob's future relationship with Esau.

3 Robert Davidson, *Genesis 12 – 50: Cambridge Bible Commentary* (Cambridge: Cambridge University Press, 1979), p. 140.

4 Heb. 12:16.

5 Gen. 25:29–34.

6 Rebekah, Jacob's mother, trained him in the art of deception.

7 Gen. 28:10.

8 Gen. 27:42 – 28:9.

9 Gen. 31:1–21.

10 Gen. 12:2.

11 Gen. 28:10–19.

12 Gen. 28:20–22.

13 Gen. 33:1–17.

14 Gen. 33:20.

15 Gen. 33:18; 34:2.

16 Gen. 34.

17 Gen. 34:25–9.

18 Gen. 35:1–4.

[19] Gen. 35:5.
[20] Gen. 35:10.

6 A Victim of Blessing

[1] Gen. 37:3–4.
[2] Gen. 37:5–10,18–20.
[3] Gen. 37:24–8.
[4] Gen. 37:38.
[5] Gen. 39:2–4.
[6] Gen. 39.
[7] Gen. 39:22.
[8] Gen. 41.
[9] Gen. 41:14–34.
[10] Gen. 41:57.
[11] Gen. 42:9–24; 44:2–44.
[12] Gen. 42:25; 43:16–34.
[13] Gen. 42:24; 43:30.
[14] Gen. 45:4–7.
[15] Gen. 47:11.
[16] Gen. 47:12.
[17] 2 Cor. 5:19–20.

Part Two: Israel and the Kingdom

7 The Stage

[1] Jer. 20:7–18.
[2] 1 Kgs 17:13; 19:9.
[3] Jeremiah (Jer. 20:7–18), Elijah (1 Kgs 19:1–4), and Jonah (Jonah 4:5–11).
[4] Isa. 20:3.
[5] Ezek. 8:3.
[6] Jonah 1:3.
[7] Joel and Zechariah.
[8] 1 Kgs 19; Jer. 38:6.

9 E.g. Ps. 137:9.

10 Gen. 15:18 says the promised land will extend from the Nile to the Euphrates River. Gen. 17:8 narrows it to the land of Canaan. Throughout the Old Testament the borders are defined in the phrase: 'from Dan to Beersheba', the settled area of the Jewish nation. The larger borders were not to be taken by force like Canaan. The world was to be won by attraction.

11 Isa. 9:1; Matt. 4:15.

12 Num. 20:17–21.

13 R. Steven Notley and Anson F. Rainey, *A Sacred Bridge: Carta's Atlas of the Biblical World* (Jerusalem: Carta, 2014). The cover of this book is a good illustration of Israel's central geographic position in the ancient Near East.

14 Ezek. 26:2.

15 Centre of the earth (Ezek. 38:12). The Hebrew text is better translated the 'navel' of the earth.

8 The Audience

1 Mesopotamia is modern-day Iraq. Mesopotamia means 'between two rivers' (the Tigris and the Euphrates).

2 The original movie was released in 1994. The continuing story ran for ten seasons on television (1997–2007). There were further adaptations in the following years.

3 Exod. 7:14 – 11:10.

4 Exod. 7:13,22; 8:19.

5 Baal is sometimes used as a generic term for 'lord' or 'owner'. It's also the specific appellation of various deities such as Hadad, the storm and fertility god.

6 1 Kgs 17:1.

7 See the first chapter of this book.

8 This is my own paraphrase. See Gary A. Rendsburg, 'The Mock of Baal in 1 Kings 18:27', *Catholic Biblical Quarterly* 50 (1988): pp. 414–17. See also *The Complete Jewish Bible* and *The Living Bible* translations of 1 Kgs 18:27.

9 1 Kgs 18:29.

10 1 Kgs 18:36–9.

11 Pokémon (Japanese for 'pocket monsters') is a hugely popular game, television and film franchise.

12 Christian Merak, *The Land of a Thousand Gods: A History of Asia Minor in the Ancient World* (trans. Steven Rendall; Princeton: Princeton University Press, 2016).

13 A sacred, or temple prostitute, either male or female, would have sex with the worshippers. This took place in the temple dedicated to the deity you wanted to act on your behalf.

14 For example, when the god Motu threatens to kill Baal, Baal repeatedly copulates with a cow and has a male child through the union to carry on his influence. The Hittites forbid bestiality with cows, pigs, sheep and dogs but they don't exclude donkeys or horses. Spring fertility rites of Babylon included a seven-day-and-night orgy with dogs and other various animals. In many areas of the ancient Near East, bestiality was connected to magic rituals. This is probably one of the reasons God told the Israelites to kill animals in certain towns and places (e.g. Deut. 13:15; 20:16; Josh. 6:21; 1 Sam. 15:2–3).

15 Deut. 18:10–14.

16 Matt. 16:18.

17 Over twenty times God said he was stepping in to show the Hebrews, the Egyptians and the entire world that he is the only God (e.g. Exod. 6:11–12; 7:4–5; 29:45–6; 8:22; 9:14; 18:11).

18 Eph. 6:12.

9 The Actors

1 Richard Dawkins, *The God Delusion* (New York: Houghton Mifflin, 2006), p. 31.

2 Paul Copan, *Is God a Moral Monster?: Making Sense of the Old Testament God* (Grand Rapids: Baker Books, 2011).

3 Helen Paynter, *God of Violence Yesterday, God of Love Today?: Wrestling Honestly with the Old Testament* (Abingdon: Bible Reading Fellowship, 2019).

4. David T. Lamb, *God Behaving Badly: Is the God of the Old Testament Angry, Sexist and Racist?* (Downers Grove: InterVarsity Press, 2011).
5. Exod. 2:1–10.
6. Exod. 3.
7. *Chutzpah* is a Yiddish word that has filtered into the English language. It means: audacity, boldness, incredible gall, guts.
8. I realise this title precedes Moses. It's a problem on many levels. I added it here because of its popularity among Christians. Scholars wrestle with this particular declaration because of what God says in Exodus 6:2. Here he tells Moses that he didn't reveal his name (Yahweh) to the patriarchs, so why does Abraham declare it in Genesis 22:14 (Yahweh will provide)? If this arouses your interest and you want a more scholarly discussion of this name, see R.W.L. Moberly, *The Old Testament of the Old Testament: Patriarchal Narratives and Mosaic Yahwism* (OTBT, Philadelphia: Fortress Press, 1992).
9. Num. 14:1–10.
10. Num. 14.
11. Num. 13:31–3.
12. E.g. Isa. 54:5; Jer. 3:14; Hos. 1 – 2.
13. Deut. 7:7–8.
14. Isa. 5:4; Jer. 2:5.

11 Does God Wear a Watch?

1. E.g. Job 38 – 41; 1 Kgs 19:1–10; Jonah 4:1–4.
2. Theologians call the answers to this kind of question a 'theodicy'.
3. Isa. 11:6; 65:25.
4. See https://en.wikipedia.org/wiki/Predictions_and_claims_for_the_Second_Coming_of_Christ (accessed 23 January 2018).
5. Matt. 24:36.
6. See Rev. 6:1–8.
7. John 3:16–18; 5:28–9; Rev. 20:11–13.

8   One of the most referenced chapters regarding the end times is Matt. 24. Notice most of the signs centre on the behaviour of people.

9   Matt. 24:36–42.

10 Matt. 24:14.

11 See Michael J. Vlach, 'Israel's Repentance and the Kingdom of God', *Master's Seminary Journal* 27 (2016): pp. 161–86.

12 Rom. 8:22.

12 Love is Patient

1   Exod. 33:18.

2   E.g. Matt. 16:22–3.

3   Donald Miller, *Blue Like Jazz: Nonreligious Thoughts on Christian Spirituality* (Nashville: Thomas Nelson Publishers, 2003), p. 30.

13 The Culture of Sodom

1   Gen. 6:11 tells us the earth was corrupt and full of violence. From God's perspective this is just another way to say the planet was void of love.

2   Lev. 18:24–5.

3   Gen. 12:3.

4   God was looking for a way to delay his judgement. If he found fifty righteous people living there, they would hopefully be a positive influence in the town. However, they were nowhere to be found; even Lot and his family, who was spared, carried the culture of Sodom with them. Lot didn't want to leave. His wife desired to return, and his daughters do unspeakable sexual acts with their father (Gen. 19).

5   Gen. 19:23–9; Deut. 29:23–4; Isa. 1:10.

6   Gen. 14:17–20; Heb. 5:5–6; 7:1–19; Ps. 110:4.

7   Melchizedek is mentioned twice in the Old Testament (Gen. 14:8 and Ps. 110:4), and eight times in the book of Hebrews (Heb. 7).

Salem is an early name for Jerusalem. It's the geographical centre of Canaan. Already God was laying claim to this city.

[8] The context of this verse is the death of the righteous but the principle still pertains to the living, being relocated for their protection.

[9] See Gen. 18:20–21; 19:27–8.

[10] Exod. 23:31.

[11] See Paul Copan and Matthew Flannagan, *Did God Really Command Genocide?* (Grand Rapids: Baker Books, 2014).

14 Living the Creed

[1] Many Jews today pray it when they get up and when they go to bed. It is also attached to the entrance of their homes; it's called a *mezuzah*.

[2] Monotheism appeared for a very short time in Egypt during the fourteenth century BCE. Pharoah Akhenaten worshipped Aten, the sun-disk god. It never caught on and it couldn't shift the culture primarily because there wasn't a large, or determined enough community to sustain it.

15 God in the Camp

[1] Exod. 20:18–21.

[2] Gen. 9:11–17.

[3] Exod. 19.

[4] Isa. 54:5; Ezek. 16; and the book of Hosea.

[5] Isa. 57:3–10; Jer. 9:2; 23:10; Ezek. 6:9; 16:32; 23:45; Matt. 12:39; Mark 8:38; Jas 4:4.

[6] 2 Cor. 6:14–16.

[7] E.g. Ps. 81:11.

[8] Exod. 34 – 40; and the book of Leviticus.

[9] Exod. 26 – 30.

[10] The outer court contained the bronze furniture. The holy place and the holy of holies contained the gold. The ark of the covenant was the most valuable piece.

[11] E.g. Exod. 25:17–22.

[12] 1 Kgs 8:27.

[13] Exod. 20:3–6; Deut. 5:7–10.

16 No Longer Single

[1] The book is a celebration of physical love, but has been interpreted metaphorically to describe the love between God and Israel. Rabbi Akiva famously defended it saying, 'For the whole world is not as worthy as the day on which Song of Songs was given to Israel, for all the Writings are holy, but Song of Songs is the Holy of Holies' (Mishnah Yadayim 3:5). Many Christians interpret it as the love expressed between Jesus and the church.

[2] Gal. 5:1.

[3] Exod. 20:3–7,14.

[4] See Talmud Makkot 23b. You can find them listed with their scriptural equivalent at http://www.jewfaq.org/613.htm (accessed 2 January 2020).

[5] http://www.latimes.com/opinion/editorials/la-ed-new-state-laws-20160102-story.html (accessed 12 May 2018).

[6] http://www.bbc.co.uk/news/uk-politics-13569604 (accessed 13 May 2018).

[7] Laws in the ancient Near East were often paradigmatic in nature. They were models to follow. For example, look at how the law in Exod. 22:1 is incorporated into the story of Zacchaeus (Luke 19:1–10). Zacchaeus wasn't dealing with oxen and sheep but he sure recognised the paradigm. The principle was the same, if you steal – pay back the victim four times as much. Zacchaeus paid up. Jesus approved.

[8] Rom. 7 and Gal. 3.

[9] Gal. 1:8.

[10] Lev. 16.

[11] Lev. 4:27–31; 5:14–19.

[12] 2 Sam. 12:13–14; 1 Chr. 21; 2 Chr. 33:1–13; Pss 32:5; 51:16–19; Hos. 14:1–4.

[13] E.g. the Code of Hammurabi, Babylon (1754 BCE).

17 The Benefits

[1] 1 Sam. 5 – 6.

[2] Lev. 10.

[3] 2 Sam. 6:1–15.

[4] Josh. 7:1–5; 1 Chr. 21:14–15.

[5] Prov. 3:11–12; Heb. 12:5–11.

[6] Mal. 3:10.

[7] Deut. 13:19–20.

[8] One difference between a prosperity gospel and kingdom prosperity is where you place the emphasis. The prosperity gospel focuses on the individual: What can I get? What can I achieve? Kingdom prosperity, on the other hand, focuses on the community: How does my prosperity benefit those around me? The kingdom of God is about love.

18 Som-adat

[1] We saw a brief episode of this when the Queen of Sheba visited Solomon in 1 Kgs 10.

[2] Deut. 28:13.

19 A Nation of Priests

[1] Lev. 20 – 21.

[2] John Wesley's Journal, 11 June, 1739.

20 Always Room for More

[1] Scripturally speaking, we have a future hope, and that hope reaches into eternity (e.g. John 3:16; Rev. 21:4). Is God offering us something we were never made for in the beginning? The tree of life was also in the garden of Eden. Whether nature was red in tooth and claw, before we messed everything up, I don't know. However in the redeemed, new, restored creation it appears the animal kingdom will no longer be violent (Isa. 11:6). Whether animals and bacteria and germs and plants will die in the new creation, I don't know. Even if they do, it doesn't mean we die. We were created in the image of God, they were not. If Jesus took on humanity for the rest of eternity, we must've been created for eternal life, not death.

[2] Eccl. 3:9–11.

[3] E.g. 1 Cor. 15:26. See also Richard Weikart, *The Death of Humanity: and the Case for Life* (Washington: Regnery Faith, 2016); Steven Cave, 'Death: Why We Should Be Grateful for It', *New Scientist* 2887 (2012).

[4] Gen. 2:17; 1 Cor. 15:26.

[5] H.G. Wells, *The Time Machine* (Portsmouth: Heinemann, 1895).

[6] The 1973 movie, *Soylent Green*, portrays the grim reality of overpopulation.

[7] Gen. 15:5; 22:17.

[8] https://www.bbc.co.uk/news/science-environment-44661979 (accessed 20 January 2019).

[9] https://en.wikipedia.org/wiki/Expansion_of_the_universe (accessed 21 January 2019).

[10] E.g. the Queen of Sheba visits Solomon (1 Kgs 10:1–13).

21 Street Cred

[1] Exod. 20:2–17.

[2] My interpretive paraphrase of Exod. 20:3–4.

[3] Early television would censor obscenities with an audible bleep.

4 Bagels are usually cooked in boiling water. Pigs are an unclean animal, especially when it comes to cuisine.
5 'Cigarettes and Whiskey and Wild, Wild Women' is the title of a song written by Tim Spencer (1948).
6 Exod. 20:8–17.

22 Fire the Boss

1 Deut. 9:6.
2 2 Kgs 22:8.
3 Deut. 7:2–4.
4 Jas 1:13–14.

23 The Morality Clause

1 https://en.wikipedia.org/wiki/Roscoe_Arbuckle (accessed 15 May 2020).
2 Isa. 42:8.
3 Luke 15:11–32.

24 The Legal Team

1 The prophets of the royal court are found in the books of Samuel and Kings: Gad, Nathan, Ahijah, Iddo, Shemaiah, Azariah and others.
2 Their story is in 1 and 2 Kings.
3 Amos, Isaiah, Jeremiah, Ezekiel.
4 1 Kgs 12.
5 1 Kgs 12:28–9.
6 The Canaanites weren't subject to the morality clause because they weren't under the Sinai contract, but they did have other warnings of what was to come. Sodom and Gomorrah was a big shout in the dark.

7   In 722 BCE, Samaria was besieged. The people were starving.
    Cannibalism broke out in the city, yet the people still refused to
    return to God. So God invokes phase five of the morality clause;
    see 2 Kgs 18:9–12.
8   Isa. 28:21.
9   2 Kgs 18:13.
10 2 Kgs 18:14–16.
11 2 Kgs 19:1–4.
12 See also 2 Chr. 32.
13 Ezekiel was taken captive ten years before the final invasion of
    Jerusalem.
14 Jer. 52:8–11.
15 E.g. Lev. 26:33–5 and 2 Chr. 36:21.
16 Isa. 42:3.

25 Snake Water

1   Erich von Däniken, *Chariots of the Gods: Unsolved Mysteries of
    the Past* (New York: Bantam Books, 1972); J.F. Blumrich, *The
    Spaceships of Ezekiel* (New York: Bantam Books, 1974).
2   See John Bright, *A History of Israel* (London: Westminster John
    Knox, 4th edn, 2000), pp. 336–7; E.C. Broome, 'Ezekiel's
    Abnormal Personality', *Journal of Biblical Literature*, 65 (1946):
    pp. 277–92.
3   The Babylonians took captives from Jerusalem in three stages: 605
    BCE (Daniel), 597 BCE (Ezekiel), and in 587–6 BCE Jerusalem/
    Judah falls.
4   Ezek. 11:14–17.
5   Exod. 33:15–16.
6   Jer. 2:5–8.

26 Religion or Presence

1   Rom. 14:17.
2   Jer. 29:10; Dan. 9:2.

3   Josephus, a contemporary historian at the time said 1,100,000 died and 97,000 were taken captive (*The Wars of the Jews*, Book 6).

4   Matt. 5:14; 13:44; Luke 17:20–21.

Part Three: Jesus and the Kingdom

27 Jesus is Reality

1   E.g. John 21:25.

2   John 4:24; 14:26.

28 Gleeful Revelation

1   This verse can be interpreted in three different ways. We either become like a child, or we receive the kingdom like Jesus received the children, or we should be as excited and expectant as a child to receive it.

2   Heb. 12:2.

3   Eph. 1:10.

4   Eph. 1:16–19.

5   Helen Keller, *The Story of My Life* (New York: Doubleday, 1905).

29 The Divine Voice

1   John 2:1–11; 4:46–54; 5:1–15; 6:5–14,16–24; 9:1–7; 11:1–45.

2   Gen. 2:7; John 20:22.

3   Heb. 1:3.

4   Num. 23:19; Titus 1:2; Heb. 6:18.

5   John 5:19–20; 12:49.

6   E.g. Phil. 1:19; Acts 16:7; Rom. 8:9; 2 Cor. 3:18.

7   Gen. 1:2–3.

30 Wisdom is a Person

[1] Gen. 1:2.
[2] Gen. 1:6–8.
[3] Gen. 1:9–10.
[4] Gen. 3:1.
[5] Gen. 2:16–17.
[6] See Rom. 8:20–22.
[7] Rev. 12:9.
[8] I find it interesting that chaos is thrown into fire and not water.
[9] Gen. 1:20–23.
[10] Rev. 20:10.
[11] Rev. 21:1.
[12] E.g. Baruch 3:36 – 4:4; Wisdom of Solomon 6:12 – 10:12; Sirach 1:1–10; 6:18–31; 24:1–34; Job 28:12–28; Prov. 1:20–33; 4:4–6; 8:1–36; 9:1–6.
[13] Prov. 3:13–18.
[14] The ancient philosopher Heraclitus said *logos* was the ordering principle of the universe. It is the divine logic that creates harmony in existence. Plato says it's what defines something, or what something truly is – its authenticity.
[15] John 1:14.
[16] 1 Cor. 1:18 – 2:16; Jas 3:14–18.
[17] Rev. 1:18.
[18] 1 Cor. 1:20–21.
[19] 2 Thess. 2:1–9.
[20] 1 Cor. 2:16.
[21] Matt. 8:23–7.
[22] Mark 4:35–41.
[23] Matt. 14:22–33.
[24] We are also elevated in the humanity of Jesus. We too are to walk above chaos. See Rom. 16:20, and Eph. 1:22–3.
[25] John 2:1–12.
[26] Eph. 1:10; Rev. 21:1 – 22:5.

31 The Soundtrack of Heaven

1   The Essenes were also around during the time of Jesus. However, they are not mentioned in the Bible. Some scholars suggest John the Baptist was influenced by them.

2   Matt. 2:1–4.

3   Matt. 26:3–4; Luke 4:28–30; John 11:45–8.

4   There were various persecutions against Christians. The religion eventually conquered Rome under Constantine. It was the ideas and conviction of the Christians that were a threat, not a military uprising, although there were a few revolts. Rome wasn't tolerant of seditions no matter how small or large they were.

5   John 19:19.

6   Ambrosius Theodosius Macrobius, *Saturnalia*, bk 2, ch. 4:11.

7   Matt. 2:16–18.

8   Luke 5:37–9.

9   In his 1892 commentary on Isaiah, Bernhard Duhm isolated four passages calling them the 'Songs of the Suffering Servant' (Isa. 42:1–4; 49:1–6; 50:4–7; 52:13 – 53:12). There have been various interpretations of who the suffering servant actually is. The two primary ones focus on Israel as a nation or Jesus as the Messiah. However, I'm using the term 'suffering servant' in its wider sense, embracing Ps. 22 and all the other messianic prophecies pointing to the cross.

10   John 13:1–17.

11   E.g. Mark 9:5; 11:21; 14:45; John 1:49; 4:31; 6:52; 9:2; 11:8.

12   John 1:13–17.

32 Earworms and Mind-Loops

1   1 John 3:8.

2   Matt. 5:17.

3   E.g. Matt. 11:27; John 17:4–6; Col. 1:15.

4   1 Pet. 2:22–5.

⁵ For example, in Luke 4:18–21 Jesus announces his mission in no uncertain terms: he is to proclaim the gospel. The only gospel Jesus proclaimed was the gospel of the kingdom. He also announces that the freedom afforded by the kingdom is taking place right now in their hearing: 'Today this scripture is fulfilled'. The priority of Jesus throughout the gospels is establishing the kingdom of God. Later on in this chapter Jesus explicitly states, this 'is why I was sent' (Luke 4:43). We can't afford to ignore the voice of Jesus when it comes to mission and the primacy of the kingdom of God.

33 The Gospel of Jesus

¹ E.g. Luke 13:1–9.

34 Guardians of the Kingdom

¹ Zech. 4:10.
² See Deut. 18:15. One of the main characteristics of a biblical prophet is someone who speaks for God and not just about him. Moses and Jesus both spoke for God. This is why the people who listened to the Sermon on the Mount were amazed at the teaching of Jesus 'because he taught as one who had authority, and not as their teachers of the law' (Matt. 7:29).
³ Acts 3:22.
⁴ E.g. Matt. 21:11; Luke 7:16; 24:19; John 4:19.
⁵ E.g. Mark 6:4.
⁶ Matt. 11:9–15.
⁷ I taught OT Prophets for seven years at Belfast Bible College and still teach the Prophets (as a guest lecturer) at Nazarene Theological College.
⁸ 1 Kgs 18; 2 Kgs 1.
⁹ 1 Kgs 17:17–24; 2 Kgs 2:8.
¹⁰ 2 Kgs 2:11–12.
¹¹ 2 Kgs 2:1–18.

12 The double portion was also the inheritance of the first-born child in a family. Elisha inherited Elijah's place of leadership among the prophets of his day.

13 2 Kgs 7:8; Matt. 3:4.

14 1 Kgs 18 – 19.

15 Matt. 14:3–12.

16 2 Kgs 2:9–14.

17 Matt. 3:16.

18 2 Kgs 6:18–20.

19 2 Kgs 5.

20 2 Kgs 4:32–7; 8:4–5; 13:21.

21 For example, Samaria was under siege and the people were dying of starvation. 2 Kgs 6:25–9 tells us a donkey's head was sold for eighty shekels of silver (very expensive and very poor meat) and a small measure of dove dung was sold for five shekels. The famine was so severe the people were eating their babies (vv. 26–9). Elisha tells the king that by tomorrow the siege will lift and there will be more than enough food to go around (2 Kgs 7:1–2). The king didn't believe him but still, this was good news. Elisha told him the finest flour will appear and cost only one shekel, and twice as much barely will go for the same price. This will take place at the city gate. 2 Kgs 7:3–18 tells us how it happened. When the lepers saw the fulfilment they said, 'This is a day of good news' (2 Kgs 7:9).

22 2 Kgs 4:8–37.

23 Luke 7:11–15.

24 John 6:8–14.

25 Rom. 8:32.

26 Matt. 6:9–10.

27 Matt. 6:33.

28 E.g. the treasure in the field, the sower and the seed, the wheat and the tares, the mustard seed, the unmerciful servant, the workers in the vineyard, the wise and foolish virgins.

29 Matt. 5 – 7.

35 Rob the Devil

[1] I apologise for my naivety even to address the subjects of 'eternity' and 'space and time', but we all touch on them somehow. Even the scientific statement that the universe is expanding begs the question: expanding into what? Into nothingness? If so, then even that nothingness is something. Space is space – it exists, empty or full; if it didn't exist, there would be nowhere to expand. I'm also intrigued that we as mere humans on this planet could come up with a word like 'infinity'. It's beyond our human experience and observation. Obviously, there is more going on around us and in us than we realise. In the few introductory paragraphs of this chapter, I'm just trying to simplify and describe a Christian's theological understanding of the subject. Biblically, we know Jesus wasn't created, and he didn't originate in space and time. We call that other reality (or dimension), 'eternity'. It is not 'space and time'. How they relate to each other is a mystery.

[2] E.g. Isa. 14:12–17; Ezek. 28:11–19; Job 1:6; Luke 10:18.

[3] Luke 10:18; Isa. 14:12; Rev. 12:9.

[4] Phil. 2:6–7.

[5] Luke 2:51; Heb. 5:7–8.

[6] Matt. 17:24–7.

[7] Heb. 4:15.

[8] John the Baptist and God the Father.

[9] 1 Cor. 15:45–9.

[10] Gen. 3:15.

[11] John 12:31.

[12] 2 Cor. 4:4.

[13] Systematic theology is an organised topical approach to Scripture. It is a discipline that categorises Scripture according to subject. For example, you will find all the verses about Jesus under the heading, 'Christology'.

[14] Luke 4:1; 4:14.

[15] My paraphrase and interpretation of what Jesus declared.

[16] See Chapter 24, 'The Legal Team'.

[17] E.g. 1 Pet. 5:8.

36 Search and Destroy

[1] Matt. 13:44.
[2] Luke 2:25,38.
[3] John 10:9.
[4] E.g. Matt. 5:21–44.
[5] 1 John 3:8.
[6] E.g. Matt. 4:9–10.
[7] The wilderness was considered the house, or the home of demons (e.g. Matt. 12:43; Luke 8:29). Also, look up the word 'Wilderness' in: David Noel Freedman, ed. *Eerdman's Dictionary of the Bible* (Grand Rapids: William B. Eerdmans Publishing Co, 2000). See also Leland Ryken, James C. Wilhoit, and, Tremper Longman III, eds, *Dictionary of Biblical Imagery* (London: Inter-Varsity Press, 1998).
[8] 1 Sam. 8:7.

37 The Painful Edit

[1] Luke 11:52.
[2] Matt. 5 – 7.
[3] Isa. 6:8–12.
[4] See Ann Spangler and Lois Trevberg, *Sitting at the Feet of Rabbi Jesus* (Grand Rapids: Zondervan, 2009), ch. 3.
[5] Luke 20:13–15.
[6] Gen. 22:2.
[7] See Heb. 10:19–31.
[8] John 19:19–22.
[9] E.g. Matt. 21:43–4.

38 Reaching for Crumbs

[1] John 4:1–42.
[2] Matt. 15:21–28; Mark 7:24–30.
[3] Exod. 15:26.

4 Luke 7:7–10.

5 John 10:7–9; 14:6.

6 The phrase 'outer darkness' occurs three times in the Gospel of Matthew (Matt. 8:12; 22:13; 25:30). In all three parables there is no mention of duration or eternal damnation. Notice also who is thrown into this outer darkness. Matthew 8:12 says it is the subjects of the kingdom. Matthew 22:12 tells us it was a man who was invited to the party and actually stepped through the door but was inappropriately dressed. He was even called 'friend'. In Matthew 25:28 the culprit is a hired servant. The servant was in the house and had received a bag of gold from his master before the eviction. There are more passages in the New Testament that speak of being 'inside' and 'outside' of the kingdom (e.g. Matt. 25:1–13; Mark 4:11; Luke 13:22–30; 1 Cor. 5:12–13; 1 Tim. 3:7). It appears there is more going on here than our traditional concepts of hell or the lake of fire. How does eternal fire correlate with darkness?

7 E.g. Exod. 34:14.

8 E.g. Rom. 11.

9 E.g. Jer. 31:36–7; Isa. 54:9–10.

10 Zech. 14:3–4 is a prophetic picture of Acts 1:9–12. It appears Jesus will return to the Mount of Olives just outside of Jerusalem. Rev. 21 tells us God will descend with the 'New Jerusalem'. I can understand spiritualising these prophetic statements, but that is not the biblical pattern. For example, as prophesied, Jesus was born in the actual town of Bethlehem (Mic. 5:2).

11 John 4:1–42.

12 Rev. 1:18.

13 1 Peter 5:8–9.

14 John 15:13.

15 Matt. 10:5–6.

39 I'm Outta Here

1 French phrase: 'joy of living'.

2 E.g. Exod. 26.

3 E.g. Exod. 40:34–8.

4 Col. 2:10; Rom. 3:22; 1 Cor. 1:30; 2 Cor. 5:21.

5 Rom. 1:17; 3:21–2; 10:4; 1 Cor. 1:30; 2 Cor. 5:21; Phil. 3:9.

6 2 Cor. 6:16.

7 Israel fell in 722 BCE. Judah fell in 587 BCE.

Part Four: The Church and the Kingdom

40 The Next Generation

1 Dan. 9.

2 Acts 2.

3 For the record, I'm not promoting gambling or card games. This is just an illustration relevant to our culture.

4 See Gal. 3:28.

5 Throughout the book of Acts, God revealed his plan to open the stage to the Gentiles. The disciples could have rejected it or permitted it. God gave them this right, but he knew their heart and he was very persuasive. They chose to work with God. They used the keys handed to them and said, 'Yes, we permit this even though it flies in the face of everything we previously believed.' Consider Acts 15.

6 This is a quote from Exod. 19:5–6.

41 Sign on the Dotted Line

1 Ps. 8:4; Heb. 2:6.

2 The covenant made with Abraham (Gen. 15:9–21) and Phinehas (Num. 25:1–15) are also considered promissory.

3 Exod. 19 – 24.

4 Gen. 9:13.

5 E.g. Gal. 3:19–22.

6 E.g. Matt. 22:36–40.

42 Embracing Change

[1]   A lot of what Jesus predicted in Matt. 24, Mark 13 and Luke 21
     was applicable to the apocalypse of 70 CE. See any major com-
     mentary on the subject.
[2]   Acts 9 – 11.

43 Messianic Prophecies

[1]   Rom. 8:1–2.
[2]   Isa. 11:6–9.
[3]   The Talmud has an interesting discussion about the Messiah's
     arrival which ties in with our discussion: 'if they [the Jewish peo-
     ple] are meritorious, [he will come] with the clouds of heaven; if
     not, lowly and riding upon an ass' (Babylonian Talmud: Tractate
     Sanhedrin, 98a).
[4]   For a more in-depth discussion see Bart D. Ehrman, *Did Jesus
     Exist?: The Historical Argument for Jesus of Nazareth* (New York:
     HarperOne Collins, 2012).
[5]   Read any major commentary on John.
[6]   E.g. *The Testament of Joseph* 19:8, or the *Book of Enoch* 90:38.
[7]   A suffering Messiah was not in the Jewish psyche before Jesus
     was born. E.g. Lloyd Gaston, *No Stone on Another: Studies in the
     Significance of the Fall of Jerusalem in the Synoptic Gospels* (Novum
     Testamentum Supplement Series 23, Leiden: Brill Publishers,
     1970), p. 292; Joshua W. Jipp, 'Luke's Scriptural Suffering
     Messiah: A Search for Precedent, a Search for Identity', *Catholic
     Biblical Quarterly* 72 (2010): pp. 255–74.
[8]   E.g. Luke 8:19–21; 11:27–8; 12:51–3; 14:26.
[9]   E.g. Mark 3:21,31–5.

44 The Full Gospel

[1]   1 Cor. 15:1–34.
[2]   Luke 17:21.

3 E.g. Acts 11:18.

4 E.g. Acts 15 and Galatians.

5 The term 'born again' could also be interpreted as 'born from above'. Both speak of the new contract. 'Born from above' relates to the Holy Spirit living inside of us, the law written on our heart. 'Born again' also relates to the new covenant. The Jews were born as a people of God at Sinai (the first contract), but to enter the kingdom under the new contract you have to sign on the dotted line a second time (born again). It's a new deal.

6 Matt. 5:17–19.

7 E.g. Jesus ascended from the Mount of Olives (Acts 1:1–12); Jesus returns to the Mount of Olives (Zech. 14:3–4). God the Father will move to earth in the New Jerusalem (Rev. 21). The battles of Revelation take place in Israel (e.g. Rev. 16:16). The 144,000 Jews are commissioned in Israel (Rev 14:1–4). Obviously, the promised land is still an ongoing promise. It seems wherever there is a tangible geography in the old and new creation the land of Israel will still be God's chosen stage. We can spiritualise it but the Bible has no problem pinpointing a physical location. It all has to take place somewhere.

46 Pentecost

1 E.g. Lev. 23 (Passover, Pentecost and Tabernacles).

2 Travel was never safe, comfortable or easy in the ancient Near East or in Israel. Oftentimes pilgrimage was a community endeavour. For safety people would travel with others from their hometown or village (e.g. Luke 2:41–4).

3 The pilgrimage psalms are quoted from the *New Living Translation*. The reason is to keep myself on the right side of copyright law, not because this is the preferred translation.

4 Acts 2:4.

5 Acts 2.

6 Matt. 27:51.

7 Jas 3:7.

8 Gen. 11:1–9.

9   Woodstock was the first major three-day rock festival. In 1969 over four hundred thousand people, mostly hippies, descended on the fields of Max Yasgur's six-hundred-acre dairy farm. It was billed as 'three days of peace and music'.

47 Pilgrimage

1   This is one of the Christian classics. It's an allegory of the Christian life written by John Bunyan in 1678.

48 The Great Divide

1   Romans 14:16–19.
2   See Chapter 21, 'Street Cred'.
3   Parables are wide open to interpretation. They are to open the heart, not just inform the mind. This particular parable could also be speaking of Jesus himself. He came to the field of Israel. The kingdom was buried in it, but no one could see it. He knew it was there. He dug it up. The Jews rejected him and his message. He buries it again, and goes to the cross and buys the field and the treasure with his own blood. The same interpretation could also be applied to the following parable about the pearl (Matt. 13:45–6).
4   Matt. 25:14–30.

49 A Paradigm Shift

1   Teen Challenge (also called Adult Challenge) is a worldwide para-church ministry facilitating the Holy Spirit's power, in the name of Jesus Christ, to free people from addictions and self-destructive behaviour. It was founded by David Wilkerson in 1960.

50 Kingdom Pastors

1 Rev. 2 – 3.
2 Rev. 2:2–3.
3 Rev. 2:14–16.
4 Rev. 2:20–26.
5 Rev. 3:1–2.
6 Rev. 2:18–19.
7 Rev. 3:15–19.
8 Rev. 2:9.
9 Rev. 3:17.
10 Rev. 1:11.
11 Rev. 1:12–19.
12 1 Cor. 12:12–21.
13 Exod. 33:15–16.

52 Through the Looking Glass

1 Lewis Carroll, *Through the Looking-Glass and What Alice Found There* (1872), ch. 5.
2 For a history of the Dock Cafe go to https://www.the-dock.org/blog/the-story-of-the-dock/ (accessed 25 November 2020).
3 In June 2019 the Dock Cafe was awarded the Tripadvisor 'Hall of Fame' badge for consecutive years of excellence (2015–19).
4 Muslims believe Jesus to be a great prophet (as mentioned in the Qur'an) but they don't believe he is God incarnate.
5 Acts 5:15–16.

53 Tipping the Scales

1 Excerpts of this chapter are taken from Richard Porter, 'Tipping the Scales', *Wild Goose Magazine; Return to Eden* 1 (Wild Goose Collaboration, 2018): pp. 38–9. www.wildgoose.ie (accessed 5 March 2020).
2 Matt. 5:44.

3 Matt. 18:21–2.
4 Phil. 2:3–4.
5 Read closely John 15:1–18. Here Jesus speaks about the mission of the church, along with the individuals participating in it. He uses the word 'abide'. We must abide in him, stay close, remain faithful, actively keep in fellowship. We have to keep him in the centre of everything. How do we do this? He repeats the answer over and over again, obey his command (vv. 10,12,14,17). What is his command? Love each other (vv. 12,17). John 13:34–5 relates this directly to the mission of the church. If we don't love each other, we aren't abiding in Jesus. If we can't love our fellow brothers and sister in the body of Christ, we are just making a lot of noise in our buildings, in our homes and on the streets; and that noise will not produce fruit or build the kingdom (1 Cor. 13:1–3).
6 Luke 21:1–4.
7 Matt. 5:38–9.
8 Rom. 12:1.

54 Heaven's Silence

1 In some Christian circles we have equated worship with singing. Singing is an expression of worship but it's not the whole package.
2 E.g. Jonathan Edwards (1703–58), sermon called, 'Why Saints in Glory Will Rejoice to See the Torment of the Damned'.
3 1 Cor. 2:9.
4 1 Cor. 2:10.
5 E.g. Matt. 5:3; 5:20; 7:21–3; John 3:5; 1 Cor. 6:9–10; Gal. 5:19–21; Eph. 5:5.
6 E.g. Rom. 6:15; Eph. 2:8–9; Titus 2:11,14; 1 Tim. 2:4; 2 Pet. 3:9.
7 Acts 2:17–21; Joel 2:18–32.
8 E.g. John 14:26; 15:26; 16:8–9,13; Rom. 8:26; 1 Cor. 2:11–12.
9 E.g. 1 John 1:9.
10 E.g. Every fifty-year cycle, Israel was to declare and observe a year of liberty and rest. The fields lie fallow, yet God provides food. Slaves are released and land is returned to its initial family. Debts are cleared and people can step into the future with a clean slate

before and behind them (e.g. Lev. 25:8–17). We find allusions to the year of Jubilee in both testaments; often it is ascribed to the ministry of Jesus (e.g. Luke 4:16–21; Matt. 11:2–5; Isa. 49:8–10; 2 Cor. 6:1–2; Mark 1:14–15).

[11] Rev. 20:11–15.

[12] Matt. 25:23; 7:23.

[13] Whenever God steps in to judge people and nations, the Bible calls it the 'day of the Lord'. The phrase also points to the final days of this creation (e.g. Isa. 2:12; Ezek. 13:5; 30:3–4; Jer. 46:10; Amos 5:18–20; Zeph. 1:14–18; 3:8; Isa. 13:9–10; Mal. 4:5; 2 Pet. 3:10; 1 Thess. 5:2–3).

[14] Joel 2:31; Acts 2:20.

[15] Rev. 21 – 22.

[16] Rev. 21:3–4.

[17] Rev. 6:12–14.

[18] Rev. 21:1.

[19] Rev. 6:14.

[20] Rev. 21 – 22.

[21] Rev. 5.

[22] Isa. 6:1–4.

[23] Rev. 4:6–9.

55 A Chip off the Old Block

[1] 2 Pet. 3:9–10.

[2] Rev. 7:1–8; 14:1–5.

[3] Rev. 11:1–14.

[4] See David Nirenberg, *Anti-Judaism: The Western Tradition* (New York: W.W. Norton, 2013); James Carroll, *Constantine's Sword: The Church and the Jews: The History* (New York: Houghton Mifflin, Mariner Books, 2002); Robert Michael, *Holy Hatred: Christianity, Antisemitism, and the Holocaust* (New York: Palgrave Macmillan, 2006); Michael Brown, *Our Hands are Stained with Blood: The Tragic Story of the Church and the Jewish People* (Shippensburg, PA: Destiny Image, 1992).

5   See Kirster Stendahl, *Paul among Jews and Gentiles* (Philadelphia: Fortress Press, 1976).
6   E.g. Acts 10.
7   See *Judaism's View of Jesus.* https://en.wikipedia.org/wiki/Judaism%27s_view_of_Jesus (accessed 21 January 2020).
8   Luke (Luke/Acts) was possibly a Gentile and perhaps King Lemuel (Prov. 31:1–9). However we have no conclusive evidence.
9   E.g. John 16:5–15.
10 I was fortunate enough to be in Jerusalem at the Feast of Tabernacles in 1980. That year many foreign embassies were moving out of the city for political reasons, but at the Christian celebration it was announced we were going to open a Christian embassy in Jerusalem in support of the Jews. Today, it is still a viable, kingdom venture. The International Christian Embassy (ICEJ) is just one example of Christians tipping the scales.
11 I once caught a tiny glimpse of what it will take to win the Jewish heart. On the kibbutz we were given seventeen dollars a month for spending money. We had to go into the office and collect it. The last time I entered that room before leaving the country, the Jewish man in charge of the volunteers said: 'I don't know what it is about you, but you always seem to bring the peace.' He knew I was a Christian, and I am humbled that he saw something of Christ in me. In so many words he was saying: 'I want som-adat.' This is as close to making the Jews jealous as I have ever experienced. It was worth serving there just to hear that.

56 The Last Hurrah

1   The word 'rapture' refers to the moment Christian believers, the living and the dead, will rise from the earth to meet Christ in the air.
2   E.g. Matt. 21:43.
3   E.g. 1 Cor. 3.
4   Eph. 1:3.
5   Gal. 5:22–5; 1 Cor. 12.
6   Rev. 20:7–10.

7   E.g. Matt. 3:12; 13:24–30.
8   Matt. 13:24–30; Ps. 2:1–6.
9   E.g. 2 Cor. 12:2–4.
10   E.g. Isa. 65:17–19.
11   1 Pet. 3 talks about the destruction of the earth by water and by fire, but both events point more to a 'deep cleansing' rather than obliteration.

The Christing

*Mining the Bible to reveal
the extravagant anointing of
the Holy Spirit*

Paul White

Do you want to fall more in love with Jesus?

The Holy Spirit is the Spirit of Jesus. The awesome power of this
'Christing' is to get the life-giving, oppression-busting, freedom-
bringing life of Jesus into the whole world, starting right where we
live.

Take a gallop through the scriptures with Paul White and discover
the different images used to describe the Holy Spirit. In a fresh
and conversational style, peppered with personal stories and the
author's own illustrations, you will see how the same dynamic
power of God seen throughout the Bible is still available to us
today.

Be encouraged to live in a deep, passionate relationship with Jesus.
Get ready to release the 'Christing'!

978-1-78893-173-1

The Good God

Enjoying Father, Son, and Spirit

Michael Reeves

Why is God love? *Because God is a Trinity.*

Why can we be saved? *Because God is a Trinity.*

How are we able to live the Christian life? *Through the Trinity.*

In this lively and refreshing book, we find an accessible introduction
to the profound beauty of the Trinity. With wit and clarity, Reeves
draws from notable teachers from church history to the present to
reveal how the Christian life is rooted in the triune God - Father, Son
and Spirit. Be encouraged to grow in enjoyment of God and see how
God's triune being makes all his ways beautiful.

978-1-84227-744-7

Authentic

We trust you enjoyed reading this book
from Authentic. If you want to be
informed of any new titles from this author
and other releases you can sign up to the
Authentic newsletter by scanning below:

Online:
authenticmedia.co.uk

Follow us: